"Richard Hamilton brings an acute report~~~~
an's sense of context to his first-~~
a fine sense of the city's compli
sexual traditions. From the my
Bowles to the music of Brian Jon~
the essential gumshoe work throu,
matic city and taken the measure, ~~~gier's myth,
magic, morality and mystery."

Iain Finlayson
Author of *Tangier: City of the Dream*

"Tangier is a city which resonates in the imagination of those who
have walked its streets, and those who have yet to do so. In 'Tangier:
From the Romans to the Rolling Stones' Richard Hamilton takes us on
a fascinating and evocative journey through this mythical city's rich
cultural history. Along the way we witness Tangier's political upheavals,
wander through its landscapes, explore its vivid psyche and meet
some of the city's famous sons and daughters, many of whom were
adopted. Hamilton is an endearing narrator. He has a delightfully comic
touch and is a gentle and unobtrusive presence, allowing his protagonists to take centre stage. He shows us a city which is simultaneously
seedy and opulent, cruel and kind, a place which attracts and repels in
equal measure. This is a captivating book, which will intrigue, enchant
and entertain any reader who accepts the invitation to travel with
Hamilton and his celebrated companions through this fabled city."

Samantha Herron
Author of *The Djinn in the Skull:*
Stories from Hidden Morocco

"This absorbing portrait of Tangier is refreshingly detailed by the
galaxy of famous artists and writers – Henri Matisse, Paul Bowles,
William Burroughs, Brion Gysin, Francis Bacon, Joe Orton, the Rolling
Stones and the stars of screen and society – who flocked to this seedy
seaport on the Strait."

John Hopkins
Author of *The Tangier Diaries*

TANGIER

TANGIER

From the Romans to the Rolling Stones

RICHARD HAMILTON

TAURIS PARKE
Bloomsbury Publishing Plc
50 Bedford Square, London, WC1B 3DP, UK
29 Earlsfort Terrace, Dublin 2, Ireland

BLOOMSBURY, TAURIS PARKE and the TAURIS PARKE logo are trademarks of
Bloomsbury Publishing Plc

First published in Great Britain by Bloomsbury Publishing Plc 2019
This edition published 2024

Richard Hamilton has asserted his right under the Copyright, Designs and Patents Act, 1988,
to be identified as Author of this work

All photographs not otherwise credited are copyright of the author

Bloomsbury Publishing Plc does not have any control over, or responsibility for, any third-party
websites referred to or in this book. All internet addresses given in this book were correct at the
time of going to press. The author and publisher regret any inconvenience caused if addresses have
changed or sites have ceased to exist, but can accept no responsibility for any such changes

A catalogue record for this book is available from the British Library

Library of Congress Cataloguing-in-Publication data has been applied for

ISBN: PB: 978-0-7556-5451-2 HB: 978-1-7845-3343-4
eBook: 978-1-7867-2647-6

2 4 6 8 10 9 7 5 3 1

Typeset by Westchester Publishing Services
Printed and bound in the United Kingdom by CPI Group (UK) Ltd, Croydon, CR0 4YY

MIX
Paper | Supporting
responsible forestry
FSC® C013604

To find out more about our authors and books visit www.bloomsbury.com and
sign up for our newsletters

To Iris and Julian

Contents

Acknowledgements

Many people have helped me write this book. I am most indebted to Otmane Benchekroun without whom I would have known virtually nothing about Tangier from the Moroccan perspective.

Others in Tangier who were generous with their time and patient with my questions include Jonathan Dawson, Josh Shoemake, Mohamed Mrabet, Gipi de Richemont, Simon-Pierre Hamelin, Lawrence Mynott, Anthea Pender, Barbara Abensur, Albrecht Jerentrup, Nadia and Suomi La Valle, Lotfi Akalay, Merieme Addou, Charles Sevigny, Gerald Loftus, Rachel Muyal, Frank Rynne, Brian J. Bowe, Mohamed Karbach, Rieko Akatsuka, Ahmed Attar, Hatmi Mohammed, Mohammed Jami, Ornella Tommasi, Nour Eddine Merini, Rachid Tafersiti, Umberto Pasti, Anna McKew, Fatiima Eirifi, Abdelmajid Raiss el Fenn, Mohamed Merini, Hicham Hassini and Ashraf. I also want to thank Nadine van Loon who accompanied me on my very first trip to Tangier in 2007. Christopher Gibbs, David Stotter and Joe Abensur, all of whom sadly passed away before this book was published, deserve special mentions. I would particularly like to thank Stéphanie Gaou, the owner of the wonderful *Les Insolites* bookshop in Tangier, for all her help and support.

In England, I owe thanks to John Hopkins, Andrew Damonte, Aziz Samih, Tahir Shah, Adam Cooper, Gered Mankowitz, David Arditti and Abdelmajid Semlali. I would also like to express my gratitude to Graham McCulloch, Simon Hawkesley, Annie Austin, Ali Bahaijoub, Benedicte Clarkson, Mina Metioui, Rosemary Askew, David Nicoll, John Wolfe, Aine Marsland, Chris McHugo, Saeida Rouass, Rozina Ahmed, Laila Agha, Latifa Rhoualmi and many others at the British Moroccan Society.

I will never forget our wonderful visit to Tangier in 2016. I am also indebted to Tatiana Wilde at I.B. Tauris and Jayne Parsons at Bloomsbury for their editorial input.

My sister Julia is a big fan of this part of the Mediterranean. I always appreciate her feedback and artistic eye.

Finally, I am incredibly grateful for the love, support, consideration and tolerance of my wife Caroline, who helped edit the final manuscript, as well as for the boundless joy that my children, Iris and Julian give me every day.

TANGIER

ONE

Hercules

Inveniet viam aut faciet (He will find a way or make one)

A battered beige Mercedes drove me west from Tangier through a spongy forest of cedar, eucalyptus, mimosa, cypress and umbrella pine along a winding, sea-sprayed road. The route, lined by grass as soft as carpet and as luminous as the mountains of the Rif, descended to Cap Spartel and the Caves of Hercules. The grand taxi pulled up outside the Cap Spartel Café, its neon signs nestling incongruously against an ancient cliff. On the northwest point of mainland Africa, looking out onto the Atlantic and the coast of Spain, was the lighthouse. Protected by a cohort of palm trees, the squat yellow tower consisted of white corner stones, and a grey metal cupola encasing its light, giving it the appearance of a Roundhead's helmet. This Spanish style building was first illuminated in 1864. It was also the first sign of co-operation between the European powers and prefigured the International Zone that was to come. It would inspire Paul Bowles' novel *Let it Come Down*. 'FARO DE CABO ESPARTEL, ENTRADA PROHIBIDA' shouted a sign that offered neither explanation nor apology. There was nothing to do but join the visitors in the café, buy a postcard of the frustratingly out of reach lighthouse or leave. We left.

Near Cap Spartel is Spartel Bank, a sunken island that vanished under the sea about 12,000 years ago, due to rising ocean levels. The geologists Jacques Collina-Girard and Marc-André Gutscher thought it might have been the lost island of Atlantis.

When the taxi stopped at the entrance to the Caves of Hercules, a worker in overalls barred the way, informing us with visible pleasure that the site was closed. A new entrance and visitor centre was under construction. There was nothing I could do but retrace my steps. It was April 2014.

What a poor start to a book and the exploration of Tangier's earliest history. I was reminded of a local saying: 'You cry when you leave Tangier and you cry when you arrive there too.'

But a year later I came back to the city, without tears and determined to see the caves. This time I was better prepared, teaming up with Otmane Benchekroun, a writer, teacher and conservationist.

The Benchekrouns are a famous Tangier family with a long history that echoes the city. They were descended from the Moors (*Moriscos*) who were expelled from Spain at the end of the fifteenth century during the *Reconquista*. Otmane's great-grandfather was an adviser to Sultan Moulay Abdelaziz, the boy king who ascended to the throne in 1894 at the tender age of 16. This earlier Benchekroun also owned a publishing house in Egypt, married an Egyptian woman and was one of the first Moroccans to write about his country's history. Otmane's grandfather owned several shops in the medina and made a fortune selling paper tissues. He also bought a large square mansion on the Marshan, where Otmane grew up. He showed it to me. Tucked in a corner of the street behind a screen of palm trees, wisteria and an ornate lamp post, the house lies empty, but with its shutters still open and roof tiles furrowed. It was inside this house that the very week his son (Otmane's father) was born, the grandfather was murdered by the guardian. The killer ran off with the family jewellery and his master's pistol, with which he had shot him.

Otmane turned out to be an enormous help as a guide, font of knowledge, companion and friend, even though he would occasionally wince when I asked him a question in mangled French. He was also a useful human fly swatter. Whenever I was besieged by faux guides, Otmane would shoo them away. It must be said that some of these hustlers were actually quite funny. 'It is better to have one mosquito following you than a hundred,' one said to me near the port.

In an area where taxis congregate impiously outside St Andrew's Church, Otmane negotiated a better price for a ride in a Mercedes, whilst I loitered out of sight on the other side of the road. 'You want taxi?' a generic voice asked. After several minutes in which the taxi hustler must have been impressed by my involuntary haggling and steely resolve, Otmane beckoned me to join him. The deal had been done, and as we drove off, I waved goodbye to the hustler with visible pleasure.

The car took us up to the Old Mountain. Along the Rue de la Vieille Montagne, I gawped at the entrances of enormous opulent villas owned by, amongst others, the antiques dealer Christopher Gibbs, the fashion designer Yves Saint Laurent and the Chilean artist Claudio Bravo. Tangerine folklore has it that Bravo was enamoured with painting dwarfs, so every day lines of them would sit outside his house hoping to be selected. There is no market for dwarf painting anymore as Bravo died in 2011 and his house was put up for sale for 20 million euros. There were also several empty villas owned by King Mohammed VI, with bored, yet scared sentries keeping guard over his unused real estate. It is said that his wife, Princess Lalla Salma, wanted two swimming pools to be built in the grounds of the royal palace there. One, she insisted, had to be filled with seawater. So, a large pump was installed to push the liquid up the steep cliff face. The first attempt was unsuccessful as algae blocked the pipes. The following year however, workers built a well next to the sea and succeeded in pumping up seawater without algae.

Up above the world, the road levelled out and we drove along a plateau where there was once a Christian cemetery. The car sped on past the former expat playgrounds: the polo pitch and golf club. In the forested Rmilat region, we spotted a Kuwaiti palace. Not to be outdone, the Saudi king had bought another white edifice, although he hardly ever went there. You could also see the wires, pylons and satellite dishes transmitting Moroccan radio signals as they peeped out of their forest nest. Voice of America had transmitters further down the coast.

From here, a 25-mile beach stretches all the way to the fishing village of Asilah. In the 1960s, Otmane explained that the beach was virtually empty as few people had cars. Along Achakar Beach we passed camels and children flying kites. We drove on past a rock where men with nets tried to catch tuna. Slightly set back from the shore, almost a whole new town is under construction, thanks to money from the Gulf. The taxi driver told us it was one of the most expensive stretches of road in the world and that paving it with gold might have been cheaper. Every year, King Salman of Saudi Arabia reportedly spends 100 million dollars here on a six week holiday.

When the taxi drew up this time, there were still construction workers guarding the entrance. Our conversation with them went like this:

'It's closed.'

'Why's that?'

'Building site.'

'But we just want to take a quick look.'

'No. It's dangerous. You need permission from the Caid.'

'When will it be finished?'

'Two months.'

My heart sank. But I decided to do what a journalist often does in these cases: lurk about. A few minutes later, a more official looking man with distinguished flecks of grey hair approached. I presumed he was the project manager. He spoke in French.

'You can't come in. The work is not finished.'

'When will it be finished?'

'Two weeks.'

I would find a way or make one. I tried phoning my hotel manager to ask if he could pull some strings, but his strings were slack. I called a number for the mayor of Tangier, but there was no answer. Then, I had an idea. In Morocco, I often carry around a letter, in English, that I once received from King Mohammed VI, about my first book on the storytellers of Marrakech. I showed it to the project manager. A tiny, almost imperceptible look of apprehension came over him. There was a pause.

'That's not the King's signature.'

Wondering if he was calling my bluff, I decided to call his. Pointing at the coat of arms on the letterhead, I insisted it was indeed His Majesty's signature. Luckily, the project manager could not read English so he began to wonder if the letter really was my *passe-partout*. There was another long silence.

'Ok . . . come in.'

We trod carefully along gangplanks on the ground that did not appear remotely dangerous and walked through a modern open piazza surrounded by white neoclassical porticoes. Builders dragged cables along the tiles and fitted lamps to unfinished shop fronts. We were escorted by the first construction worker in his yellow bib. We looked out to sea. From here the Spanish coast is 20 miles away. One early traveller, the fourteenth-century German priest, Ludolph von Suchem, remarked that the Strait of Gibraltar was so narrow (at its narrowest point, it is only nine miles wide), that 'upon one bank there stands a Christian woman and on the other bank a heathen woman washing their clothes, and wrangling and quarrelling with one another.' Medieval Arab geographers also thought that beneath the Strait there was a bridge that joined the two continents.

Feeling like Orpheus in the Underworld, I followed a twisting, newly restored path that descended slowly between corridors of rocks, which might have squashed us if they had moved, like the clashing Symplegades or something out of Doctor Who, made of polystyrene.

Suddenly, the surly workman turned into an eager, ready-made tour guide, complete with winning smile. 'I am an archaeologist,' he informed us.

By this point I would not have cared if he was a gynaecologist. I was just so delighted to be inside the elusive Caves of Hercules, that I could have hugged him. The temperature had dropped dramatically and the silence was broken only by drips of water from the stalactites above, but I felt like singing in the rain. It was a strangely aquatic experience, like being inside a large fish. Floor lights threw yellow and blue shapes upon ribbed columns of calcium that supported the rocky ceiling, which looked as if it had been sculpted not by thousands of years of salt water but by giant ice-cream scoops. The ground was neatly laid out with a mosaic of tiles in arched patterns that echoed the cavernous walls. And there, in front of us, was one of the most famous sites in Africa.

The mouth of the main cave is shaped like the continent of Africa itself. In the distance you can see a seawater horizon, which appears to fill up the hole, like an advert for a delicious blue liqueur splashing into an ornate goblet about two-thirds full. The rocks emitted spray like miniature volcanoes spitting flames. The Atlantic stretched out before us. 'When Greek sailors approached the Strait of Gibraltar they discovered the vastness of the Atlantic,' the Moroccan novelist Lotfi Akalay wrote. 'They thought Tangier was the end of the world.'

The map of Africa at the cave entrance is almost uncannily realistic, except it has a smaller hole on its lower left flank. 'Madagascar is on the wrong side,' the 'archaeologist' informed me, but when I asked for an explanation, his reasoning became incoherent. I did not mind. I was still euphoric to have a private view of this subterranean world and I gave him an enormous tip. I found out later that the aperture looks more like Africa if viewed from the sea.

He also said that Phoenicians lived in the cave and controlled the Strait before the Romans defeated them in the Punic Wars. It is believed that the Phoenicians actually created the sea opening as well as some markings on the wall in the shape of eyes that constitute a map of the local area. The water comes in from the Atlantic, the Mediterranean and a river that runs all the way from Larache further south. The cave itself is part natural and part man-made. The latter section was also used by local Berber people to cut stone wheels from the walls and make millstones. Before the caves became a tourist attraction, it was rumoured they were brothels.

Real archaeologists will tell you that the caves show evidence of occupation as far back as the Neolithic age around 10,000 years ago and fossils discovered in another nearby grotto suggest that Neanderthals roamed the region nearly 200,000 years earlier.

Legend has it that Hercules slept in the caves before performing the eleventh of his Twelve Labours: retrieving the apples from the Garden of the Hesperides in the westernmost corner of the world.

In Greek and Roman mythology, Hercules (or Heracles) was the son of Zeus and a mortal woman, Alcmene. Like Tangier itself, he was a multifaceted figure with contradictory characteristics. The Hellenic hero is known for his incredible strength and is the ultimate symbol of manhood, but he is also a flawed character, who acts on impulse rather than intellect. His many adventures took him to the edges of the known world including the mouth of the Mediterranean. One cycle of these adventures is the Twelve Labours, or dodecathlon, the most famous of which are: slaying the Nemean Lion, killing the nine-headed Hydra, cleaning the Augean stables, capturing the Cretan Bull, and bringing back Cerberus, the dog that guarded the Underworld.

Zeus had seized power from the Titans, the monstrous sons of Uranus (Sky) and Gaea (Earth) by giving Cronus a poisoned cup to drink that made him vomit out the gods he had swallowed: Poseidon, Hades, Hestia, as well as Zeus' future wife and sister Hera. The gods waged a terrible battle for supremacy with the Titans, which ended when the gods threw the monsters into the depths of Tartarus. With his father Uranus dead, Atlas, the general of the Titans, was forced to hold the heavens aloft on his shoulders as a punishment.

Hera had been blessed with the power of prophecy and foresaw a time when the giants would storm Mount Olympus and overthrow Zeus, just as he had deposed Cronus, but she also had a vision that there would come a saviour of the gods. He would not be divine, but a man born of a mortal mother and wrapped in the skin of a lion, however Zeus and Hera could not agree on who this saviour would be. Hera insisted it would be the heir to the throne of Mycenae, Eurystheus, a descendant of Zeus via Perseus. The latter had two sons, Electryon and Sthenelus, the father of Eurystheus. Electryon took the throne of Mycenae and had a daughter Alcmene, who was so stunningly beautiful that as Hesiod remarked, 'her face and dark eyes wafted such charm as comes from golden Aphrodite.' Her husband, the soldier Amphitryon, threw a club at an ox but missed and killed his father-in-law Electryon by mistake. For this, Amphitryon and his wife were exiled to Thebes.

As he watched this tragedy unfold from his vantage point on Olympus, Zeus could not help noticing that Alcmene was indeed stunningly beautiful and he burned with passion for her. He also wanted to fulfill the prophecy about the saviour of the gods. So, Zeus came down in the form of Amphitryon, slipped into Alcmene's bed and brought her to the heights of ecstasy as only a true Olympian can. When her real husband came to bed later expecting sex, Alcmene must have been surprised, but complied anyway. In due course, Alcmene bore twins: Hercules and Iphicles, fathered by Zeus and Amphitryon.

When Hera learnt about her husband's latest infidelity, she was incandescent with rage. Not only had Zeus thrown his support behind a rival of her pick for the gods' champion, but he had also fathered the illegitimate child himself. Hera tried to prevent this offspring from ever being born. When that did not work, she sent a pair of enormous slithering serpents to slay the baby in his crib, but the infant throttled them with his tiny hands. Curious about this incident, Amphitryon consulted the blind seer Tiresias who pronounced that Zeus, not Amphitryon, was the boy's father. In an attempt to placate the raging queen of the gods, Alcmene named her son 'the glory of Hera,' Heracles, or as the Romans would call him, Hercules. But Hera's life-long vendetta against the boy would continue.

When he was a child tending cattle on a mountain, two nymphs appeared and offered Hercules a choice. The first nymph, Pleasure, offered him an easy, simple and pleasant life. The second, Virtue, offered him a harsh existence that would eventually lead to glory. He chose the latter.

Many years later, after the death of his father Sthenelus, Eurystheus ascended to the Mycenaean throne. Hercules went to Thebes, defeated the city's enemies and married King Creon's daughter Megara, who bore him three sons. This displeased Hera though, and she sent a fit of madness to visit Hercules. In his delusional state, he thought his house was full of enemies and went from room to room slaughtering as he went. When he came to his senses, Hercules found that the corpses were those of his wife and children. In despair, the demi-god fled Thebes and wandered the edges of the world until he came to the Oracle at Delphi. She told him that the path to atonement was for him to be enslaved by Hera's champion, Eurystheus, for twelve years and perform ten labours for him. Only then, the Oracle said, would the hero be cleansed of his sin and become immortal.

Eurystheus consulted Hera and together they chose tasks so impossible they thought would crush Hercules' spirit. So began the ten labours, the first of which was to slay the Nemean Lion. After three more of these tasks: killing the many-headed Hydra, as well as capturing the Golden Hind and the Erymanthian Boar, Hercules went off on a brief tangent to join Jason and the Argonauts in search of the Golden Fleece. He returned for his fifth labour, cleaning the Augean Stables and carried on, via the Stymphalian Birds, the Mares of Diomedes, the Girdle of Hippolyta and the Cattle of Geryon, until he had completed all ten tasks as requested.

Just when he thought he could finally put his feet up, Eurystheus annoyingly moved the goal posts and added two more tasks, claiming, rather pedantically, that neither the Hydra nor the Augean Stables really counted because Hercules had received extra help. It was a sort of *Monty Python and the Holy Grail*, 'we are now no longer the knights who say Ni,' moment (not content with a shrubbery, the knights demanded that Arthur 'cut down the mightiest tree in the forest with . . . a herring') and it must have been extremely frustrating. Hercules remained undaunted however. The first of these two extra labours was to steal the golden apples from the Garden of the Hesperides.

But Hercules first had to find out the location of the Hesperides, since the garden was situated beyond the knowledge of men and no map showed where it was. To get help, he travelled to the far north to consult the nymphs of the River Eridanus. They were not much help however, saying they did not know. Luckily, they thought they might know a man who did. This was the Titan Nereus, the eldest son of Pontus, the Ocean. He was also a shape-shifting sea god, referred to in Homer's *Iliad* as the 'Old Man of the Sea.' Nereus said he would tell Hercules where the garden was, if the hero managed to maintain a grip on him.

Hercules travelled, like a message in a bottle, in a giant goblet given to him by the Sun god, Helios. The vessel drifted and bobbed west across the Mediterranean until it reached the grotto of Nereus. The Titan was easy to recognise, because he was impossible to recognise. Even as Hercules set eyes on him, Nereus would change form. His features were in constant flux and, like Tangier itself, he was always in the process of becoming something else.

Hercules pounced on the Old Man of the Sea as he lay asleep in the cave. The Titan tried to wriggle out of the hero's grasp by changing from a slippery eel to a sea anemone, via a crab. Others say he changed into a lion, a writhing serpent, then fire and water, but still the hero held firm, until the Old Man of the Sea relented.

Nereus told Hercules to go west. He explained that the Garden of Hesperides could be found where the sun chariot of Apollo fell below the horizon at the end of every day, on the lower slopes of Mount Atlas. Some ancient Greek writers believed that the Hesperides were actually located at Lixus, to the south of Tangier.

Inside the garden was an orchard and inside the orchard was a tree. On the tree were golden apples. Yet these were no ordinary apples; Gaea, the Earth, had given them as a wedding gift to Zeus and Hera. Their sweet flesh would give eternal youth to those who ate them. The Hesperides were the daughters of Atlas who were entrusted with looking after the apple tree. Their life's work was gardening and they lived in a state of permanent bliss.

But one day, Hera caught the Hesperides eating the tree's fruit, so she sent a one hundred headed dragon called Ladon to the garden. Ladon was the brother of the dreadful Gorgons, who themselves were said to live on the furthest shores of the western ocean. Ladon's role was to wrap himself around the trunk of the apple tree as an extra burglar alarm system that could deter even the Titan himself. Atlas took great pride in his daughters' garden and when Thetis, the muse of Truth warned him that there would come a time when a son of Zeus would one day strip the tree of its gold, Atlas surrounded the orchard with an absurdly high wall and swore he would stamp to death anyone who dared to enter the compound.

So, Hercules came upon Atlas standing firm with the sky resting on his shoulders. Hercules followed Nereus' advice and decided that rather than stealing the apples himself he would trick Atlas into giving them away. 'I can help you,' said Atlas, 'but what will you do for me in return?' Hercules made several offers, none of which impressed the Titan. 'I tell you what,' Atlas finally suggested, 'I will get the apples for you myself, if you shoulder my burden while I'm away.'

Hercules agreed and as a sign of goodwill he fired a hydra-laced arrow, which flew like an Exocet missile over the wall, instantly killing Ladon, who was still wrapped around the tree. Groaning under the strain, Atlas then transferred the heavens onto the shoulders of Hercules, whose knees buckled under their weight. Then, Atlas reached over the garden wall and grabbed three apples, but his new found sense of freedom was too pleasurable to give up, so the Titan slyly informed the hero that he himself would even deliver the apples directly to the court of Eurystheus, if Hercules would not mind holding up the stars for just a couple more weeks?

Hercules knew this was a trick, but did not show it. Saying he would gladly accept the request, he first asked Atlas to just hold the heavens for a tiny bit longer while he rearranged his cloak on his shoulders, so it provided a bit more padding.

Atlas, who was probably even less bright than Hercules, agreed. No sooner had he lifted the Milky Way aloft again, the demigod snatched the apples and ran off down the mountain towards his giant goblet. The screams and curses of the Titan echoed across the Mediterranean, but rang hollow in the hero's ears.

Hercules did not return to Mycenae straightaway, but explored more of North Africa. He came upon the tyrant Antaeus, a son of Poseidon and Gaea. Nothing was more amusing to Antaeus than to challenge strangers to wrestling matches and murder them when they lost and even his temple to Poseidon was made out of the losers' bones. Hercules was not one to be intimidated by a bully however and accepted the challenge. The two contestants threw off their tunics and faced off against each other in the town square. In true Graeco-Roman style, the hero smeared oil over his body but was surprised to see his rival covering himself in sand. This helped Hercules grab hold of the king and bring him to the ground, yet when he did this, Hercules was even more surprised to find that the limbs of his opponent showed 'explosive muscle growth', as many television adverts have since promised. Springing up again, Antaeus ran towards Hercules. Just in time, it dawned on Hercules, that as long as his adversary maintained contact with the earth, the giant's mother Gaea was giving him super-human strength. The oil-smeared hero then slipped from the grasp of Antaeus, and lifted the latter off the ground, snapping his spine in the process. According to Herodotus, on his way back to Mycenae via Egypt, Hercules took even greater revenge on Antaeus by slaying his brother King Busiris, who had been sacrificing travellers to Zeus.

Yet another slight twist to this legend is that on his way to the Hesperides, the hero spotted a lovely young woman sleeping in the sun. The problem was, as is so often the way in these cases, that the woman, called Tinge, was already married. In fact she was Antaeus' wife. Antaeus found Hercules ogling his wife and challenged him to a duel. Once Hercules had crushed the giant to death, he buried him at the exact spot where Tangier stands today. Antaeus was the god of losers, which is perhaps appropriate given that the city has been a haven for many washed-up people ever since. Some say Hercules went on to marry Tinge and they had a child named Sophax, who founded the city of Tinge in honour of his mother. The city has, at various points in history had many names: Tinge, Tingis, Tingi, Titga, Tandja, Tanger and Tangier. Some researchers have suggested that the name Tinga, which is engraved on Phoenician coins, had Berber origins as 'Tin Ga' which means heights, so Tangier is really another word for 'high town.' Indeed, later visitors may have interpreted the meaning of 'high town' in another sense.

One way or another, Hercules completed his eleventh labour, and so after many a summer, Eurystheus gained the famed apples. Thus, Hercules was ready for his final official chore, capturing and bringing back Cerberus, the Hound of Hell. When Hercules brought the creature to the king, Eurystheus, who was a bit of a weakling, was so scared that he ordered Hercules to take the dog back to the Underworld. All that is of course another story, but the apples did not stay long with Eurystheus either. Athena declared that they were too sacred to be part of this shabby, transient world and took them back to the fairyland of the Hesperides. Humans have been looking for the secret of eternal youth ever since.

That is in any case the generally accepted version of the story in Greek mythology, but the Roman writers tell it differently. According to Seneca and Pliny, while Hercules was on the way to the garden, he had to cross a mountain that had once been Atlas. This situation came about because Hercules' great-grandfather, Perseus had defeated Atlas by showing him the head of the Gorgon, whom he had killed. Atlas was so stunned that he immediately became petrified and was transformed into a mountain, his hair a forest and his shoulders cliffs.

So the demigod found that his way was blocked by this immoveable object, but as Seneca noted in *Hercules Furens* (*The Madness of Hercules*): 'He will find a way or make one.' Instead of climbing or trekking over the mountain as you or I might do, depending on our fitness levels, Hercules used a mace and his superhuman strength to smash his way through it, splitting the mountain in half. In doing so, the hero rent asunder the continents of Europe and Africa and connected the Atlantic with the Mediterranean. One section of this ruptured mountain was the Rock of Gibraltar and the other was *Jebel Musa* (the Mountain of

Moses), east of Tangier. Thus, were the Pillars of Hercules and the Strait of Gibraltar created.

Writing around 50 BC however, the Greek historian, Diodorus of Sicily, dismissed this theory of the continents being split apart as palpable nonsense. Diodorus maintained that there was already an existing wider strait. It was just that Hercules squeezed the mountains slightly nearer to each other, which made the waterway narrower and stopped Atlantic monsters from entering the Mediterranean. Obviously.

For a long time it was believed that the Caves of Hercules were actually bottomless and formed one end of a mysterious subterranean Ley tunnel that stretched for 15 miles before finally emerging at St Michael's Cave in Gibraltar. The story goes that the Barbary macaques that steal your crisps at the top of the Rock of Gibraltar came there from Morocco via this tunnel, just as nowadays people pop up in Dover from Calais, via the Eurotunnel.

Around 500 BC the geographer Scylax of Caryanda wrote that the waters between Africa and Europe were very shallow and contained two islands, upon which were built an altar and a temple in honour of Hercules. These islands then disappeared at the time of the Roman Empire, although the Greek historian Strabo claimed that two large sand bars could still be found between the two continents.

In a bizarre twist, the Caves of Hercules entered the *Guinness Book of Records* on 23 October 1995, when the heavy metal band Def Leppard performed inside. They had set themselves a Herculean task. Playing that same day in London and Vancouver, they became the first rock group to perform three concerts on three continents in 24 hours. It is a record that still stands. Inside the grotto, they performed some of their own hits as well as a cover version of The Rolling Stones' 'You Can't Always Get What You Want' – something they came to appreciate at first hand. The start of the show was delayed by half an hour because of a power cut, prompting the band's lead singer, Joe Elliott, to introduce the gig with the words: 'Sorry about the delay folks, someone forgot to put a shilling in the meter.'

TWO

Quintus Sertorius

He forced to a surrender the city of Tingis

The *Rue des Siaghines*, or Silversmith's Street, leads from the Grand Socco down towards the sea. It is lined with cafés, bars and shops selling unconvincing trinkets and kitsch souvenirs. It seems to have always been a busy market street. In 1893 an English traveller, A.J. Weston, described its atmosphere.

> There are shoppers and merchants, sight-seers and idlers, buying, selling, walking, riding, working, loafing. Burnooses . . . and gabardine – sashes, turbans, fezes, cowls and skull caps – the red, yellow, blue, white, apple-green and purple of the various garments softly blending or sharply contrasting with the bronze, mahogany or yellow complexions of the moving throng.

It was once, at the time of the Roman Empire, the *Decumanus Maximus*, the main thoroughfare that connected the centre of the city to the harbour. Being supremely well organised, the Romans arranged their cities around such an east-west orientated road and another perpendicular axis, the *Cardo Maximus*, from north to south. At the intersection of these two, they placed the Forum, or market place; probably where the Petit Socco lies today.

As it descends, the *Rue des Siaghines* turns into the *Rue de la Marine* and here on your right is the Grand Mosque Mohammed V. This large building, topped with green roof tiles and white minaret, is actually newer than it looks (nothing in Tangier is quite what it seems). The mosque was erected in 1977, but sits on the site of a Portuguese cathedral, which in turn lies above a Roman temple. Otmane remembered that it was called the *Campo de Romanos* and that he and his friends would play football here, using chunks of Roman columns as impromptu goalposts.

Much of Tangier's history is a chronology of foreigners and exiles. Nearly 3,000 years ago the Phoenicians set up trading colonies on the coast and ever since, the local inhabitants have, much to their bemusement seen waves of successive civilizations come and go, imposing their lifestyles upon them. Carthaginians, Romans, Vandals, Byzantines, Arabs, Portuguese, British, Spanish and French have all occupied the region in their time.

It is thought that the Phoenician port came under Roman rule following the destruction of Carthage in 146 BC. 'The Phoenicians settled in Tangier,' the local historian Rachid Tafersiti told me, 'but they were not warriors. They negotiated with the natives. But the Romans, no, they colonised, occupied and protected Tangier with their walls. We know the ramparts of the city have their origins in the Roman era.' The Romans adapted the town's name from the Berber Tinga. Later, Tingis grew in importance first as a free city under the Emperor Augustus and then as a colony, called *Colonia Iulia Tingi*, under Claudius, who made it the capital of Mauritania Tingitana.

Near the Café Hafa on the Marshan is an empty patch of overgrown lawn which has as a backdrop the ramparts of the Kasbah and various multicoloured tumbledown houses. The roof terraces of these are cluttered with washing lines and satellite dishes. To the left is a rocky promontory facing the sea. Here, Moroccan families sit in the long grass and wild flowers to admire the view. Some dream their Tangerine dreams of one day getting to Europe, which looks so tantalizingly within reach. This plateau, called the *Gharsa Ghanam*, has been walked upon for centuries and polished smooth underfoot. Here, about two dozen oblong shapes are indented in the rock, some of them filled with stagnant water, sweet wrappers and cigarette butts. In all, 98 Phoenician graves were discovered in archaeological digs that began in 1910.

The Phoenicians arrived in North Africa at the beginning of the first millennium BC and remained there until the second century BC.

Carthage emerged as the largest of the Phoenician colonies. By 500 BC the city of Dido and Hannibal became the richest metropolis the Mediterranean had ever seen. Carthage's maritime empire lasted for nearly four centuries – longer than the land empire of Alexander the Great.

The downfall of Carthage can be traced back to a strangely symbolic act involving clothing and fruit. When the elder Cato visited Africa in 153 BC he was struck by the fecundity of Carthaginian agriculture, as Plutarch wrote.

Cato, the famous Roman orator, shook out the folds of his toga and contrived to drop some African figs on the floor of the Senate. When the senators admired their size and beauty, he remarked that the country which produced them was only three days' sail from Rome.

By revealing the figs from his toga, Cato inspired his fellow senators with an insatiable lust for the wealth of Carthage. 'Delenda est Carthago,' Cato proclaimed. 'Carthage must be destroyed' became Rome's death sentence on one of the greatest ancient empires. When the city finally surrendered in 146 BC, its centre was levelled and 50,000 traumatised citizens were enslaved. We know very little about Carthaginian civilization today, and that is exactly what the Romans wanted. 'Great Carthage drove three wars,' wrote Bertolt Brecht, 'After the first one it was still powerful. After the second one it was still inhabitable. After the third one it was no longer possible to find her.'

Otmane and I took a stroll up to the Marshan along the Avenue Ibn Al Abbar, which used to be called the Paseo del Doctor Cenarro, after a Spanish philanthropist. Dr Severo Cenarro founded the Spanish Hospital where he battled against a cholera outbreak in 1895. The doctor himself lies buried near the Grand Socco on the edge of the Mendoubia gardens. When we saw his tomb, someone, perhaps unaware of his philanthropy, had vandalised it. Red paint had been splashed onto his marble portrait, as if, like Oedipus, he was bleeding from his eyes.

On the left of the Avenue Ibn Al Abbar, across the road from the Institut Pasteur, we found a rectangular area sunk into the ground and framed by a white concrete border. These are the remains of Roman tombs, some of the very few visible signs of that civilization in the city itself. 'Whatever remains of Tingis,' remarks Ethel Davies in *North Africa: The Roman Coast*, 'is hidden under 1,600 years of subsequent living.'

A French archaeologist, Maurice Euzennat, believed that the outer limits of the ancient Roman settlement could be traced according to the remains of such necropolises. These are to the northwest on the Marshan, to the west at the Mendoubia and to the south at Bou Kachkach. There were also some baths underneath the Kasbah and the confused remains of a monument, probably a basilica, had been uncovered in the *Rue de Belgique*. 'Among the few antiquities that have been discovered,' Euzennat concluded, 'the only noteworthy finds, aside from inscriptions and a few mosaic fragments, are a statue of a woman of indifferent workmanship and a mutilated head of the emperor Galba.'

There certainly was not a lot to see here in the Marshan; just worn stone blocks partially covered in grass. To add insult to injury, someone had splashed red paint on some of the stones, so that they too suffered the same fate as poor Doctor Cenarro. The authorities in Tangier had not done much to protect the site nor provided any information signs for visitors. Otmane told me there are probably more ruins lurking beneath the adjoining houses, but that there is no political appetite for further excavation. 'For Moroccans, history starts with the Islamic era,' he murmured.

There are however more interesting relics in the Kasbah Museum, inside the palace of Sultan Moulay Ismail, Dar el-Makhzen. Among the artefacts is an astonishingly beautiful head of Bacchus, discovered in the Marshan cemetery. There is also a bronze cauldron handle, an ostrich egg lit up in its cabinet like a full moon, a bust of Eros, a Winged Victory and a mosaic of Venus from Volubilis. There was also a cracked amphora from around AD 300. Nothing unusual about that you might think, until you read the inscription, which explains that a small child was, and still is, buried inside. It was common practice in Roman times to bury dead babies in this way. Particularly small containers, shaped like a uterus, were used for perinatal infants. The neck of the jug was broken off and then replaced after the baby was placed inside. This unbelievably sad relic was dug up at Cotta near the Caves of Hercules.

It is difficult to visualise Roman Tangier since it lies buried like a sleeping corpse beneath layers of later civilizations. To have a better view you would perhaps need to be a flying alien with X-ray vision. Instead, we took a day trip outside the city to see Morocco's oldest and largest Roman ruins at Lixus, about 50 miles further south. This is, after Volubilis, the most important Roman site in the country.

As we had done for our trip to the Caves of Hercules, Otmane negotiated the fare for a grand taxi near St Andrew's Church. This time we hired an upright, modern Fiat, which resembled a Popemobile. It was less romantic than a Mercedes but a lot more comfortable. We drove through the southern districts of Tangier, which Otmane explained were, until the 1960s, just fields. On the outskirts of the city, near the airport, lay a new sports complex and an enormous football stadium; a testament to the Tangerine obsession with 'futbol', 'La Liga' and 'El Clasico' (games between Barcelona and Real Madrid). Our journey took us though the Diplomatic Forest along the route national N1 towards Asilah. 'C'est dégueulasse!' Otmane muttered as a new development of apartment blocks flashed past us. He would point out other blocks that looked equally incongruous, as if they had been dropped from a great height onto the earth. 'We have a saying in Arabic,' Otmane added, 'that things that are not put in the right place, are like a nose on a face.'

We drove past Tahaddart Beach where a narrow bridge scaled the river of the same name, marking the outermost limits of the old International Zone. On the banks of the estuary, gangly anglers waved long fishing rods above their heads like antennae. A group of camels looked at them with the air of insouciance through which they seem to have regarded mankind since the dawn of time.

The road between Tangier and Larache used to be a Roman road. It stretched on, bordered by yellow flowers and green hills as perfectly rounded as those from the *Teletubbies*. Clouds swirled above the horizon like inverted commas or intricate Arabic calligraphy. Every now and then, a minaret from a mosque would peep out from the folds of the hills. We passed a small town. Like so many here it was made of brown breeze blocks with crates of Coke stacked outside the shops and signs for *La Vache Qui Rit* cheese. Construction was also underway for a new superfast TGV railway that now whizzes people from Tangier to Casablanca in just two hours (it used to take about five).

Before we reached Asilah, I saw an abandoned *complex touristique* where soulless apartment blocks huddled around an empty swimming pool like thirsty giants. Otmane informed me that in the 1980s many blocks like this were built by money-laundering drug barons. The traffickers were eventually put in jail, but their strange legacy of half-built construction sites remains. Now that the north of Morocco has been embraced by King Mohammed VI, the drug barons have been brought into line.

In Asilah we stopped for a coffee at an old establishment by the sea called Café Zrirak (it means 'a little blue'). Pestered by feral kittens, we sat on wicker chairs at a little blue table beneath a corrugated iron roof festooned with fishing nets and red buoys. It was a slightly subaqueous experience and I half expected to be served drinks by a mermaid. 'They have all the time in the world,' Otmane remarked of the old men playing dominoes and smoking pipes or *sebsis* at the tables next to us. Outside the Zrirak was an old car for sale. 'Happiness,' the sign on the rear windscreen informed us philosophically, 'is owning a Renault 4.'

About two miles before Larache, we turned off the main road and arrived at Lixus, nestling above the River Loukos which snakes through a flat salt marsh towards the sea. It was here, legend has it, that Hercules came to steal the golden apples. Both the Roman philosopher Pliny the Elder and the Greek geographer Strabo say that on an island in the estuary Antaeus had a palace, behind which stretched the famous garden. Perhaps the golden apples were in fact Moroccan tangerines expanded in the minds of travellers and subsequently raised to legendary status.

We do not know how old Lixus is. Megalithic stones and flint tools found here hint at prehistoric origins. The Romans believed the town existed before Byblos, around 5,000 BC. The earliest mention of Lixus or Lixos is in a fourth-century BC manuscript known as a *periplus* that charts a clockwise circumnavigation of the Mediterranean, by the Greek writer Pseudo-Scylax, who said it was a Phoenician settlement. A century later the Carthaginian explorer, Hanno the Navigator, referred to a river named Lixos and the local inhabitants as Lixites. Pliny the Elder said Lixus dated back to the twelfth century BC. Archaeological research in the 1950s supports Pliny and suggests that there was a temple dedicated to Hercules (the Phoenicians called him Melkarth) here in the twelfth century. Shards of red pottery from the eighth and seventh centuries BC show that the Phoenician city occupied a large part of the acropolis, but no Phoenician architecture remains.

Greek vases and bronzes from Cyprus were found there, showing how Lixus traded with other cultures. Ancient carvings of grapes and tuna suggest that wine production and fishing were the main sources of income. Inscriptions on Roman coins from Lixus also show that the Romanization of the city began in the first century BC. But it was only in AD 42, during the reign of the Emperor Claudius, that Lixus officially became a colony of the Romans. They called it the Eternal City.

Lixus thrived under the kings of Mauretania, Juba II and his son Ptolemy. When the latter was assassinated by Caligula in AD 40, the city was swallowed up into the larger Roman province of Mauretania Tingitana, ruled from Tingis.

Lixus was a vast industrial complex, of about 150 acres, thought to be the largest and most important in the Mediterranean. Here the Romans built public monuments, such as temples, an amphitheatre and baths decorated with frescoes and mosaics. But by the fourth century, the fortunes of Lixus began to fade. In the fifth century, 200 years after Diocletian had withdrawn the empire's administration from the region, it was finally abandoned.

Nevertheless Arab texts say that a city called Tuchummus later established itself on the ruins of the ancient city and Arabic coins have been excavated here. When the Arabs arrived, they called it Shimish (the sun) and their queen was called Shimisa (little sun). Today, you can still see the remains of an ancient mosque, which now looks more like a garden patio, shaded by three olive trees and pointing east towards Mecca.

Each civilization has made their mark on this sunny hilltop and turned it towards their gods. The Romans built their temples on top of earlier ruins which were orientated towards the sun. The Phoenicians called it Makom Shemesh (City of the Sun). The Phoenicians believed in the supreme God El, the sun and the king of the west, who was married to Asherat, the mother of earth and the queen of the sea. As you watch the sun set on the Atlantic you can follow the benign El as he sinks into his wife Asherat.

Accompanied by a local guide whose English was virtually incomprehensible (he kept saying 'ADD' instead of AD), Otmane and I made our way up from the entrance site at the side of the road. Here we could see a honeycomb of oblong stone pits. These are the remains of factories that produced salt, as well as a strange rancid sauce, called *Garum*, made from the tuna which flap about on Lixus' coins. The factories were built in the first century AD and remained until the Romans left.

We walked up a track about a hundred yards long that leads to the acropolis, via the theatre and amphitheatre which was adapted for gladiator fights. The audience was protected from the animals by four-metre high walls. Morocco, 'the wild beast country' as Herodotus called it, was the major source of animals for circus games.

Built into the side of the theatre are the remains of a public bath from the third century AD. Until 1998, the floor of the *tepidarium*, or warm room, featured a famous mosaic depicting the head of the sea god Oceanus on the body of a lobster. It was irreparably damaged when the son of one of the site's guards tried to dig it up and sell it.

We climbed above the theatre and passed through ramparts to the main fortifications of the acropolis; a network of walls, foundations, villas and temple sanctuaries. The largest of these had underground cisterns and priests' quarters. In the villas, mosaics were discovered depicting Helios, Mars and Rhea and the Three Graces, as well as Venus and Adonis, but they are all now housed in the archaeological museum in Tetouan, to prevent them suffering a similar fate to Oceanus. The ruins of the temple span more than a thousand years and the separate parts are difficult to disentangle. Excavations have unearthed the forum and the temple of Melkarth, where the god was served by barefoot priests, who would construct a fire around the altar.

Besides the Garden of the Hesperides, there is another story about Lixus. It was said that the Roman commander Quintus Sertorius uncovered the tomb of Hercules' adversary, Antaeus here. In his *Lives*,

Plutarch tells us that once Sertorius sailed from Spain to North Africa, the residents of Tingis told him where the burial site was.

> In this city the Libyans (Africans) say that Antaeus is buried; and Sertorius had his tomb dug open, the great size of which made him disbelieve the Barbarians. But when he came upon the body and found it to be sixty cubits (feet) long, as they tell us, he was dumb-founded, and after performing a sacrifice filled up the tomb again, and joined in magnifying its traditions and honours.

There has however been further speculation about the resting place of Antaeus. 'His magnifying,' writes the classicist Robin Lane Fox, 'did not stop a subsequent dispute. Some of our sources placed the actual find on the west coast of Morocco near Lixus. Others made Tingis the site both of the grave and the initial information.'

Lane Fox believes that neither Sertorius nor the locals were fantasizing about the size of the skeleton, which may have actually been the bones of extinct prehistoric beasts such as Neogene elephants, mammoths or giant giraffidae, all of which have been discovered in Morocco. Plutarch writes that Sertorius found Antaeus' tomb on a 'high hill' which today's Tangerines believe is the one known as the Charf. Writing in AD 43, the Roman geographer Pomponius Mela described an enormous round shield made out of elephant hide that Antaeus is said to have carried.

Quintus Sertorius was a Roman statesman and general who defied the Senate to become the independent ruler of Spain for eight years. There are not many people in history who have a war named after them (the Sertorian War). He was also the de-facto governor of Roman Tangier. There was something else quite distinctive about him. 'The most warlike of generals,' says Plutarch, 'and those who achieved most by a mixture of craft and ability, have been one-eyed men – Philip, Antigonus, Hannibal and the subject of this Life, Sertorius.'

He was born in 123 BC in the town of Nursia in Umbria. His family was of Sabine origin and 'of some prominence.' His father died while he was very young and he was brought up by his mother, Rhea.

In Rome, Sertorius built up a reputation as a jurist and an orator before embarking on a glittering military career, fighting in Gaul against the Cimbri and Teutons, Germanic tribes who had invaded the province in 105 BC. The first Roman army sent out against them was heavily defeated. At the battle of Arausio, Sertorius lost his horse and was wounded but managed to swim to safety across the Rhone. When another army was dispatched under the consul Gaius Marius in 102 BC, Sertorius volunteered to go in disguise, mingling among the enemy as a spy – 'putting on a Celtic dress and acquiring the commonest expressions of that language' – according to Plutarch. His mission was successful and Marius promoted him. After this he fought at the battle of *Aquae Sextiae* (Aix-en-Provence) in which the Romans crushed the Teutons.

In 97 BC, Sertorius served as a military tribune in Spain, winning an honour known as the Grass Crown. He became famous for recapturing the city of Castulo on the same night that it had been taken from an inebriated Roman garrison.

When Sertorius returned to Rome he was elected as a public official or *quaestor* and served in Cisalpine Gaul (in northern Italy) in 91 BC. At this time a row was brewing over whether Rome should grant citizenship to its allies. The row escalated into a full-scale conflict, known as the Social War (91-88 BC) between Rome and other Italian cities. It was at this time, Plutarch writes, that Sertorius was injured again.

He displayed astonishing deeds of prowess and exposed his person unsparingly in battle, in consequence of which he got a blow that cost him one of his eyes. But on this he actually prided himself at all times . . . the marks of his bravery remained with him, and when men saw what he had lost, they saw at the same time a proof of his valour.

In Rome, he stood for election as a tribune, but was thwarted by the Roman general and later dictator, Lucius Cornelius Sulla. This caused a longstanding enmity between them.

No sooner had the Social War come to an end than another one erupted. The Civil War of 88-7 BC broke out between a faction supporting Sulla and another backing Marius. Sertorius supported the latter. This turned out to be a poor decision, as Marius lost and was forced into exile.

Violence then erupted between Sulla's men and the revolutionary *Populares*, led by Lucius Cornelius Cinna. Sertorius declared his allegiance to Cinna. When Marius returned from exile to join Cinna's forces, they divided their army into three sections commanded by Cinna, Marius and Sertorius and laid siege to Rome. In what became known as the Reign of Terror, Sertorius is said to have done his best to moderate the others' lust for vengeance. 'Sertorius alone,' writes Plutarch, 'neither killed anyone to gratify his anger, nor waxed insolent with victory.'

When Sulla came back from fighting in Anatolia in 82 BC, another series of clashes ensued. Sertorius decided that backing the anti-Sullan forces was hopeless and he left Rome. He made his way to Spain to take up the post of *praetor* and formed an alternative power base representing the *Populares*. He won the local population over, but Sulla sent Caius Annius to Spain to pursue the renegade commander. Annius advanced with his troops across the Pyrenees, scattering all those who stood in their way.

It was at this point that Sertorius abandoned Spain and sailed to North Africa. His fleet was attacked while stopping to refill its water supplies and Sertorius tried to return to Spain. After a sea battle with Annius, Sertorius retreated to the Canary Islands. As many an expat has done since, Sertorius would have been quite happy to settle here but got embroiled in yet another conflict. Pirates who had been helping him, sailed off to Mauretania where they hoped to restore a local prince, Ascalis, to the throne.

> Sertorius did not despair, but resolved to go to the aid of those who were fighting against Ascalis . . . The *Maurusians* (Moors) were glad to have him come, and he set himself to work, defeated Ascalis in battle and laid siege to him. Moreover, when Sulla sent out Paccianus with an army to give aid to Ascalis, Sertorius joined battle against Paccianus and slew him, won over his soldiers after their defeat, and forced to a surrender the city of Tingis, into which Ascalis and his brethren had fled for refuge.

Unfortunately we know little about Sertorius' time in Tingis, but Plutarch tells us that he was well liked by the local population.

Sertorius, then, having made himself master of the whole country, did no wrong to those who were his suppliants and put their trust in him, but restored to them property, cities and government, receiving only what was right and fair in free gifts from them.

After this the Lusitanians (who occupied modern Portugal and western Spain) were so impressed by Sertorius' capture of Tingis that they sent ambassadors asking him if he could lead their struggle against the occupying Roman forces. So, in 80 BC Sertorius crossed the straits to Spain again, with 2,600 Roman and 700 North African soldiers. These forces were later increased. The Lusitanians admired his bravery and called him the 'new Hannibal.' Another of Sertorius' hallmarks was a white pet fawn. This was a gift from a local peasant, but Sertorius said it came from someone else.

In time, after he had made the animal so tame and gentle that it obeyed his call, accompanied him on his walks, and did not mind the crowds and all the uproar of camp life, he gradually tried to give the doe a religious importance by declaring that she was a gift of Diana and solemnly alleged that she revealed many hidden things to him, knowing that the Barbarians were naturally an easy prey to superstition. Whenever he had secret intelligence that the enemy had made an incursion into the territory which he commanded, or were trying to bring a city to revolt from him, he would pretend that the doe had conversed with him in his dreams . . . They believed that they were led, not by the mortal wisdom of a foreigner, but by a god.

By introducing Roman weapons and tactics, Sertorius, who by now commanded about 8,000 men, managed to hold off around 130,000 Roman soldiers. In an unusual demonstration, he pointed out that small forces could defeat larger enemies.

He called a general assembly and introduced before it two horses, one utterly weak and already quite old, the other large-sized and strong, with a tail that was astonishing for the thickness and beauty of its hair. By the side of the feeble horse stood a man who was tall and robust, and by the side of the powerful horse another man, small and of a contemptible appearance. At a signal given them, the strong man seized the tail of his horse with both hands and tried to pull it towards him with all his might, as though he would tear if off; but the weak man began to pluck out the hairs in the tail of the strong horse one by one. The strong man gave himself no end of trouble to no purpose, made the spectators laugh a good deal, and then gave up his attempt; but the weak man, in a trice and with no trouble, stripped his horse's tail of its hair. Then Sertorius rose up and said: "Ye see, men of my allies, that perseverance is more efficacious than violence, and that many things which cannot be mastered when they stand together yield when one masters them little by little."

Sertorius had an early understanding of what modern-day occupying forces call 'winning hearts and minds.' He was said to be strict and severe with his soldiers, but considerate towards the local population. He provided a school for the children of native families. He was also very cunning. While besieging the people known as the Characitani, who lived in caves in the mountains, he ordered his men to build a mound of earth opposite the entrance to their dwellings. When the wind blew into the caves, the Characitani were choked and blinded by the dust.

At the time, Roman Spain was divided into two provinces: Hispania Ulterior and Hispania Citerior (Further and Nearer Spain). Sertorius defeated the governors of both. Quintus Caecilius Metellus was sent out from Rome against Sertorius in 79 BC, but Metellus' conventional tactics proved useless against Sertorius' guerilla warfare. When Metellus failed to defeat Sertorius, Sulla sent out another heavyweight to try to conquer its troublesome foe in Spain. Gnaeus Pompeius Magnus, better known as Pompey, was one of the greatest Roman commanders and statesmen, but he too was to struggle against Sertorius who contemptuously called him 'Sulla's pupil.'

Sertorius managed to trick the great Pompey at the battle of Lauron. He seized a hill which had a good view of the city. Pompey approached, in Plutarch's words, 'believing that Sertorius was caught between the

city and his adversary's forces.' But Sertorius, shouting out that a
general must look behind him rather than in front, pointed to 6,000
men whom he had left behind at the camp. Pompey was surrounded
and the people of Lauron surrendered to Sertorius, who let them go,
but burned down their city. In one incident during the siege, one of
Sertorius' men tried to rape a local woman. When Sertorius heard what
had happened he had the whole cohort (about 500 soldiers) executed.

Sertorius very nearly captured Pompey himself at the battle of
Sucro. The latter only escaped because Sertorius' North African troops
had started fighting amongst themselves over the gold ornaments
worn by Pompey's horse.

When fighting stopped for the winter, Pompey wrote to Rome
asking for reinforcements. Without these, he said, he and Metellus
would be driven out of Spain. Metellus even offered a reward for
anyone who killed Sertorius. This was seen as an admission that
Sertorius could not be defeated by conventional means.

Sertorius offered to lay down his arms and return home if he was
allowed to go quietly and live out the rest of his life in peace. As
Plutarch writes: 'he said he preferred to live in Rome as her meanest
citizen rather than to live in exile from his country and be called
supreme ruler of all the rest of the world together.' The proposal was
rejected.

By 74 BC, the tide was turning against him. Pompey was gaining
the upper hand and began to capture city after city. Sertorius was not
only losing the war but also losing his tactical acumen and, like many
a Tangerine after him, he descended into drunkenness and debauchery.
The morale of the Iberians declined and Sertorius' authority was on
the wane.

Those Roman commanders who had supported Sertorius in the war
went on to become 'seized with envy and foolish jealousy of their
leader.' The general Marcus Perpenna Vento, together with men by the
name of Manlius, Aufidius, Gracinus and Antonius, plotted to kill
Sertorius in an assassination that prefigured that of Julius Caesar. In a
very Tangier twist, both Manlius and Aufidius were 'enamoured of a
beautiful boy.' Things came to a head in 72 BC, when Perpenna
invited Sertorius to a banquet.

But when Perpenna, after taking a cup of wine in his hands, dropped it as he was drinking and made a clatter with it, which was their signal, Antonius, who reclined above Sertorius on the couch, smote him with his sword. Sertorius turned at the blow and would have risen with his assailant, but Antonius fell upon his chest and seized both his hands, so that he could make no defence even, and died from the blows of many.

Just as Caesar's treacherous killing was dramatised by Shakespeare, the death of Sertorius was embellished by Pierre Corneille in his tragedy of the same name and performed in Paris in 1662. In a very French way, Corneille added additional romantic interest by placing Sertorius in a complicated love triangle.

At the time of his death, Sertorius was on the verge of successfully establishing an independent Roman republic in Spain, but it crumbled under the onslaught of Pompey and Metellus, who eliminated the remaining opposition.

For nearly 600 years the Romans governed northwest Africa. The region consisted of ancient Mauretania, east Mauretania and Numidia (northern Algeria) and Africa Proconsularis (Tunisia). A land that they had conquered almost inadvertently became their most profitable acquisition. Although they controlled less than 140,000 square miles, the territory contributed far more to the agricultural wealth of the Roman Empire than anywhere else. At the height of its prosperity, during the second and third centuries AD, northwest Africa was the granary of Rome and produced more olive oil than the whole of Italy. Throughout the region the Roman genius for building was readily apparent. They constructed 12,000 miles of roads and hundreds of aqueducts in North Africa, most of which can still be seen today.

But the Romans, as later occupiers would find, were often led astray by the seductions of Tangier and beyond, as the American historian Susan Raven explained.

Traditional Roman honesty soon deserted its representatives abroad surrounded by the temptations offered by rich provincial cities; speculation and the worst forms of usury were to become so

commonplace, that even a man like Cicero did not hesitate to line
his pockets with a fortune.

The Emperor Claudius changed the kingdom into two provinces:
Mauretania Tingitana and Mauretania Caesariensis (Algeria). Most
Roman historians considered all of Morocco north of the Atlas Mountains
part of the Roman Empire, but some, like Leo Africanus, believed that
the Roman frontier reached as far as modern day Casablanca, founded
by the Romans as a port named Anfa.

Roman legionary fortresses were model towns; the streets ran at
right angles and the buildings were orderly and precise; in the words
of Raven, 'the typical geometric pattern following the logic of set-
square and ruler.' As in Lixus, the Romans usually built fortresses,
camps and veterans' towns on rising ground overlooking a plain.
Looking at the view across the wide plains from Lixus, it is difficult to
believe that this was a purely pragmatic choice and not an aesthetic
one.

There were four kinds of city in Roman North Africa. Firstly, there
were the old Phoenician coastal towns, which were cosmopolitan and
had large immigrant populations. Tingis was one of them. Secondly,
there were old native settlements such as Volubilis and then there
were purpose-built Roman veterans' colonies. Finally, there were market
towns of the interior, which grew organically out of native hamlets
and villages. By the third century, there were 500-600 cities. The
inhabitants built their towns of stone and embellished them with
temples, forums and public baths, whilst arches, tombs, basilicas and
theatres were cut into the hillside.

By the second century AD, Rome was in terminal decline. Of the 26
Emperors who ruled from AD 235 to AD 284, only one had died a
natural death. By the end of the third century the Romans finally
withdrew from the far west, leaving Mauretania Tingitana to be
governed by local chieftains. The remaining Roman province, a small
area around Tingis, was administered as part of Spain.

Mauretania Tingitana continued to be a part of the Roman Empire
until AD 429, when the Vandals overran the area and Rome's admin-
istrative control finally came to an end. The Vandals crossed the strait
of Gibraltar that year and occupied Tingis in 425. From there they

swept across North Africa. It is hard not to think of the Vandals in slightly comic book terms. They would hardly have been heard of by most people today if their name had not been resurrected by an eighteenth-century bishop in central France to form the French word *vandalisme*. 'The bishop's coinage gave it a wider currency,' wrote Raven 'and saddled the Vandals with a reputation for whole-sale destructiveness which they hardly deserved.'

Certainly in Africa the Vandals did not live up to their name. They did not tear up the legacies of the Roman Empire. Instead they maintained Roman law, minted Roman coins, made Latin the official language, employed Roman architects and built baths, 'taking to the delights of civilization,' as Raven wrote, 'with Teutonic enthusiasm.' In fact, this hard-nosed Germanic tribe went soft and, foreshadowing other sybarites who would come to Tangier later, they had an absolute ball, as the Greek historian Procopius observed.

> The Vandals, since the time when they gained possession of Libya (Africa), used to indulge in baths, all of them, every day, and enjoyed a table abounding in all things, the sweetest and best that the earth and sea produce. And they wore gold very generally, and clothed themselves in garments of silk and passed their time, thus dressed, in theatres and hippodromes and in other pleasurable pursuits, and above all else in hunting. And they had dancers and mimes and all other things to hear and see which are of a musical nature or otherwise merit attention among men. And most of them dwelt in parks, which were well supplied with water and trees; and they had great numbers of banquets, and all manner of sexual pleasures were in great vogue among them.

'Their new wealth sapped their barbarian virtues,' wrote Raven, 'the fleshpots of Carthage . . . proved as enervating to their energies as King Gaiseric had feared, when he tried to close down the most notorious district of the great seaport.' The same was presumably true of Tingis, where fleshpots have never been too hard to come by.

When an Egyptian bishop told the Byzantine Emperor Justinian that Christ had appeared to him in a vision instructing the Emperor to reconquer Africa, Justinian took the omen seriously. So in AD 533, five hundred ships sailed from Constantinople under Count Belisarius. When Belisarius defeated the Vandal king Gelimer, the latter made a strange request. Procopius, who worked as Belisarius' secretary, said Gelimer asked for, 'a lyre, a loaf of bread and a sponge. He longed for freshly baked wheat bread; the sponge was for an inflamed eye and the lyre was to accompany an ode he had composed on his misfortunes.'

In the blink of a swollen eye, the Vandals lost their kingdom and disappeared without trace. Procopius noted that the Byzantines were also seduced by what was on offer in their new territory. They were, he said, 'becoming all of a sudden, masters of great wealth and of women both young and very comely.'

The first of the Arab invasions swept through northwest Africa in the seventh century, although Roman influence was only eliminated by the second wave, four centuries later. 'The Arabs found much to admire in their new conquest,' writes Raven at the end of her book.

They, like the Vandals, were delighted to enter into the Roman inheritance. Unlike the Vandals, they brought gifts of their own. Under them, Africa was to flourish anew, but not in the Roman way.

THREE

Ibn Battuta

Travelling — it leaves you speechless, then turns you into a storyteller

The airport at Tangier is a large beige box that looks as if it has just been dumped onto the tarmac from above, sitting on the runway like the object of a cargo cult. This box is supported by external steel cantilevers in the style of a football stadium. Inside is an airless void contained by slippery fake marble floors and polished concrete columns engraved with Berber patterns. Muzak is piped through to this charmless chamber to try to add atmosphere. It fails.

On one of my research trips in 2016, I flew into Tangier and took my place in the queue for security. 'They got quite a shock when they opened my suitcase,' the man behind me whispered, 'and found my *Playboy* magazines.' I was not sure how to reply. 'I think they were pleasantly surprised,' he added reassuringly.

I also heard of another incident at the airport customs involving Patrick Thursfield, a writer who retired to Tangier. He showed his passport to an eager young security official, whose expression quickly changed from routine boredom to uncontainable excitement. Without any explanation, Thursfield was whisked away to a private room, where he was stripped down to his underpants. The junior officer then called in the Head of Customs.

'I've got him!' he said proudly to his superior.

'Who?'

'The spy.'

The Head of Customs looked at Thursfield and then at his passport. There was an awkward silence. 'Please excuse me,' he said softly to Thursfield. He then turned to his underling, as if he were Basil Fawlty addressing Manuel and boxed his ears. 'Get out of the room you idiot!' he shouted, before apologizing to Thursfield. It transpired that the Englishman's passport number ended in 007 and the young Moroccan thought he had accosted James Bond.

In the arrivals hall ancient and redundant porters slump over trolleys, hypnotised by conveyor belts which slither slowly beneath pictures of Riffian warriors, wide-hatted peasant women and adverts for Maroc Telecom. Towards the exit is a café called 'Jetlaags' with a pink wall supporting a portrait of Mohammed VI, who sips mint tea thoughtfully.

The airport is named after one of Tangier's most famous citizens, Ibn Battuta. He has also bestowed his name upon the ferry from Spain, the football stadium, a square, a street and an insalubrious hotel.

Marco Polo was just 17 when he embarked on his travels in 1272. He was away from Italy for 23 years. The Venetian traveller died in 1324, just when a contemporary, Shams al-Din Abu Abdallah Muhammad b. Abdallah b. Ibrahim al-Luwati al-Tanji, better known as Ibn Battuta, was preparing to set out on his voyages of discovery. Over a period of nearly 30 years, the Tangerine visited most of the known Islamic world and beyond. His journeys covered Africa, Eastern Europe, the Middle East, South and Central Asia as well as the Far East. He is considered one of the greatest travellers of all time. His journeys inspired Daniel Defoe, who also visited Tangier, to write *Robinson Crusoe*.

Ibn Battuta was born in Tangier on 25 February 1304 during the Merenid dynasty and came from a family of Islamic legal scholars. Tangier had been an Arab city following their invasion of North Africa in the seventh century. The city itself had fallen to Musa bin Nusayr of the Umayyad Caliphate some time around 707. Very little is known about Ibn Battuta's early life in the city. We do know that he was of Berber descent, from the Lawatah people, who are descended from the Lebu, an ancient Berber tribe from which Libya derives its name. By the ninth century the Lawatah had settled in southwestern Morocco. After the coming of Islam, they conveniently claimed to be of Arab origin.

It is not easy to trace Battuta's family ancestry, but Tim Mackintosh-Smith, the author of *Travels with a Tangerine*, has attempted to do so.

> One theory explains 'Battutah' as a Maghribi diminutive of the Arabic *battah*, 'duck', and a pet version of the girl's name Fatimah. The notion that 'IB' should mean 'Son of the She-duckling' is charming enough to be plausible. But then so are the various other suggestions that have been put forward: Son of the Father of a Tassel/of an Egg-Shaped Bottle/of a Bad Woman with an Ellipsoid Body.

As a young man he would have studied at a Sunni Maliki jurisprudence school, the dominant form of education in North Africa at the time. He worked as a religious judge or *cadi* on many occasions. Lotfi Akalay is a Tangerine novelist and broadcaster who wrote a biography of Ibn Battuta. He agrees that we know hardly anything about Battuta's life in Tangier, but said that his writings reflect his urban background.

> He never mentions the countryside in the places he visited. He really is the product of the city. He is a true citizen. He talks about markets, monuments and mosques; never fields, forests or mountains. Tangier is an open city and Tangerines have always looked outwards. In this sense, Ibn Battuta is a typical Tangerine. Tangier is a town where people talk of elsewhere. There is a local saying: "Tangerines have one eye on the sea, one ear on the news and one buttock on the rocks."

I met Lotfi on the terrace of a café in the centre of town near the Cinema Roxy. When I asked what inspired him to write about the great traveller, he said it was 'by chance.' His French boss at Radio Medi1 had commissioned him to tell stories from Battuta's voyages on the airwaves every week, for eight months. 'I gave Moroccans the opportunity to get to know Ibn Battuta,' he said. Ibn Battuta was himself inspired by Ibn Jubayr, an Andalusian traveller, who made the journey to Mecca more than a century earlier.

> If you are a son of this Maghrib of ours and wish for success, then head for the land of the East! Forsake your homeland in pursuit of

knowledge . . . Seize the chance of freedom from the cares of the
world before family and children ensnare you, before the day comes
when you gnash your teeth in regret for the time that is gone.

So in 1325, at the tender age of 21, Ibn Battuta set off from Tangier
to Mecca. This journey would take him 16 months, but he would not
set eyes on Morocco again for 24 years.

I set out alone, having neither fellow-traveller in whose compan-
ionship I might find cheer, nor caravan whose part I might join, but
swayed by an overmastering impulse within me and a desire long-
cherished in my bosom to visit these illustrious sanctuaries. So I
braced my resolution to quit all my dear friends, female and male,
and forsook my home as birds forsake their nests.

'It is remarkable that he should speak of saying goodbye to female
and male friends,' Lotfi added.

Few Moroccans would put it in those words even today. Ibn Battuta
was a very modern man and in many ways the fourteenth century
was more enlightened than the twenty-first. He was not shocked by
anything. He told the sultan how different people in different countries made love and you wouldn't do that today.

Twenty-nine years after Ibn Battuta forsook his nest he settled down
again in Tangier, to a life of scholarly obscurity. He spent 44 per cent
of his life outside Morocco, visited the equivalent of 44 modern
nations and travelled more than 73,000 miles – about three times the
distance covered by Marco Polo. 'The Italian was not interested in
how people think. But Ibn Battuta was curious,' Lotfi said.

He wanted to know what was inside people's heads. Can you imagine
an American or a European coming over here today to find out
what Moroccans are thinking? Yet this is what he did. He listened
to people. He travelled more with his ears than with his eyes. He
wanted to know exactly what made Turks, Syrians and Africans tick.
That is what is unique about him. Not even Marco Polo did that.

As the British writer Barnaby Rogerson explains, what started off as a simple pilgrimage to Mecca would evolve into a massive, haphazard, globetrotting odyssey.

> His journeys, if traced on a map of the Middle East, look like a disordered cardiograph, as he whizzed backwards and forwards, seeking wisdom from scholars and employment from sultans, while continually allowing himself to be distracted by women, food, dervish mystics and an itching *wanderlust*.

Ibn Battuta wandered as far south as Tanzania, as far north as the Volga and as far east as Quanzhou in China. He did not reject his homeland, but saw Morocco as another point on the perimeter of a vast sphere of Islamic influence.

Just as Marco Polo recounted his tales to Rustichello in a Genoese jail, so 60 years later in 1356, Ibn Battuta related his adventures to the writer, theologian and poet, Muhammad Ibn Juzayy who acted as his editor, trying to convert a mass of information based on the explorer's memories into a coherent narrative. Like the writings of Herodotus, *The Travels* are quirky, amusing, colourful and unreliable. Just as the future founder of the BBC, Lord Reith, would recommend, Ibn Battuta wanted to inform, educate and entertain, but not necessarily in that order. To verify every detail of this written work would, as the scholar, Amikam Elad, points out, take the lifetimes of several researchers. *The Travels* are long; four volumes of 1,000 pages. The writings seem to mix fact with fiction, reportage with mysticism and offer the reader an early form of magical realism. They bring to life a medieval world bulging with marvels and mysteries. They do not reveal much about the traveller himself, except, as Mackintosh-Smith observes, that 'he had a beard . . . a soft heart, a big head, a huge libido.'

Ibn Battuta first travelled to Mecca by following the North African coast in modern day Algeria and then Tunis where he stayed for two months. He set off in the searing summer heat and was exposed to death, fever and homesickness. At one point he strapped himself into his saddle to stop himself falling to the ground in his fevered state. To avoid the risk of attacks by Bedouin, Ibn Battuta usually joined a caravan. He wed a girl in the town of Sfax about 170 miles south of Tunis, the first of his many marriages.

In the spring of 1326, after a journey of 2,200 miles, Ibn Battuta arrived at Alexandria. Here, the man who would have gazed lovingly at the Mediterranean from Tangier, quoted the long prayer known as the 'Litany of the Sea.'

Subject to us every sea that is Thine on earth and in heaven, in the world of sense and in the invisible world, the sea of this life and the sea of the life to come.

In the Egyptian port he encountered two ascetics who predicted his destiny. Sheikh Burhanuddin told him, 'You will visit my brothers Fariduddin in India, Rakunoddin in Sind and Burhanuddin in China. Convey my greetings to them.' Ibn Battuta then dreamt that he had been swept away on the wings of a giant bird that bore him first to Mecca, then Yemen and finally to distant Oriental lands before the bird abandoned him in some dark country. The second pious man, Sheikh Murshidi interpreted this to mean that Ibn Battuta was destined to be a world traveller.

You shall make the Pilgrimage to Mecca and you shall travel through the lands of Yemen and Iraq, the land of the Turks, and the land of India. You will stay there for a long time and you will meet there my brother Dilshad the Indian, who will rescue you from a danger into which you will fall.

East of Alexandria, Ibn Battuta visited the town of Damietta. Here, he heard the strange tales of the Jamal al-Din, who had gone there before him and lived in a cemetery. Originally from Persia, Jamal al-Din was the leader of a wandering Sufi dervish sect known as the Qalanders. Legend has it that a woman fell madly in love with Jamal al-Din. She asked him into her house where she tried to persuade the mystic to forsake his vow of chastity. Pretending that he was willing, Jamal al-Din first said he needed to go to the toilet, but when he emerged some time later having shaved off his beard, eyebrows and all other facial hair, the horrified hostess told him to leave. The Qalanders followed their master and shaved their beards, much to the outrage of a society in which beards were the norm. They also gave up other social norms including polite conversation.

From Alexandria, Ibn Battuta journeyed to Cairo where he stayed for a month before taking many detours within the Mamluk Sultanate, including the Nile Valley and the Red Sea, where he was forced to turn back by a local rebellion in which all the boats in the harbour had been destroyed. 'He had made the elementary mistake,' Mackintosh-Smith comments, 'of ignoring that inexorable tour operator, Fate.'

In the township of Minya on the outskirts of Cairo, Ibn Battuta entered a bathhouse where he noticed naked men. He complained to the local governor and a by-law was immediately introduced to prevent such a practice. Despite his love of the flesh, the Moroccan was actually somewhat prudish. Mackintosh-Smith says that the bathhouse was often a place for misbehaving, remarking that another ancient scholar, al-Jammaz, described having sex in the bath as one of the three greatest pleasures in life. The other two are 'pissing in a washing bowl and slapping a bald man on the pate.'

His second detour was from Cairo to Damascus. Near Damascus he visited several holy shrines. 'For many Muslims,' adds Mackintosh-Smith, 'tomb visiting is something to be done regularly, like changing the oil in a car: it ensures the smooth running of history.' One such tomb was the Cave of Hunger, where 70 prophets had died after taking refuge with only a loaf of bread between them. Each one, it is said, preferred not to take a bite, but passed the loaf to his neighbour, until they all died.

In Damascus, Ibn Battuta noted, the governor had removed all the frogs, as he could not bear their croaks. In northern Syria he visited several mountain fortresses. Some were out of bounds as they belonged to the dangerous eleventh-century Shia sect, the Nizaris, better known as the Assassins. Ibn Battuta called them the Arrows of the Sultan al-Nasir.

When he desires to send one of them to assassinate some foe of his, he pays him his blood money. If he escapes after carrying out the deed, the money is his, but if he is caught it goes to his children. They have poisoned knives with which they strike their victims.

The Assassins' infamous reputation spread to medieval Europe via the Crusaders. They told tales of how these killers were led by the mysterious Old Man of the Mountain, who sent them off on deadly missions under the influence of hashish (from which the word assassin derives). Like Al Qaeda or Islamic State, the Assassins would become the stuff of nightmares. Mackintosh-Smith notes this haunting effect on the Western psyche.

Their mountain territory was a semi-fictional world where the medieval imagination ran wild. Picture a plot by Frederick Forsyth, enacted by members of the Branch Davidians on drugs, then translated into troubadour Provencal and you will have a fair idea of how the Middle Ages viewed the Assassins.

For about two centuries, the Assassins specialised in contract killings. Sometimes the murders were conducted in broad daylight and in full view of the public to try to terrorise their enemies. But at other times the Assassins carried out covert operations. Sometimes they did not kill their targets, but preferred to threaten their foes, with a dagger and a note left under a pillow for example. Tales of the Assassins were further embellished by Marco Polo. Their legend lives on to this day, not least in the computer game, *Assassin's Creed*.

From Syria, the Tangerine left behind a pregnant wife and joined a caravan that took him 800 miles to Medina and from there to Mecca. The caravan passed through what was known as the Valley of Hell, travelling day and night in order to avoid the fate of many who had died of thirst in the hot, dry wind, the *Samum*. He saw an inscription on a rock recording an occasion when the wind had dried all the water sources, making the cost of a single mouthful of liquid 1,000 *dinars*, the last surviving vendor and buyer both perishing in the act of exchange. In Mecca, Ibn Battuta was particularly taken by the women.

They are of rare and surpassing beauty, pious and chaste. They too, like the men, make much use of perfumes, to such a degree that a woman will spend the night hungry and buy perfume with the price of her food.

Ibn Battuta left Mecca in November 1326. By now the travel bug had truly set in, so, instead of returning to Tangier, he headed north, joining a group of pilgrims going back to Baghdad via a circuitous route that included parts of modern-day Iran. In Basra, he climbed the minaret of the large mosque having heard that one of them would tremble whenever the name of Ali, the prophet's cousin and son-in-law was mentioned. Ibn Battuta repeated the ritual but called out the name of Abu Bakr, the first Caliph, since Basra was a Sunni town. The minaret did indeed tremble.

Ibn Battuta was almost like a modern-day anthropologist but for him travel was also a spiritual journey. What drove him on was the desire to achieve blessing or *baraka* from proximity to the saints, dead or alive. 'IB was intrigued by the world beyond the senses and by the holy men who could look into it,' Mackintosh-Smith says. 'In his day there were a lot of them about and a disproportionate number of holy men came from the Maghrib . . . IB was surfing a wave of sanctity.'

In Baghdad in 1327, Ibn Battuta joined the royal retinue of the Mongol ruler Abu Said before turning north along the Silk Road to Tabriz and Mosul where he was the guest of the Ilkhanate governor. In Mosul, he joined another feeder caravan heading to Baghdad and then on to Mecca for his second pilgrimage. Although there is confusion as to how long he stayed in Mecca, he later made his way to the Red Sea port of Jeddah and followed the coast in a series of boat trips. Once again he could not help noticing the local women.

> They are of exceeding and pre-eminent beauty . . . They have a predilection for the stranger and do not refuse to marry him, as the women of our country do. When he wishes to travel, his wife goes out with him and bids him farewell; and if there should be a child between them, it is she who takes care of it and supplies what is needed for it until its father returns.

From the port of Aden, Ibn Battuta boarded a ship for Somalia, where in 1331, he visited Mogadishu at the zenith of its prosperity. From here, he made his way south to Mombasa and then Kilwa in today's Tanzania.

In 1332 Ibn Battuta completed his third *hajj* and in the autumn set off for Anatolia, hoping to take an overland route to India. He stayed in more than 25 Anatolian hospices of the semi-religious *fityan* associations. Historians believe he did indeed visit many towns in Anatolia, just not in the sequence he described. He found the Turks welcoming, but said they consumed too much hashish. He was also drawn to the town of Konya, where in the previous century the Persian mystic poet Rumi had lived. Rumi was lecturing as an academic in Konya when a cake seller came into the room. He disappeared with her and, as the Tangerine recounts, something very strange happened. 'After many years he returned,' Ibn Battuta wrote, 'but he had become demented, and would speak only in Persian rhymed couplets which no one could understand.'

Rumi, or Mevlana as the Turks knew him, would utter his couplets while dancing or rotating around a pillar. He founded an order known as the Mevlevis who, after Rumi's death, continued this tradition. This was how the Whirling Dervishes came about, with Konya as their spiritual home. Battuta recalled how the voices of the Mevlevis 'work upon men's souls and at which hearts are humbled, skins creep, and eyes fill with tears.'

In Ladhiq, he berated the inhabitants for their practice of buying beautiful Greek slave girls and renting them out as prostitutes. But his outrage may not have been that deep, as he himself bought slave girls. Ibn Battuta decided that female company was important on the road, so he indulged himself with these girls, treating them as concubines. In Ephesus he bought 'a Greek slave girl, a virgin, for 40 gold *dinars*.' In total, ten wives are mentioned in *The Travels*, although he rarely took them away with him.

As a respected scholar who had collected so much knowledge, the further Ibn Battuta travelled, the more he was showered with gifts. 'In Birgi,' writes David Waines in *The Odyssey of Ibn Battuta*, 'they hit the jackpot.'

The sultan insisted on entertaining the company in two of his residences . . . Their stay of two weeks was with full board plus extras, and upon leaving Ibn Battuta alone was presented with

100 mithqals of gold, 1,000 silver dirhams, a complete set of clothes,
a horse and a second Greek slave.

In Kastamanou in northern Anatolia, the Tangerine met a sheikh
who was, on account of his great age, perhaps justifiably shaky.

I found him lying on his back. One of his servants helped him to sit
up, and another raised the eyelids from his eyes. On seeing me the
shaykh addressed me in pure Arabic, saying, "You are heartily
welcome!" I asked him his age and he said, "I was an associate of
Caliph al-Mustansir, and at his death I was 30 years old. My age now
is 163 years."

From Kastamonou, the traveller ventured to Sinop on the Black Sea,
famous as the home of Diogenes, the Cynic of Sinop (described in
Travels with a Tangerine as 'a celebrated al fresco masturbator'). Battuta
noted that the inhabitants of Sinop, like latter-day Tangerines, had a
penchant for drugs.

I saw here several high-ranking officers, with an orderly in front of
them holding a bag filled with a substance resembling henna. As I
watched, one of the officers took a spoonful of it and ate it. I had no
idea what it was, but the person with me told me it was hashish.

From Sinop, Ibn Battuta took a route across the Black Sea to the
Crimea. The voyage was unpleasant.

A storm blew up against us. We were in sore straits, with destruction
staring us in the face. I was in the cabin, along with a man from the
Maghrib named Abu Bakr, and I bade him go up on deck to observe
the state of the sea. He did so and returned, saying, "I commend
you to God."

Kaffa or Theodosia in the Crimea was Ibn Battuta's first taste of what
is now modern-day Russia. He noted that its people had 'red hair, blue
eyes and ugly faces.' In Kaffa, he lodged in a mosque, but in the
morning was startled out of his wits when he heard, for the first time

in his life, the sound of church bells. He and his companions climbed the minaret to recite the call to prayer to try and drown out the sound of the bells.

From the Crimea, the Tangerine made his way to the mobile metropolis of the Uzbeg Khan, the ruler of the Golden Horde, the northern part of the great Mongol Empire and a descendant of Genghis Khan.

In the eyes of Ibn Battuta, the Islamic world was divided among seven mighty rulers. He met five of them. Uzbeg was the last of these. Although he used his capital, New Sarai, on the River Volga, as his base, Uzbeg moved his court around to keep a close eye on his vast realm. On his journey across the steppe, Ibn Battuta bought wagons. These vehicles were an important means of transport in the Mongol Empire. Ibn Battuta said they had four large wheels and were pulled by at least two horses, oxen or camels. The wagons also carried the passengers' sleeping quarters. He bought several wagons of different sizes, one for himself and a slave girl and others for his travel companions.

The Turkish travel routine was similar to that of the Arab caravans on the pilgrimage to Mecca. They would set off after the dawn prayer, stop for lunch, resume in the afternoon and travel until sunset. When Ibn Battuta finally met the sultan's travelling residence (ordu) it was one enormous tented city, continually on the move and escorted by thousands of Mongolian horsemen.

> With its inhabitants, mosques and bazaars in it, the smoke of the kitchens rising in the air (for they cook while on the march) and horse-drawn wagons transporting the people.

Ibn Battuta made his way to Bolghar, on the banks of the Volga, the most northerly point that he ever reached on his journeys, yet he actually wanted to go further north into the 'land of darkness' (northern Siberia). It was said that there lived a mysterious people who were reluctant to show themselves. Southern merchants would leave their goods out on the snow at night and return to their tents. The next morning they would find that their merchandise had been taken by the mysterious people, who left animal skins and furs for them in return. Neither the merchants, nor the mysterious people ever set eyes on each other.

Travelling with Uzbeg Khan was enjoyable, but the Tangerine disapproved of his copious alcohol consumption. When the retinue reached Astrakhan, Uzbeg Khan gave permission for one of his pregnant wives, Princess Bayalun, the daughter of the Byzantine Emperor, to return to her home city of Constantinople to give birth. Ibn Battuta joined this expedition, his first beyond the boundaries of the Islamic world. Uzbeg Khan's parting gift to the Moroccan was 1,500 gold dinars, as well as ingots of silver, horses, robes and furs.

His itinerary from Constantinople back to New Sarai is one of the most confusing passages in *The Travels*, but we know that it was very cold. 'Not a drop of water fell,' he said, 'without being frozen on the instant. When I washed my face, the water ran down my beard and froze.'

Ibn Battuta continued on past the Caspian Sea to Bukhara and Samarkand, where he visited the Mongol king Tarmashirin. He journeyed south to Afghanistan and crossed into India via the Hindu Kush. In September 1333, he reached the Indus. In western India, he came across a sect, the *Haydariyya* and noted in particular that they wore iron rings on their hands, necks, ears and sometimes even on their penises, so as not to have sex.

In Delhi he met the wealthiest man in the Muslim world, Sultan Muhammad bin Tughluq. The sultan was impressed by Ibn Battuta's years of study and appointed him as a religious judge, but the sultan's moods were erratic and the Moroccan oscillated between living the high life and being suspected of treason. 'This sovereign is, of all men, the most addicted to the giving of gifts,' Battuta recalled, 'and the shedding of blood.'

The Sultan of Delhi was like a precursor to the seventeenth-century Moroccan Sultan, Moulay Ismail. At one point Battuta was horrified to see the mutilated bodies and stuffed skins of executed prisoners dangling from the tops of the city walls. Muhammad bin Tughluq attempted to get a respected Sufi sheikh, Shihab al-Din, to work for him, but the sheikh rejected the offer. The sultan later had the man force fed with human excrement and then beheaded. It was Ibn Battuta's friendship with the Sufi that caused the Tangerine to fall out of favour with the sultan. Battuta's chance to escape finally came in 1347, when an emissary arrived from China asking for permission to rebuild a temple.

The Indian ruler proposed that the Moroccan traveller be sent as his special envoy to the King of China. On his way from Delhi, Ibn Battuta recorded encounters with yogis and in the town of Parvan he heard of man-eating tigers. Later, someone explained to him that it was not really a tiger, but a yogi who would appear in the shape of a tiger. Another of the yogis' tricks was to abstain from food and drink for months, spending most of the time buried under the earth with only a small gap for breathing. In the southern city of Madurai, Ibn Battuta, met the local Muslim sultan, Ghiyath al-Din, who took a special pleasure in killing his Hindu captives. One day, a yogi prepared some pills for the 80-year-old sultan as an aphrodisiac. The pills contained iron filings, but the sultan was so delighted with their effect on his libido that he took an overdose and died. Ibn Battuta remarked that it was unclear whether Ghiyath al-Din's death was from the iron filings or excessive copulation.

The explorer then sailed to Calicut on the Malabar coast, preceding Vasco da Gama by two centuries. In Calicut harbour, Ibn Battuta was left stranded. Most of the gifts were boarded onto a junk and the slaves were placed on a smaller vessel, a kakam. Battuta had remained on shore for Friday prayers and intended to board the next morning, but an overnight storm destroyed the junk and killed everyone on it. The captain of the kakam set sail with Ibn Battuta's possessions but without Ibn Battuta.

From Calicut he boarded another ship bound for the Maldives. He stayed here for 18 months, was appointed as a judge again and married several times. For Ibn Battuta the islands were, and some modern holidaymakers would agree, Paradise on Earth. He noted what happened when you ate the local fish and coconut.

> An amazing and unparalleled effect in sexual intercourse, and the people of these islands perform wonders in this respect. I myself had four wives there, and concubines as well, and I used to visit all of them every day and pass the night with the wife whose turn it was.

If Tangier was later to attract sex tourists, then the city's most famous traveller went forth from that city to become one himself. He went on to take two more brides so that, out of his total of ten wives, he found six of them during his relatively short stay in the Maldives.

> It is easy to get married in these islands on account of the smallness of the dowries and the pleasure of their women's society . . . I have never found in the world any women more agreeable to consort with than they are . . . They do not cover their heads, not even their ruler the Sultana, and they comb their hair and gather it to one side. Most of them wear only an apron from the navel to the ground, the rest of their bodies being uncovered. It is thus they walk abroad in the bazaars and elsewhere. When I was a religious judge there, I tried to put an end to this practice and ordered them to wear clothes, but I met with no success.

From the Maldives Ibn Battuta went to Ceylon. Here there was a conical shaped mountain known as Adam's Peak. This was thought to contain a footprint on the spot where Adam came down to earth after being expelled from the Garden of Eden. His ship almost sank when he left Ceylon and then his rescue vessel was attacked by pirates. Stranded onshore, he worked his way back to the southern Indian kingdom of Madurai, where he was a guest of the sultan (Ghiyas-ud-Din Muhammad Damghani), but he left India again, boarding a Chinese junk. He reached the port of Chittagong in present-day Bangladesh, intending to travel to Sylhet to meet the Shah Jalal, who was so well renowned that Ibn Battuta made a one-month journey through the mountains just to see him. When he finally met Shah Jalal in 1345, Ibn Battuta noted he was tall, lean and fair and lived by the mosque in a cave, subsisting on goat's milk.

That year, he travelled on to Samudra Pasai in modern-day Aceh in Sumatra, at the edge of the Muslim world. From Java, the Moroccan voyaged by sea for 88 days. He set foot in China at the city of Zaitun. He found this name very amusing as it means 'olive' in Arabic and yet he could not find a single olive anywhere. He did however see local cuisine that involved cooking frogs and dogs. In China, as predicted all those years ago, he also met the prominent Persian scholar Burhanuddin. Their coming together had involved a bizarre series of implausible coincidences. In the mountains of Bengal, Ibn Battuta had set out to meet an aged saint. When he encountered the holy man he was struck by his odd clothing, as he was wearing a goat-hair cloak, which he gave to the Moroccan. Much later in China, a government minister spotted Ibn Battuta wearing this garment and presented him to the local governor. This official admired the cloak so much that he swapped it for ten robes, money and a horse. The following year when Ibn Battuta was in the Chinese capital, he met Burhanuddin and found him wearing the same goat-hair cloak. Ibn Battuta was even more amazed when the Persian scholar produced a letter from a friend in Bengal, predicting that the garment would reach him by the same route that Ibn Battuta had experienced.

Ibn Battuta seems to pinpoint China as a region that is beyond the known world and antithetical to normality. His China narrative is separated from the rest of his travels as it is bookended by two strange tales. The first is about Princess Urduja of Tawalisi, whom the Moroccan encountered on his way to China. The princess invited Ibn Battuta and those on board his ship to dinner. Here, he found females in attendance as well as the princess' female ministers. Many kings and princes were said to have tried to marry her only to be rebuffed with the remark that she would only wed a man who could defeat her in a fight. When the Tangerine told the princess that he had been to India, she replied 'I must invade India and take possession of it. Its wealth and soldiers please me.'

The second story occurs on his return from China when his boat was lost in an unknown sea, out of which a mountain arose into the air. His crewmen told Ibn Battuta that the mountain was actually a rukh, the giant bird that occurs in the story of Sinbad the Sailor, and which Marco Polo claimed lived near Madagascar.

In Beijing, the Tangerine referred to himself as the long-lost ambassador from the Delhi Sultanate. He believed that the Great Wall of China was built by Dhul-Qarnayn to contain Gog and Magog as mentioned in the Qur'an. He also experienced further examples of weird and wonderful wizardry, involving a young man being followed by an older one, each clambering up a rope that vanished into thin air. The old man then began to throw down the severed

limbs of his younger companion. When he came down from the
rope, the elder man started to attach the limbs together again and
kicked the younger performer, who promptly stood up with his body
assembled correctly.

From China, he headed for Southeast Asia but was unfairly charged
a large sum of money by the crew and lost most of what he had saved.
Details of his homeward journey are scant, but he travelled back
via Kawlam in southern India and Zafar on the Arabian coast. By
January 1348, he was in Baghdad and from there he headed towards
Damascus, where he learned about the death of his father some 15 years
earlier. The Black Death had struck and spread through Syria, Palestine
and Arabia, whilst in Europe the Jews and the Moors were accused of
deliberately spreading the disease. One of Ibn Battuta's sons had also
died from the plague, but his mother was still alive. He arrived in
Damascus intending to retrace his very first route on the *hajj*. He set out
on his final pilgrimage and reached Mecca in November 1348. He
finally decided to return to Morocco nearly a quarter of a century after
leaving home, hit by a rather belated sense of homesickness. He talked
of 'affection for my people and friends, and love for my country,
which for me is better than all others.'

On the way, Battuta made one last detour to Sardinia before returning
to Tangier in 1349. But within only a few days of his arrival he
embarked on a trip to Al-Andalus. He set off in 1350 with the intention of defending Gibraltar from King Alfonso XI, but by the time he
arrived there, Alfonso had also succumbed to the plague and the threat
of a Spanish invasion had receded, so Ibn Battuta turned the occasion
into a sight-seeing holiday in Valencia and Granada. After that, he travelled through Morocco discovering that Marrakech too had been
devastated by the Black Death. The Red City was a ghost town and the
capital had been transferred to Fes. On the road to Fes in November 1349,
Ibn Battuta learnt that his mother had died from the plague and after
paying his respects to the Sultan of Morocco, he visited her grave in
Tangier.

In the autumn of 1351, the explorer made his way to the town of
Sijilmasa on the southern edge of the Sahara. After 25 days in a desert
caravan he arrived at the salt lake of Taghaza in northern Mali, which
he noted was riddled with flies. In Niani, the capital of the Empire of

Mali, he was appalled to see a variety of women who, 'appear naked, exposing their genitals.'

Of all the women Ibn Battuta admired, those of the nomadic Berber tribe, the Bardama, probably took the biscuit. 'They are the most perfectly beautiful of women and have the most elegant figures,' he said, 'They are pure white and very fat.'

From Niani he went to Timbuktu, which was, at the time, relatively unimportant. It was on this journey that he first encountered a hippopotamus. He travelled on down the River Niger in a canoe carved from a single tree to Gao, where he received a message from the Sultan of Morocco to return home immediately. He did so accompanying a large caravan transporting 600 slave girls and arrived back in Morocco in early 1354. 'I had laid down my travelling staff in this noble country after confirming with superabundant impartiality that it is the best of countries.' His last comments in The Travels were to describe a pass through the Atlas Mountains.

> It was a time of intense cold and a great deal of snow had settled on the road. I have seen difficult roads and much snow in Bukkara, Samarkand, Khurasan and the country of the Turks, but I never saw one more difficult than this.

Here ends Ibn Battuta's work. It was, he said, his 'gift to those who contemplate the wonders of cities and the marvels of travelling.'

Frustratingly little is known of Ibn Battuta's life after the completion of his travelogue in 1355, as David Waines writes.

> In the years left to him, a decade or so at least, there is no certain evidence as to his whereabouts or activities. Did he expect to enjoy fame and fortune or was he disappointed and bitter at his failure to achieve either? Did he withdraw into relative obscurity, perhaps serving his community as a religious judge? Or did he retreat more completely, to be left alone with only his memories?

Even the date of Ibn Battuta's death is not certain – either 1368 or 1369. We know that he was appointed as a judge and that he outlived his patron, the Sultan Abu Inan and his editor, Ibn Juzayy. The latter remarked however that the author was satisfied with all that he had accomplished.

> I have indeed – praise be to God – attained my desire in this world, which was to travel through the Earth, and I have attained this honour, which no ordinary person has attained.

I asked Lotfi Akalay what lasting influence Ibn Battuta had left on the cultural life of Tangier today. 'Nothing,' he replied. Ibn Battuta, it seemed, was a prophet who was not accepted in his hometown.

> The Moroccans know absolutely nothing about Ibn Battuta. At the time that he went to see the sultan, other Moroccans were jealous of him and said he told nothing but lies. But if the sultan had not ordered Ibn Juzayy to write down *The Travels*, Ibn Battuta would have been a complete unknown. It is the same today. I wrote my book about him and then in 2004, I presented it at conferences to celebrate 700 years since his birth. I gave talks in Paris, Washington, Rome and Madrid but was never invited to do so in Morocco. When I presented my book in Paris, the auditorium was completely full, but there was not a single Moroccan there. They have no interest in him and they know nothing. Here we are in an ocean of ignorance about him. It is as if we have been plunged into the middle of the night.

At this point, Lotfi concluded our interview. 'No, Moroccans have never been interested in him,' he said. Then he nudged me gently on the shoulder, smiled and pointed at Otmane, 'Just like now for example!' Otmane, who had been sitting in a chair opposite us, had fallen asleep.

Finding Ibn Battuta's tomb is not easy, but Otmane shepherded me through the medina to look for it. We walked across the Grand Socco and down the Rue d'Italie before taking a right turn beneath Bab Teatro. We then took a left and ascended a backstreet called Rue Jnan Kabtan or Capitaine, named after a seventeenth-century English military officer. After this, we walked up another alleyway actually called the Rue Ibn Battuta, which was so narrow that larger men would have become stuck there. Up to shoulder height, the walls of the houses were painted blue or pink and had dented brown metal doors. Otmane explained that the blue pigment keeps the flies away and does not show up the dirt when people stand, like flamingos, with one foot against the wall. Above that level, shuttered windows laced with dangerously exposed cables punctuated yellow and mouldy plaster-work. As the gradient became steeper, the steps also contained a central stone ramp useful for wheelbarrows and trolleys. I had first been introduced to Otmane on Facebook via a mutual friend and it was at this point that he compared the narrow passages in Tangier to Facebook's own 'medina of alleyways.' As we approached the tomb at the summit of the lane we encountered a limping black cat and two small children. The girl was skipping and teaching her little brother to count each skip.

It was soon fairly obvious that the mausoleum did not date to the fourteenth century. It was a white and blue wedge-shaped block with a small dome on one side and Andalusian tiles on the roof. One wall was embedded with coffee-coloured hexagonal tiles. An arch, pointed like the hood of a djellaba, provided a frame for a cheap looking wooden door. It was locked. My hopes were prematurely raised when we saw a mobile phone number for the tomb's guardian on the door, but the number was out of service. By a lucky coincidence, Otmane, as he would do many times, came to the rescue. He had taken a video of the interior with his mobile phone and sent it to me later, via Facebook, with a message: 'a coincidence is better than a thousand rendezvous.'

The tomb chamber looked slightly bigger on the inside than it did on the outside, but it was still slightly disappointing. The floor is covered in a thick white carpet and the ceiling is decorated with a silver arabesque frieze. Shelves attached to the walls support copies of the Qur'an, candles and prayer beads. The coffin itself is protected by a metal railing, which looks like a wrought iron bedpost, and is draped with a green and yellow shroud inscribed with Arabic calligraphy.

Most academics do not think that this is actually Ibn Battuta's tomb. One Moroccan expert, Dr Abdelhadi Tazi, believes he was buried at Anfa, an old Berber port, which was destroyed by the Portuguese in 1468 and is now itself buried beneath the concrete of Casablanca. It is a typically Moroccan ending for the man who travelled across the world.

FOUR

Samuel Pepys

God almighty should lose no time at all in destroying this city

'We were very naughty then,' 97-year-old Charles Sevigny told me as he showed me around his house, Dar Zero, in the Place de la Kasbah.

'Are people less naughty now?' I asked him.

'Oh yes, terribly boring.'

Dar Zero is a small box-shaped white building with a necklace of pink azaleas creeping over its parapet. The previous owner was an English painter, Jim Wylie, who would answer the door wearing a mask. When the visitor asked for him, he would reply that Mr Wylie was currently unavailable, as he had gone mad. For me, it had been one of those Moroccan mornings and getting inside nearly drove me mad. At first, no one opened the heavy wooden door when we knocked. Otmane and I came back a few hours later to be told that Charles was unavailable, not because he was mad, but because he was not there. Nor was he available when we tried a third time; he was taking his afternoon nap. In total, three different servants answered the door and it was only the last of these who finally brought his master, who eyed me with suspicion.

'Why are you knocking on my door?'

'I'm writing a book about Tangier.'

'That will be difficult. What do you want to know about me?'

'I would like to see inside your house.'

'So you're not interested in me? You must know me if you knocked on my door.'

'Well, I'm interested in your house . . . but I'm sure you're very interesting too!'

At this point, in a panic, I reeled off as many names of potential mutual acquaintances as I could think of. Surprisingly, it worked. Charles let us in. Like the Tardis, Dar Zero seemed larger on the inside than on the outside. An unfinished game of solitaire lay on a desk along with a set of headphones and a pint of beer. Charles flicked through his photo album, a sort of Who's Who of Tangier in the 1960s. 'That's me there,' he said, pointing to one picture, 'I was very slender then.' There were photos of parties at the adjoining building, York Castle, frequented by Christian Dior, Malcolm Forbes, Barbara Hutton, Paul Bowles and, almost everywhere, assorted young men in skimpy swimming trunks. 'This is pretty much the look of Tangier in those days,' he said. Charles came here in the 1950s when the International Zone was at its zenith. He and his partner, Yves Vidal originally lived in York Castle but later moved into Dar Zero.

Dar Zero was practically a ruin. It was leaking, the electricity had been cut off and it was lit by candlelight. Poor Jim had no more money, so we helped him out a bit. And after he died we bought it to save it. We had the whole thing renovated. Yves was a great host. We had some wonderful parties.

Now York Castle is itself a ruin. In 1996 a drought was followed by a severe storm. A crack appeared in the walls. It grew and grew, eventually splitting the building in two. 'It's a wreck now,' Charles said.

'Who lives there?'

'Squatters.'

Dar Zero has a long history. Before Jim Wylie, Richard Hughes, who wrote *A High Wind in Jamaica*, had bought the house in 1930 for two donkey-loads of silver. 'The man Hughes bought it from was so excited,' it says in the introduction to Hughes' *In the Lap of Atlas*, 'that he didn't go to bed for two days and two nights, but sat up biting every piece to make certain it was good.'

If 97 seems a good age, it is nothing compared to the fig tree in the courtyard. The gnarled trunk was twisted and held together by an iron chain. Charles said this was the work of Jim Wylie, who noticed that the trunk was also in danger of splitting in two. 'That tree is more than 300 years old,' he said proudly.

Beneath the branches of the fig tree a certain Samuel Pepys wrote up his diaries on a visit to Tangier in 1683. 'God Almighty should lose no time at all in destroying this city,' wrote Pepys, who was appalled by the debauchery of the British garrison. Four centuries earlier St Francis of Assisi was equally scathing, labelling it as a 'city of madness and delusions.'

In 1660, at the time of Charles II's restoration, England was one of the great world powers, with colonies in North America and the East and West Indies, yet it wanted more. For fresh slices of the New World cake however, England had to compete with the Dutch, French, Spanish and Portuguese. Charles' foreign policy was inextricably linked with his marriage plans, as three of those European powers were keen to arrange weddings to cement alliances. For Portugal, such a match would help it maintain its newly-won independence from Spain. The Queen Regent was desperate for a union between Charles and her daughter, the Infanta Catherine of Braganza, whom the British consul in Lisbon described as having, 'as sweet a disposition as ever was born, and a lady of excellent partes.'

The Portuguese ambassador offered Charles a package he could not resist: a dowry of £500,000, free trade in Brazil and the East Indies, the island of Bombay and, last but not least, Tangier. When he saw the dark eyes of the Infanta staring out of her portrait, Charles was sold on the idea. He was convinced she 'could not be unhandsome' and was certainly not 'dull and foggy' as he had described the German princesses. So on 8 May 1661, in front of Parliament, Charles II announced a marriage treaty with Portugal. 'The recent acquisition of Tangier,' Charles told MPs, 'must be regarded as a jewel of immense value in the royal diadem.'

Portugal had acquired Tangier nearly two centuries earlier. In 1437 Henry the Navigator had besieged the town for 25 days without success, but then suddenly, during a revolution in Morocco in 1471, the Portuguese entered Tangier without a drop of blood being spilt.

Charles II clearly envisaged Tangier as a prosperous city with a harbour that would transform it into one of the best trading stations in the Mediterranean. He also thought having the port would maintain

England's naval supremacy and become the key to unlocking new colonies in the African interior. It was also vital that the English had a base in the Straits to protect its ships from pirates. Barbary Corsairs operated from Algiers, Tripoli, Tunis and Sale (the dreaded 'Sale Rovers') and privateers preyed on smaller trading vessels like vultures. Every year hundreds of Christian prisoners were kidnapped and sold into slavery, as Enid Routh observed in *Tangier 1661–1684, England's Lost Atlantic Outpost*.

> Warfare carried on against these pirates assumed the character of a post-medieval crusade, and the acquisition of Tangier was welcomed in England as a means of putting down the terror of the Mediterranean, and of advancing the interests of Christendom . . . many a sea-faring family must have hoped that Tangier might prove a haven of refuge to those who were braving the dangers of pirate-haunted waters.

Pirates were not the only problem. Danger also lurked from inland as Tangier was almost completely encircled on land by neighbouring Moors. The Portuguese garrison had made a sortie against the Moors, but it had ended so disastrously, that on 14 January 1661, the governor asked for English help. Charles II entrusted Admiral Edward Montagu, the First Earl of Sandwich, with securing Tangier, settling 'the business of Algiers' (pirates from Algiers) and bringing the Infanta to England from Lisbon. Sandwich arrived at Tangier Bay with seven or eight ships and landed a detachment of soldiers. While he was guarding English interests in the Mediterranean, preparations were being made to send a garrison to Tangier and in September 1661, Henry Mordaunt, the Earl of Peterborough was appointed as the city's first English governor. In January the following year, Peterborough set sail with 3,000 men, as well as the wives and families of two or three hundred soldiers, and a hundred horses. At the end of the month 27 ships were anchored in the Bay of Tangier. There was no visible sign of anything but peace. Sandwich handed over the citadel to Peterborough, giving him the keys to the city on 30 January 1662. The latter probably thought he was holding the keys to Africa, but, in the words of Routh, the English were 'doomed to an abrupt awakening.'

One of the first challenges the new garrison encountered was learning how to defend their outpost from scratch; the Portuguese had left no handover notes. In fact they had left nothing at all. Like spiteful outgoing tenants removing every light bulb from a flat at the end of their lease, the Portuguese had taken everything with them, including the doors and windows of their houses. Sandwich left Tangier on 18 February to escort the young queen to England, but before doing so he conducted a survey of the bay to assess the feasibility of a stone breakwater, which became known as the 'Mole of Tangier.'

Begun in 1663, the Mole was 1,425 feet long and 100 feet wide. Nine years later it was over budget and still under construction. The man who oversaw the project, Sir Hugh Cholmley, had to fork out some of his own money to keep the work going. The huge expenditure would be one of the reasons for England's eventual withdrawal.

Charles was hoping that as Governor of Tangier, Peterborough would also expand his remit to neighbouring areas, but this commission was over-optimistic and fundamentally flawed; Charles did not have the money to see it through. One suggestion, was that convicted criminals should be sent to Morocco to turn them into honest people: 'There must be speciall care had that weomen be amoghst them . . . otherwise no governor will be able to rule them.' Another proposal was to deport one third of the people of Scotland to Morocco.

English relations with the Moors were not easy, and not made any simpler by a cultural chasm between the two. Most Englishmen knew nothing about the natives of Morocco and some very weird ideas prevailed. As they had failed to defeat the Portuguese, the Moors were considered 'a very effeminate people.' One writer wrote that a child who lived near Tangier was born 'with Eagle's Bill, Claws and Feathers too.' The English had arrived in Morocco during a period of great political upheaval. The Saadian dynasty was coming to an end and a power struggle ensued between Mohammed and his brother Rachid II of the emerging Sharifian dynasty. Among Mohammed's supporters was the warlord Ghailan. With ambitions to carve out his own northern kingdom, Ghailan was the first enemy that the English garrison had to deal with, and he embarked on a campaign of intermittent guerrilla warfare. He declared his intentions early on by advancing towards Tangier with an army of around 5,000 horsemen. Peterborough managed to make peace by giving in to Ghailan's demands for gunpowder, but as Enid Routh remarked, it was a Faustian pact.

During the next few months the garrison suffered every possible annoyance from Ghailan's people, who were incessantly on the watch to drive off cattle, to surprise foraging parties and to cut off every man who ventured far from the walls.

This was a pattern that would be repeated over the years of occupation; attacks on the citadel would be followed by promises of peace that would inevitably be broken. Making deals with the treacherous Ghailan was about as easy as agreeing on weapons inspections with Saddam Hussein.

On 3 May 1662, an English force of 500 men was ambushed by Ghailan at what is known as Jews' River, which trickles out into Merkala Beach to the west of town. It was said that the Jews landed here after their expulsion from Spain in 1492. The English suffered heavy losses and over the next nine months 650 Englishmen were to die at the hands of the warlord, who was also fighting other Moroccan tribes and later agreed to peace.

Maintaining a garrison that was by now 2,000 strong proved a huge drain on English resources and cost the country around £70,000 a year. There were problems getting the cash to Tangier and a lot of unnecessary extravagance. To address this disturbing haemorrhaging of finances, in November 1662 Charles created a Tangier Committee with Thomas Povey as its first treasurer. It also included the Earl of Sandwich, Sir Hugh Cholmley, Lord Peterborough and a clerk of the Acts of the Navy: Samuel Pepys.

Although he had hardly ever been to sea, the famous diarist of London during the Great Fire, the Great Plague and the Dutch Wars, had at this time made himself an indispensible expert on naval matters. His biographer, Claire Tomalin, says he is still revered by naval historians.

Pepys embarked on the study of everything he needed to know to carry out his service to the navy, from its early records to its recruiting methods, from the multiplication tables and the use of the slide rule to the best methods of timber measurement, from rope manufacture to victualling and ships' pursuers' accounts, from sea charts to tide tables, from flag-making to the language of sailors . . . The romance of the navy came to him not through wind, water and tides but through papers, contracts and ledgers, rows of figures and dockyard visits.

Pepys became increasingly impatient with the way the accounts for Tangier were managed by Povey, and in 1665 Pepys took over his post. He was very thorough with the governor's requests for more money and scrupulous with the accounts. It was a lucrative position and Pepys received many unofficial offerings from contractors on top of his official salary.

Less than a year after he had been appointed as governor, Earl Peterborough was replaced by Earl Teviot. On 30 March 1663 the new governor signed a contract with Cholmley to build the Mole. Teviot still had to deal with Ghailan who was preparing to besiege the city with scaling ladders. Teviot built stone redoubts beyond the town as an outer layer of defence. In the words of the ambassador to Lisbon, Teviot was adding 'as many skins to it, one without another, as there are of an onion.'

On 14 June, Ghailan advanced with 4,000 horsemen and 2,000 foot soldiers, but the garrison repelled them. Ghailan's troops then lit fires hoping that the smoke would get in the eyes of the gunners, but the scheme backfired when the wind changed and hindered the Moors. On 21 July 1663 a six-month peace treaty began.

Tangier was being transformed from a tiny military outpost into a city. By 1668 it would be declared a free city, administered as a corporation with a mayor, aldermen, councillors and a recorder who could hear criminal and civil cases. It was attracting traders from Morocco, Spain, France and Holland and as trade increased, the civil population grew. Among them were Jewish merchants who faced discrimination as they were suspected of passing on intelligence to the Moors. There was a sense of paranoia (just as there would be in the city amongst the military officers, spies and general assorted misfits during World War II) that incoming foreigners might sell information on to other European powers.

A truce with Ghailan that was due to end in January 1664 was extended with the offer of 50 barrels of gunpowder and an assurance not to build any new fortifications. Teviot inspired a sense of confidence among the English as he was prepared to lead from the front, at times staying up all night with his soldiers in the trenches.

In February that year Ghailan broke his promise and led another assault on the town. Teviot managed to defend it with the help of mines laid outside the walls. On 3 May 1664, he marched three miles out of Tangier to Merkala Beach (the site of the ambush exactly two years earlier). He did not know that he would be marching to his death. A day later he was attacked by 3,000 Moors and only nine out of several hundred English soldiers survived at what became known as Teviot Hill. The incident was recorded by Samuel Pepys on 1 June.

Southwell tells me the very sad newes of my Lord Teviot and nineteen more commission officers being killed at Tangier by the Moores . . . which is very sad, and he says afflicts the King much.

After the disaster at Teviot Hill, a dozen new forts were built around the town by a Swedish engineer at a cost of £800 a year. All the time, from their positions outside the town, the Moors looked on, waiting to pounce. Despite the sense of unease, a newly installed governor, Lord Belasyse wrote optimistically about Tangier in April 1665.

His Majesty would have a greater esteeme off it than any other off his dominions weare he heare to see the prospects off the streights uppon Spain, the shipps that pass, the frutefull mountaynes off Afrique, the fragrent perfumes off flowers, rere frutes and sallads, excellent ayre, meates and wines.

In early 1666 Ghailan again offered peace. This time it was agreed that the treaty would last forever, but Belasyse need not have bothered. He did not realise he was dealing with the wrong man. By now, Ghailan was little more than an outlawed fugitive. As his power had waned, that of the Emperor Moulay Rachid II was on the rise. In 1668, after seven years of intermittent warfare, promises and lies, the Moorish warlord fled his base in Asilah and arrived in Tangier to seek asylum.

As Routh noted, he 'at last passed as a fugitive through the gates of the city, which he had so long hoped to enter as conqueror.' Ghailan turned up with around 300 followers including women. They were something of a novelty to the officers who found 'some amongst them were very pritty.' Ghailan could not completely swallow his hatred of the English and fell out with them over a Portuguese girl who had been captured and sold to him as a slave. Back in Tangier, the girl re-converted from Islam to Christianity. This drove Ghailan into a fury and he left in a huff, for Algiers, harbouring his resentment for the rest of his life. He died several years later when Rachid's successor, Moulay Ismail, attacked Ghailan near Alcazar to the east of Tangier. The warlord was shot by a musket ball and his head was stuck on a lance.

Rachid himself came to an equally unhappy end in 1672. After a bout of drinking in Marrakech, he went for a horse ride in the Agdal Gardens, but was caught by the neck in the fork of a tree and strangled.

Meanwhile, life in the garrison was hard. England had amassed huge debts from the war with the Dutch and by 1673 the garrison had not been paid for two years. The lack of cash meant that supplies had to be shipped out from England at great expense. Many soldiers suffered from ill health. Unlike the Portuguese, who had lived on a local Mediterranean diet of fruit, herbs, fish, bread, and cattle from the Moors, the garrison depended on English rations of salted beef and pork. A survey in 1669 discovered 127 casks of beef and pork that had been sitting in the king's stores for three years. To prevent waste, these were shipped off to Tangier, but the garrison refused it. In 1673 Lord Middleton wrote that he found, 'the beife soe extreamely badd . . . I found great sicknesse creeping amongst our people', whilst in 1682, a further 24,000 pounds of beef and pork had become so rotten they were thrown into the sea.

The Irish aristocrat William McMurrough O'Brien, the Second Earl of Inchiquin, succeeded Lord Middleton as governor from 1675 until 1680. In 1676 the commander of the garrison, Sir Palmes Fairborne became the Lieutenant Governor and had the fortifications improved, but pay was still in arrears. One hundred men were in hospital with scurvy and a mutiny was looming. As he prepared for war, Fairborne opened negotiations with Moulay Ismail's deputy, the *Alcaid* Omar of Alcazar, who would prove to be as slippery as Ghailan.

In 1680, Tangier would face its biggest crisis, and the Sultan Moulay Ismail would come closest to achieving his long-held dream of driving the Christians into the sea. Things were not looking good; the fortifications were in disrepair, the garrison was depleted, soldiers were ill and morale was low. The English could not possibly hope to hold out against the enemy at the gates. Reports were coming of an enormous force that included 'several thousands of the king's army of blacks,' from Sudan. The siege began on 25th March with the Moors digging trenches around the city and by 6 April the forts were isolated. Just 250 men held them, communicating with the main castle every night by speaking trumpets – men who reported the movements of the enemy in Gaelic – so that the Moroccans would not understand the messages.

After the Moors laid out their plans and their land mines, Inchiquin defended forts from behind the lines with mortar, 'fire-balls throw'd downe from the fort.' The invaders suffered heavy losses however and made no direct assault for another two weeks. On 29 April they placed a mine next to Charles Fort and demanded the surrender of those inside, but the English refused. The mine was sprung, but failed to reach the fort.

The *Alcaid* was undeterred. He hanged the man responsible for the failed mine, laid three more and pressed on with the siege. Fairborne wrote to London that without reinforcements Tangier could not be held and rather than lose it to the Moors he would advise the King to blow it up. 'It was a desperate chance,' Routh said, '176 men against 3 or 4,000 – but they took it rather than wait on, trapped in their fort, until the inevitable end.' By 14 May, the trenches, which were between 12 and 20 feet deep, were partly filled with water and Fairborne wrote that 'there was furious fighting in their muddy depths.'

The *Alcaid* demanded the total surrender of Tangier but Inchiquin refused. On 21 May renewed proposals for peace were made and a truce of four months was agreed, but on fairly humiliating terms for the English; all the ground taken during the English occupation was to be given up. The governor feared that the Moors would be able to fire into the Upper Castle and set fire to the houses crowded into the narrow streets around the market place. Fairborne wrote home warning that unless 4,000 soldiers were despatched immediately, 'his Majestie had better resolve to quit and leave both the Towne and Mole in a ruin.'

The Moors considered the city as good as taken. The ruinous ramparts were left in 'a very crazy position' and Lord Inchiquin was recalled home in June 1680 leaving Fairborne in command. This was a wake-up call to the government in Westminster. Preparations were made for relief, but Charles' adviser The Earl of Sunderland told the King that this force would fail. Although not all the promises were fulfilled, the prospect of reinforcements emboldened the garrison, but on 15 September the Moors attacked again. A ship, the Swiftstakes, was anchored in Tangier Bay with 135 men. Five days later the English advanced and after more than seven hours of battle, the Moors gradually gave ground. On 24 October 1680, Fairborne was mortally wounded by a bullet and three days later, the whole garrison, with 1,500 soldiers and 300 cavalrymen advanced out of the town and went on the offensive. Fairborne, who had been carried onto his balcony on a chair, watched the fighting and lived long enough to witness success on the battle-field, but there was great loss of life. From 20 September to 27 October nearly 700 British soldiers died, as did 2,000 Moors.

After this, the Alcaid agreed to another six months of peace in return for gunpowder, muskets and cloth. It was also a condition that no further fortifications were to be built outside the town wall.

In 1681, Colonel Percy Kirke, who would be made governor the following year, was sent out to meet Sultan Moulay Ismail in Meknes. In spite of his hatred of foreigners, Ismail took a strange liking to Kirke, who spent three weeks in his court. Kirke in turn had nothing but praise for the sultan and was giddy with his own apparent diplomatic success.

The Emperour telling me that for his sake . . . he would give foure yeares peace for Tanger, and swore by God, that as long as I was Governor here, he would cut off the Alcaydes head if he gave us any the least suspicion of a breach of peace.

Ismail was the most successful tyrant who ever sat on the Moroccan throne, but he was, in modern terms, a psychopath. The walls of Fes and Meknes were adorned with the heads of 10,000 of his victims and he also made a bridge out of rushes interwoven with the bodies of prisoners of war. Rival tribes and international powers regarded him with fear and awe. Even Kirke, who had initially been seduced by his charm, was becoming more aware of his true nature. 'He excels all mankind in barbarous and bloody actions, massacre and murder being his Royal game,' he wrote, 'he invents every day a new pastime of cruelty.' Ismail was known to have speared 20 or 30 black slaves for no reason, and on one single day he strangled 30 women in his harem. Not even his own sons or pets were spared. A favourite cat was tied to a mule's tail and dragged to death, for stealing a rabbit. Besides 30,000 of his native slaves, Ismail also owned 2,500 Christians, including 70 English soldiers from the Tangier garrison.

In 1681 the *Alcaid* died. He had come to Tangier for treatment by an English doctor after a mystery illness. Some thought he died of poisoning, while others, imagining what it must have been like to be answerable to Ismail, put it down to anxiety. He was replaced by his brother, Ali ben Abdallah. On 9 December the Moorish embassy set sail and arrived 20 days later at Deal in Kent. On 11 January 1682 the *London Gazette* recorded a meeting at Banqueting House between the ambassador, Mohammed ben Hadou, and King Charles and Queen Catherine. They exchanged letters and the ambassador gave Charles ostriches. This somewhat confused the king. The monarch 'knew nothing more proper to send by way of return than a flock of geese,' noted Sir John Reresby. In London the arrival of the Moors caused a great commotion and they were viewed as exotic celebrities. Banquets were held at Whitehall and horse parades in Hyde Park, whilst the ambassador enjoyed himself so much that he stayed for more than six months. All good things must come to an end however and eventually he was persuaded to go home, arriving back in Tangier at the end of August. He had agreed to a maritime truce of four months, but Moulay Ismail refused to ratify treaties agreed in Whitehall and broke his promise about the release of English slaves.

At the beginning of the English occupation Tangier was viewed as a gem, but, as Routh observed, 'by degrees enthusiasm gave way to indifference and indifference to disesteem.' In Parliament there was a suspicion that Charles II was falling under the influence of Louis XIV and wanted to sell Tangier to France. When the legislature convened in October 1680, Charles insisted on keeping the town and increasing the size of the garrison, but a storm of religious excitement was sweeping the country during the 'Popish Plot' and Tangier was caught in the blast. The town contained many Irish Catholics and in Parliament Sir William Jones claimed that 'Tangier has a Popish Church.'

On 4 January 1681 Charles made an appeal to parliament to 'enable him to preserve Tangier.' Unfortunately, by this time pleas for reinforcements were starting to irk the MPs, who were sick of hearing the city's name. As Routh wrote, it had been 'the brightest jewel of his crown' and Charles could 'not be persuaded to let it stand in the diadem of another monarch. So he preferred to cast it into the sea.'

Samuel Pepys was 50 when he set sail for Tangier in 1683. He had been born in Fleet Street in 1633, at fifteen had witnessed the execution of Charles I and at 26 began to write arguably the most celebrated diary in history. His journal stretched to more than one million words but it was to remain in obscurity until more than a century after his death. Although he had resigned from the Tangier committee four years earlier, he was sent to the city to assist his friend Lord Dartmouth, a naval commander serving under Charles II, with a secret mission. Dartmouth was to evacuate the city's English inhabitants and then destroy Tangier. Pepys would be paid £4 a day and if all went well he would back home within two months.

Since his resignation as Secretary of the Admiralty Commission in 1679, Pepys had known dishonour, prison, fear of death and constant anxiety, but now he was in good health and had even begun writing a diary again. He sailed in a fleet of 21 ships. On board the lead vessel, the *Grafton*, were two of his closest friends, his former manservant, Will Hewer and Henry Sheeres, another engineer who had worked on the Mole at Tangier. Other passengers included the scholar Dr Trumbull, the physician Dr Lawrence and the fleet's chaplain, Dr Thomas Ken.

On Friday 24 August 1683, the *Grafton* plunged off the Lizard peninsula and entered the Atlantic. Pepys celebrated his first day at sea by going to bed early. He did not rise the next morning until the ship's tailor had finished altering his doublet according to the naval fashion. Not for nothing had the little man been called 'Dapper Dicky.' Sadly his clothing could not stop him being seasick and all that Sunday he stayed in his cabin making notes on his Tangier mission. In the evening he walked the quarterdeck and watched the moon rise above the restless sea. Four days into the voyage, Dartmouth finally told Pepys the purpose of their trip.

> In the afternoon my lord in his cabin first broke to me in discourse the truth of our voyage for the destroying and deserting of Tangier. The first moment he ever spoke or I ever knew that to be the intent of our going.

Dartmouth told Pepys that he, with the help of Trumbull, would be entrusted to value the properties of Tangier and compensate their outgoing owners.

> The part which is particularly reserved for me herein . . . is the inquiring into, and stating the business of the several properties of the inhabitants . . . in the lands and houses . . . for which His Majesty proposes most graciously, just reparation.

Pepys passed his time on the *Grafton* stargazing, reading the Bible and arguing with Dr Ken. On 10 September he recorded a long discussion with him about the existence of ghosts. Pepys coming down firmly in the disbelievers camp while Ken was on the opposite side. Then, on the morning of 13 September, Pepys was awoken with the news that Cap Spartel was in sight.

> Thursday – Capt. Villiers waked us early with news of his making the land of Cape Spartel, so up to see it. Then to my cabin to finish my collection of arguments for the destroying of Tangier . . . I upon the quarter deck where we were come now fair in sight of the entrance into the Straits between the two shores . . .

Cap Spartel is frequently, but incorrectly, referred to as the northernmost point in Africa, but that accolade actually belongs to Ras ben Sakka in Tunisia. From the rolling green hills above the African shoreline, Pepys could make out a variety of pleasant scents: 'a most odiferous smell like the fume of cedar or juniper.'

At approximately ten o'clock on 14 September the fleet came into Tangier Bay. By the water's edge was a little town of dwellings with flat roofs huddling together behind protected walls that climbed up a steep hill towards a fortress reminiscent of the Tower of London, that stood together with a smaller castle. To Pepys the scene was not romantic but slightly pathetic. Here was this much-vaunted imperial outpost into which England had poured so much money and which he could see was unsustainable.

How could ever anybody think this place fit to be kept at this charge, that by its being overlooked by so many hills can never be secured against an enemy?

On those hills was the Moorish army, waiting for a chance to drive the infidels back into the sea so it could reclaim all of Barbary.

The castle guns gave out their salute and the governor Colonel Percy Kirke came on board, where Dartmouth briefed him about the mission. 'Dapper Dicky' then set foot on African soil on 17 September with Dartmouth at his side. From the quayside, along alleyways lined with welcoming troops clad in red coats and green sashes they made their way up the hill to the castle and dined at the governor's house. Pepys set eyes on the governor's wife, Lady Mary Kirke. Although he enjoyed looking at her, as well as eating the grapes and Spanish pomegranates on offer, he remained unimpressed with the town itself. 'An ordinary place,' he wrote. That night he was bitten by bed bugs.

Those who had visited Tangier during the English occupation had found it utterly charming. With a temperate climate, the town was abundant with foliage. In spring, the gardens, trees and plants spilled over into its otherwise dirty streets, filling them with blossom and aromatic scents, like applying perfume to a seventeenth-century armpit. Nature had endowed it with plenty to eat such as chickens, geese, ducks, asparagus, melons, apricots and peaches, but Tangier, as it always did, offered both light and dark. It was a beautiful place and a den of iniquity. Pepys, being weary and cynical, was not easily seduced by its charms. In fact, as Tomalin writes, 'he found himself dispatched to a place that had almost nothing to interest and much to disgust him.' He was dismayed by the residents and disturbed by the behaviour of the garrison. Under Portuguese rule the city had been thoughtfully laid out with castles, churches and narrow streets of whitewashed houses complete with manicured gardens and orchards of olives, lemons, mulberries and figs, but the English and Irish soldiers, who were low on discipline and high on alcohol, neglected the town and burnt down the trees. From the outset, the British alienated the Portuguese population, destroyed some of the Catholic churches and drove out the Jews.

Pepys was relieved to throw himself into work valuing properties. The owners were summoned to the Town House and on 20 September, Pepys, Trumbull and the Admiralty Judge of Tangier, Frederick Bacher, opened proceedings. They asked what rent the owners had paid the Crown and how much they still owed to it. Pepys was used to such tasks, but 'reckoned however without the proverbial indolence and carelessness of the Tangerines.' When the commission opened, scarcely any English inhabitants turned up. The indifference of the English proprietors depressed Pepys and his hopes of being home by Christmas looked increasingly bleak. He asked Dartmouth to provide him with a dozen clerks to prepare questionnaires for the proprietors.

Two days later, Pepys' attention turned again to ghosts, as something went bump in the night.

Saturday – Mighty talk of spirits in York Castle, mighty noises being heard by the minister and most intelligent men and particularly Dr Lawrence, who told me that he was now begun to be convinced of spirits, this having continued for some time past and appearing every three or four nights, but nothing since we came to this being Saturday, a good argument against Dr Ken's argument from the silence of the oracles.

On 23 September, his first Sunday in Tangier, all thoughts of the ghosts of Tangier banished, Pepys shaved for the first time since leaving England so that he could look his best for the Holy Spirit.

Thence with my lord attended by all the officers of the garrison and Mayor and aldermen of the town to church, where Dr Ken made an excellent sermon that is full of the skill of a preacher but nothing of a natural philosopher . . . I saw very few women of any quality or beauty in the place . . . But above all that was remarkable here, I met the Governor's lady in the pew (a lady I have long admired for her beauty, but she is mightily altered. And they do tell stories of her on her part, while her husband minds pleasure of the same kind on his).

The next day the commissioners took their seats again, equipped with 120 beautifully copied questionnaires, but so few of the owners appeared, that a further proclamation had to be drafted giving them until the following Thursday. Even with this new deadline, less than ten residents turned up and they had filled in the questionnaires so badly that Pepys thought the whole process of settling their claims would take longer than it would to blow up Tangier. 'Never surely was every town governed in all matters both public and private as this place has been,' he lamented.

That Friday, Pepys, who loved a military spectacle, awoke early and set off for the hills above the town to watch Dartmouth, backed now by 4,000 'red-coats' meet the *Alcaid*. 'For once in the troubled history of British Tangier,' Arthur Bryant remarked in *Samuel Pepys: The Saviour of the Navy* 'the Moors were confronted with a display of force greater than their own.' This succeeded in securing yet another truce until the English were to depart.

On the same day, Pepys discussed the business of blowing up the Mole. It was an inadequate structure as it had given larger ships very little protection from strong westerly gales. Pepys told his masters that some of those he spoke to doubted the Mole could be blown up in less than six months. The following extract reminds me of builders arguing with a foreman on a modern-day construction site.

Kirke and I did go aside to see some hand grenades shot off and flung about 300 yards with an instrument lately invented for that use . . . I was doubtful because of the different judgements I meet with in our people that are to execute the business of blowing up, which I said they did some of them declare could not be done in 4, others 6 months. My lord presently replied to me very short that they understood not the business, for he had a way of his own in reserve that should do it within a fortnight without fail, to which

Kirke immediately added, God damn him, he would do it all in a
fortnight . . . my mouth was stopped, and so said no more.

Two days later, Pepys attended church twice. The Sunday service
seemed to have been a focal point for Pepys, as the weekly gatherings
at St Andrew's are today for the British expat community; they seem to
be a source of both spiritual fulfilment and gossip. Pepys' assessment of
the preaching abilities of poor Dr Ken and others was always scathing,
but he was delighted to set eyes again on the fragrant Lady Kirke.

Sunday — So to church and heard a very fine and seasonable but
most unsuccessful sermon from Dr Ken in reproof particularly of
the vices of this town, so as I was in pain for the Governor and the
officers about us in the church, but I perceived they regarded it not.
From church to the office again till dinner and immediately from
dinner thither till church time and so to church, where we had a
foolish sermon of Hughes, but had the pleasure of seeing fine Mrs
Kirke again better dressed than before.

Despite his obvious disdain for Tangier and its debauched denizens, by
October Pepys had settled into a fairly pleasant routine of writing up his
property valuations and checking the progress of blowing up the Mole.

Monday (1 October) . . . All this morning . . . preparing and getting
signed by my lord the commission we his other commissioners do
advise him to about surveying in general all the houses pretended
to be in propriety in the whole town . . . Towards the evening Dr
Trumbull and I walked down to the Mole and there saw the pontoon
launched but most bunglingly, and so to the head of the Mole and
saw the beginnings of mines digging in one chest . . . but it is very
hard and slow work.

Pepys seemed to be both wary of, and fascinated by, the local
Moroccans he spied outside the walled fort.

Wednesday — Up and to walk the first time into the fields over
Fountain Fort, seeing the Moors' sentries, and people treating at the

stockades, and the folly of this place in being overlooked everywhere, I seeing the very soldiers going in and out of the Castle gate,
the strange diligence and patience of the Moors . . .

But his frustration with Tangier, was not abating. 'Nothing but vice
in the whole place of all sorts for swearing, cursing, drinking and
whoring,' he wrote. Even his admiration for Lady Kirke was tempered
with his knowledge that she too was no angel.

The governor is said to have got his wife's sister with child, and that
she is now gone over to Spain to be brought to bed. And that while
he is with his whores at his little bathing house which he has
furnished with a jade a-purpose for that use there, his wife, whom
he keeps in by awe, sends for her gallants and plays the jade by
herself at home . . . It is plain that the women of the town are,
generally speaking, whores.

The following week, Pepys persevered with trying to untangle the
mess of the townsmen's claims. Dartmouth had decided to ignore the
threat of the Moors, believing their bark was probably worse than
their bite, and on 4 October, he finally came completely clean with
everyone about his mission. Writing to his friend James Houblon,
Pepys said he was looking forward to coming home via a short holiday
in Spain 'while our sulphur-mongers are preparing a Doomsday for
this unfortunate place.'

The work of valuing the residents' claims was finally finished on
18 October. In total the English received £11,000. Pepys felt immensely
irritated believing that he had done all the work and his colleague
Trumbull had done nothing. Although in his official correspondence,
Pepys was courteous about him, in his diary he could not disguise his
contempt for the younger man. From the day he set foot in Tangier,
Trumbull had moaned about all the money he could have been earning
back in Westminster, so Pepys suggested he take an early passage back
to England and Trumbull could not have been more pleased.

Sunday – Dr Trumbull being very ill of the flux, but more in his
mind, and so my lord resolves with me to send him presently

home, as being but a trouble to him, and a man of the meanest mind as to courage that ever was born.

Friday – Dr Trumbull, who is impatient with my lord to be gone to-day . . . So home again to my letters and then to my lord to supper, where everybody laughing at Dr Trumbull's foolish impatience to be gone.

Much to everyone's relief, the homesick Dr Trumbull finally left Tangier on 20 October.

Dr Trumbull still playing the fool and making himself ridiculous in his impatience to be gone . . . and then my lord and all of us with all seeming respect took our leaves of him, my lord giving himself the trouble to treat him with all the respect in the World because of his going, that he might be useful in England, and therefore came with him to my chamber and there drank a parting bottle to his good voyage . . . and so we all, my lord and all, walked down and saw him in the boat and gave him several guns from the town. And so the fool went away.

Although a Moorish attack could have occurred at any time, Pepys was generally less fearful than Trumbull and thought the fleet would keep them safe. From his very first outing on 10 October, Pepys made almost daily trips beyond the walls of the fort and his innate curiosity overcame any fear. It was during these solitary rambles that his poetic side blossomed again.

I went alone in the boat round the bay and saw the ruins very plain of old Tangier and the river of Tangier and several Moors all along upon the shore gathering driftwood . . . Coming back upon the water, I first saw how blue the remote hills will look in the evening about the Sun's going down, as I have sometimes seen them painted but never believed it natural painted.

Meanwhile, work on the Mole was progressing; just not very well. On 19 October he watched Captain Leake, the Master Gunner of England make an unsuccessful attempt to destabilise it.

Friday – About 5-a-clock I went to the Mole to see the first trial by
Capt. Leake of two bombs under the arches in the Mole blown up,
but by the looseness of the earth above they did little or no
execution.

Towards the end of the month, Dartmouth was taking advantage of
the moonlit nights and he brought all the men who had been involved
in the easier work of blasting the fortifications to the harder job of
destroying the Mole.

Saturday . . . we have news brought us of hurt done this morning at
the Mole by ground falling in, so that two or three men are killed
quite outright and several spoilt in their limbs and carried to the
hospital.

But over the next two weeks, Pepys witnessed 'some very good
execution, even to wonder with so little quantity of powder,' and
seemed to be enjoying the impromptu firework displays from various
vantage points.

Wednesday . . . At noon to dinner and notice brought us of Mr
Sheeres' mine going to be blown up, so we up to [the] top of the
house to see it, but I down to the water-gate and saw it blow up, and
it was a wonderful distance [the] stones did fly to the endangering
all the small vessels in the harbour. Going down to the Mole I saw
the effects of the blow, which was very great, some parcels of the
iron cylinder making their way quite through the side of the Mole
and making a crack in one place quite across the Mole from side to
side, and yet there was not full a barrel and a half of powder . . . it
being a fine evening, and saw the whole camp of the Moors and
their huts and manner of walking up and down in their *alhaques* that
they look almost like ghosts all in white.
    Wednesday . . . to look upon the great chest at the head of the
Mole that is to be blown up to-night . . . my lord and I standing
looking out at our dining room window, we observe the going off
of the great chest, which though four chambers yet made but one

blow and that no great one, but the stones flew up and down upon the top of our house very plain, but no hurt done.

Thursday (1 November) . . . After dinner down with my lord to the Mole, and there surprised to see the mighty effect of the last night's blowing up of the great chest, it tearing it up from the very bottom.

Monday . . . Yesterday in the afternoon, being the 22, the guard house at the end of the Mole was blowed up in my sight at my window with very good success, yet no great noise at the blowing up, and now the Mole do begin to look indeed as in a way of destruction, this being a great mark of its standing all this while, but is now gone.

To demolish every trace of a construction that weighed 167,000 tonnes was no easy task, especially with seventeenth-century tools. Cholmley and Sheeres had done their work extremely well. When the rains set in again in mid-November, the work of destruction on the Mole was still far from complete.

By 25 October Pepys had completed a report on every petition against the commissioners' findings. Perhaps his biggest problem was not the chaotic townsmen, the Mole, or even the Moors but the governor himself, Percy Kirke, whom Pepys loathed. Pepys was alarmed to hear reports of soldiers under his command breaking into houses, robbing their owners and assaulting town clerks. Pepys began to keep a private record of all Kirke's misdemeanours. Dr Ken reported that Kirke had made sure that his mistress' brother was a reader in church, despite the fact that he was 'a fellow who swore, drank and talked bawdy.' Kirke had also put two of his men to death for threatening to complain about his injustices and had tied a sergeant to a post and thrashed him. Then there was the case of a poor Jewish refugee and his wife, who Kirke sent back to Spain to be burned by the Inquisition.

By the end of November 1683 Pepys was probably too exasperated to carry on writing his diary, but his miscellaneous notes included plenty of complaints about Kirke, whom he considered responsible for the generally low moral standards of Tangier. At night, officers and ordinary soldiers could be seen lying drunk in the streets.

And to show how little he makes of drunkenness . . . I have seen a
soldier reel upon him as he has been walking with me in the
street as drunk as a dog, and at this busy time too, when everybody that is not upon the guard is at work. And he has only
laughed at him and cry "God damn me, the fellow has got a good
morning's draught already," and so let him go without one word
of reprehension.

Dartmouth asked Pepys to look into a petition by a townsman
called Fox who said he had been beaten and taken to the guardhouse.
He said that when his wife came to visit him there, she was raped by
three soldiers and his house was burgled. Kirke's response was characteristically dismissive.

Fox replied that he had no reason to lie with another woman, for he
had a wife of his own. "Yes," publicly says Kirke, "and a handsome
one, but that is no argument, for I have a wife too, and yet I lie with
other women." . . . There was too much confessed to show the
bestiality of this place.

It was not surprising then, that over dinner Pepys and Dr Ken
agreed it was 'time for God Almighty to destroy the town.' Pepys
expressed the same sentiments in letters to James Houblon.

With sorrow and indignation I speak, it is a place of the world I
would last send a young man to, but to Hell. Therefore, on God's
account as well as the King's, I think it high time it were dissolved.

In his notes he mentioned how a recorder of the town had left his
estate to a servant 'on condition that he never married a woman of
Tangier.' By now, the diarist had no doubt that holding onto the city
was impossible.

Lying in his bed on 27 October, Pepys heard the mayor and others
take their leave of Dartmouth. At dawn the next day they sailed for
England. By 5 November all the townsmen had gone and only the
soldiers, engineers and members of the fleet were left. The greater
part of that month, the diarist was confined to his chamber with a

cold. His main concern was how to get to Spain, but before he went he had one last argument with the governor. Pepys was also horrified to find that ships' captains were asking to go to Cadiz or other ports on the pretence of getting repairs done, when in fact they were making money from private trading. Dartmouth however, seemed to accept it as inevitable. 'And the chief contributory cause of it all,' Bryant concluded, 'was Tangier – that accursed town far out of reach of every decent influence and check.'

Pepys' last days in Tangier passed in a downpour of rain: 'Such weather for wind, thunder, lightning, rain and hail all together for eight or ten days, I never saw in my life.' On the night of 28 November, a great storm swept the bay and several ships lost their moorings, just as the inhabitants seemed to have done some time ago. The Montagu was severely damaged after a collision with another frigate and needed repairs. This provided Pepys with his opportunity for a lift to Cadiz. The departure seemed auspicious, as the storms, while delaying operations on the Mole, removed the danger of a Moorish attack. On the last night of November, Pepys wrote his final letters to England, washed his feet and thighs with brandy and went to bed.

The next morning he collected his belongings, intending to leave aboard the damaged frigate, but storms further delayed his departure.

December 1 – Saturday Up and to get my things together to be gone this morning on board the Montagu towards Cadiz, the weather rainy, but by and by it become so stormy.

Here Pepys' Tangier notes come to an abrupt end. It was not until the evening of 6 December that the storm finally abated and Pepys sailed for Spain.

On 6 February 1684, this strange mission came to an end when Lord Dartmouth himself set fire to the very last mine and left Tangier on board the Grafton. He was depressed to see the town abandoned and the Mediterranean left to pirates, although his sense of failure did not stop there. He had only managed to secure the release of 54 out of 130 English slaves from Ismail. The fleet set sail on 21 February but, on the voyage home, the Grafton was damaged in high seas and three frigates were lost, while another ran aground.

Pepys finally disembarked at Spithead near Portsmouth on 3 April, having earned £992 for 248 days' work. His mission was deemed successful and a month later he was appointed First Secretary of the Admiralty, in effect the minister for the navy, answerable only to the king.

The loss of Tangier caused far less public outcry than had been expected. There was just a sense of indifference and regret that so much money had been wasted. But England's loss would turn out to be France's gain. 'This mistake,' wrote the French historian Jean Sibieude, 'unique in the colonial history of England, inexplicable on the part of a country so far-seeing and realistic, was ultimately profitable to France in that she was able to install herself in North Africa.'

If England had held Tangier after the death of Ismail – she might have extended her empire, and the history of Africa might have been different, but this loss cost England a decrease in prestige that coincided with her eclipse as a naval power. As Routh concluded, it took the reign of two more monarchs before the British would use Gibraltar 'the rock which England took, instead of the shifting sandhills of Tangier, to be her watch-tower at the gates of the Mediterranean.'

Back at Dar Zero, we prepared to bid farewell to the 97-year-old Charles Sevigny.

'Oh by the way, why is it called Dar Zero?' I asked.

'Don't ask silly questions. It's a Moroccan thing. Only in Morocco does a house start with a zero.'

For the second time Charles informed me that the fig tree was 300 years old. I told him I hoped he would make it to one hundred and we said our goodbyes. 'Well, I hope you got to know a bit about me,' he added, 'I won't be around much longer and now I feel a little tired.' I thanked him again and left him to his headphones, pint of beer, game of solitaire and endless array of staff. He was a lovely old man, lost inside his little palace.

FIVE

Walter Harris

The palace itself resembled the palace of a dream, haunted by ghosts

'I came to Tangier to write an article for the *Daily Mail* about the expats, the bunch of freaks that lived here,' Jonathan Dawson said, 'as soon as I stepped off the plane, I knew I fitted in perfectly.'

Jonathan's apartment was perched on the top floor of a 1940s Spanish stone building on the Avenue Prince Moulay Abdellah, off the Boulevard Pasteur, above a seedy cabaret club. 'This used to be the Rue Goya but now it's known colloquially as Zankat Shiatan, the 'Street of Satan,' it's full of bars, drug dealers, prostitutes and of course I'm here too! If you ask a taxi driver at the airport for Zankat Shiatan, they will laugh their heads off but they'll take you here.' The apartment had three leafy roof terraces. The interior, with cracked leather armchairs and cedar bookshelves stuffed with ancient leather bound tomes, would not have looked out of place in a large English country house. On the crimson walls hung portraits, etchings and antique maps. One of these was *Mapp of the Citty of Tanger with the Straits of Gibraltar* by Wenceslaus Hollar dating from 1664, showing the walled English garrison town. Where we were standing now, Jonathan pointed out, was in those days just yellow sand. A friend of his, James Chandler, had researched seventeenth-century Tangier and worked out that its dead inhabitants were buried beyond the walls of the garrison, beneath what is now a saucepan shop in the Grand Socco. Jonathan gave me several names and numbers of people to contact. 'I didn't know Pepys at all,' he said when I told him I was also writing about the English diarist, 'so I can't introduce you to him.'

My host was dressed immaculately in pressed cream flannels, navy linen jacket, striped shirt, cufflinks, spotted tie and matching silk kerchief in his top pocket. 'You must excuse the chicken shit,' he said, as I almost fell into an enormous red sofa. 'Birdie' was his pet chicken. Our conversation was intermittently interrupted by cock-a-doodle-doos. I asked him why he lived with a chicken. 'I suppose I just like fowl,' he said, 'having grown up on a farm in Australia.' Birdie slept in the bathroom. 'He doesn't like the outdoors, he's a freak too.' Our interview was also punctuated by the barks of his dog, which sang in tune with the muezzin from a nearby mosque.

Jonathan is not the only Tangerino to enjoy living with pets. In the 1950s, the Countess Phyllis della Faille, an Anglo-American woman married to a rich Belgian, lived with many more. 'At one point,' recounts Michelle Green in *The Dream at the End of the World*, 'her inventory was said to have included 376 creatures – including 75 dogs, 33 cats, 17 birds and 28 horses.' A rare tropical fish brought from a remote part of China was flushed down the toilet by mistake.

Jonathan said he had been a 'hack reporter' in London, writing 'poofy sorts of stuff about houses and gardens.' But he came out here in 1992 and quickly made Tangier his home. Lunch was served by smiling Moroccan staff, who seemed to emerge from and disappear silently into cupboard doors, like *Mr Benn*. We retired to the lounge for coffee and cigars. 'Morocco is not a police state, but it's very well policed,' whispered Jonathan, 'they probably know you're lighting a cigar right now! My phone is probably bugged. I don't mind of course, I have nothing to hide. I'm not a terrorist, a paedophile or a money-launderer. I sometimes wish I was, but there's no money to launder.' I asked him why Tangier seemed to attract eccentrics.

I don't think people look at a map and say to themselves "I'm eccentric, I will go and live in Tangier." It's a small place, so you notice the eccentrics more. I suppose if you choose to live in a country with a slightly challenging environment, you have a different mindset. The Moroccans are very kind and they celebrate their own people who are a bit mad. They think that God took the good bits of us into safekeeping and left the sort of remaining potty husk to be looked after.

'Oh, I almost forgot this,' Jonathan said as I was preparing to leave, pointing at a heavy chunk of white stonemasonry. 'It's from Walter Harris' house.' It was a section, shaped like three anvils on top of each other, of a crenellated wall that used to encompass the terrace at Villa Harris, where the British correspondent lived. Jonathan told me that James Chandler had been working on a book about Harris, but when Chandler died and his house went up for sale, the manuscripts were stolen.

Almost exactly a year later, Otmane asked if I would like to see Villa Harris. 'All the taxi drivers know where Villa Harris is,' he said, as we were driven along the corniche, that had once rivalled the likes of Nice or Beirut, 'but none of them can tell you who Harris was.' He shook his head, not for the first time, at the philistinism of some of his fellow Tanjawis. When we squeezed out of the car, I could see that the whole surrounding area, set back from the sea, was mainly under construction. Opposite, nestling among the metal cranes and steel rods protruding from layers of concrete were advertising boards for a new development. 'Entreprise Riad' looked more Saudi Arabian than Moroccan. All of this was at such an early stage in the build that it was as if the trajectory of progress was going the other way, towards a state of demolition and decay; Tangier's Ground Zero. Everything in the city seemed to be under construction, in a state of suspended animation, as if there were labels above the skyline saying: 'to be continued' or 'back in five minutes'. It is not clear when, if ever, the works will finish.

We clambered over weeds, piles of rubble and a ditch, to find the remains of an Olympic sized swimming pool. In the 1970s, this was the Club Med hotel, but now it looked like something out of modern-day Libya, maybe Gaddafi's bunker after it was bombed. 'When we were teenagers,' Otmane reminisced with misty eyes, 'we used to go inside the Hotel Malabata on the other side of the road, take the lift to the top floor and look down on the topless sunbathers and nude swimmers in the pool.'

We moved on, leaving the abandoned pool to its skinny-dipping ghosts. On the left we gazed down on a concrete amphitheatre and cylindrical turret. The whole dusty complex brought to mind images of the Third Reich or the Berlin Olympics. We pushed on further, penetrating into the lush, luminous, forested gardens, past a thick tree trunk that might have been felled by elephants, and there, half hidden in a dense ring of palm trees, bougainvillea and other overgrown shrubs, like a lost world in a film, stood Villa Harris.

The land here is owned by the king, who hopes to rebuild Villa Harris in all its original detail, but he is not in a hurry and in the meantime, the Moroccan authorities are not savvy enough to preserve the site and stop someone like me scrambling over the rubble, or someone like Jonathan taking a memento from the Villa for his mantelpiece. At night there are other intruders; the gardens are used by drug addicts, delinquents and drunks.

The white building was surrounded by fallen columns, abandoned plinths and broken paving slabs. On the first floor, half a French shutter still swung from its hinges like a remnant from the Alamo. Below, a crescent shaped Moorish arch with two five-pointed stars invited us into a broken network of interior rooms that had only blue sunlight for ceilings. Horizontal markings on the walls, akin to watermarks after the tide has gone out, indicated where the floorboards had once been. The walls were white, but occasionally mottled by mould. Brown brickwork poked through the stucco, leaving holes in the façade, as if the building were a piece of cheese, nibbled by an enormous mouse. On one of these walls were two keyhole shaped windows, resembling a silhouetted pair of nuns. Next to the nuns, Hassan, Hamza, Abdul and Elena had insisted on telling us that they had been here on 3 March 2013. Their visit and the house itself, was frozen in time, but there was something beautiful and peaceful about the ruins of Villa Harris, which lay, in the soft shade of tropical trees, like a reclining Buddha.

When he lived here, more than a hundred years before Elena's visit, Walter Harris had an unencumbered view of the sea; there were no Entreprise Riads or Club Meds to block out that sight. Unlike other foreigners, Harris wanted to live among Moroccans and not look down on them from a remote mountain. The Moroccans loved him for that.

On the way out, we saw a black Land Rover that was on its side, having been driven, who knows how long ago, into a ditch. New lamp posts had been planted along the road. Perhaps the driver was so surprised to find them that he wrapped his car around one of the posts, à la Marc Bolan.

Walter Burton Harris was born in London on 29 August 1866. His father was a wealthy shipping merchant and his mother came from a landed Scottish family. They lived on the Chelsea Embankment, near Oscar Wilde and James McNeill Whistler, who were family friends. At Harrow he was nicknamed the Liar because of his penchant for telling fibs, something that he used to good effect in his memoir *Morocco That Was*. In Harris' colourful life it was always difficult to extract fact from fiction, as they were so closely intertwined. It is said that the life of Walter Harris was the inspiration for *Indiana Jones*.

Not wanting to be tied down to office work, Walter Harris, like Jonathan Dawson, came to Tangier by accident in 1886 and stayed there for the rest of his life, working mostly as a correspondent for *The Times*. He was a tireless traveller, having already visited Madeira, Malta, Athens, Constantinople, Egypt, India, South Africa and Archangel. It was thought that only three Christians had ever been to the town of Chefchaouen: one was poisoned, one came for an hour disguised as a rabbi and the other was Walter Harris. It was also said that he had hardly any enemies in his life, but few close friends. His compassion and skills as a raconteur earned him the respect of the myriad of people he met, from the sultans to the daughters of his servants. He married in 1898, but the union was a failure, probably because of Harris' homosexuality.

When he arrived, Harris quickly set about exploring Morocco, travelling to Fes and Marrakech, as well as the countryside outside Tangier on shooting expeditions. Beyond there the Rif Mountains were even wilder and in his second year, Harris set off disguised as a Moor for Chefchaouen with his servant Selim. At this time the town was fanatically hostile towards infidels and although his colouring could have been Moorish, his Arabic let him down, so he became nervous and left after one night.

When I was a correspondent for the BBC in Morocco from 2006 to 2007, I lived in almost perpetual fear that there would not be enough news to pay my bills. Somehow, *Inshallah*, something always came up.

It was the same for Harris. Although his first article was published in
1887, it would be years before *The Times* took regular articles from him.
The headline of this first piece was not exactly eye-catching: *Troglodyte
Remains in Southern Morocco*. Little of interest to English readers was actually happening in Morocco, so Harris would travel almost anywhere
at a moment's notice and from 1903 he was put on a monthly salary.
Harris was, however, in the right place at the right time. Up until the
country became a French protectorate in 1912, there was huge interest
in which of the Great Powers would take it; what became known as
'The Morocco Question.' In Harris' later years, Morocco was no longer
of great importance to the newspaper, but they kept the correspondent
on for old times' sake.

Harris came to know three successive Moroccan sultans: Moulay
Hassan, Moulay Abdelaziz and Moulay Hafid. His descriptions of the
Moorish court in *Morocco That Was* provide a rare insight into a vanished
era. Harris' first encounter with Moroccan royalty came in 1887, when
he accompanied a British mission to visit Moulay Hassan. Harris is
rather cynical when writing about the dealings between the British
and the Moors, but then perhaps little has changed in modern diplomatic circles.

> From time to time the European governments despatched special
> missions to the sultan – gigantic picnics to one or other of the capi-
> tals, during which the pending claims would, or would not, be
> settled; a commercial treaty was possibly discussed; eternal friend-
> ship was sworn where only hatred on one side and indifference
> on the other really existed.

In 1894, while on an expedition among hostile tribes, Moulay
Hassan suddenly died. 'Any inkling of the Sultan's death,' wrote Harris,
'would have brought the tribes down to pillage and loot the imperial
camp.' So, the death had to be covered up until his successor was
announced. Only his chamberlain, Bou Ahmed, who would later act
as regent to the boy Sultan, Moulay Abdelaziz, and a few other servants,
knew the secret. Over the next couple of days the royal entourage
hurried home, still pretending the sultan was alive.

Another of the sultan's distractions was cycling.

Moulai Abdul Aziz was an expert bicyclist, and there were often great games of bicycle-polo of an afternoon in one of the court-yards of the palace. The only other Moor who played was Menebhi [the minister for war], then at the height of his power and influence. The sultan was a plucky but careful rider, seldom coming to grief, and handling his machine with the most perfect judgment. Menebhi was equally plucky, but much more excitable, and I have seen him in pursuit of the ball, charge at full speed into the palace wall, to be rescued from what looked like a lot of broken umbrellas a minute later, as he shouted wildly for a new bicycle.

The tragedy of Abdelaziz's reign was that the Europeans exploited his love of luxury. Even when he came of age, he was too immature to put away childish things. The monarchy spent as if there was no tomorrow and for Morocco there was no tomorrow. It was suicide by shopping.

'He spent,' Harris observed, 'not only the whole revenue of his country, but also the savings of his predecessors.' The sultan was told that ordering expensive products from European countries gave great satisfaction to their governments. This was not surprising; Britain, France and Spain did not have to spend money invading Morocco, they just flooded it with toys.

Grand pianos and kitchen ranges; automobiles and immense cases of corsets; wild animals in cages, and boxes of strange theatrical uniforms; barrel-organs and hansom-cabs; a passenger lift capable of rising to dizzy altitudes, destined for a one-storeyed palace; false hair; cameras of gold and of silver with jeweled buttons; carved marble lions and living macaw parrots; jewels, real and false; steam-launches and fireworks; ladies underclothing from Paris, and saddlery from Mexico; trees for gardens that were never planted, or, if planted, were never watered; printing presses and fire-balloons – an infinity of all that was grotesque, useless, and in bad taste. As each packing-case gave forth its contents they were looked at, perhaps played with, and the majority speedily consigned to rust and rot in damp stores and damper cellars.

After the coronation of King Edward VII, the young Sultan insisted on having a crown, so one was brought to him from Paris. He also demanded a coach. This was made of crimson lacquer and lined with green silk and cloths of scarlet and gold. Harris remarked that the crown and the coach, 'formed an ensemble as expensive as it was utterly useless, for there were no roads in Morocco.' There then unfolded a decadent, tragicomic scene, which you might envision taking place in President Mobutu's palace in Zaire or Michael Jackson's ranch, Neverland.

The sultan invited the Consul of a great foreign power . . . and the writer, to come and inspect his newest purchase. In the centre of an immense field of swampy grass, surrounded by high crenellated walls, stood the scarlet carriage. In this field of many acres were opened all the packing-cases which were too large to pass through the gateways that led into the interior courts of the palace; it served also as a grazing-ground for His Majesty's menagerie. In a wide circle at some little distance from the state coach stood a ring of zebras, emus, wapiti, Hindu cattle, apes, antelope, and llamas, with a background of more timid flamingos and strange storks and cranes – one and all intent on examining, from a position of safety, the extraordinary scarlet addition to their numbers which had suddenly appeared among them.

"We will ride in it," said the sultan; and beckoning to the Consul of a Great Power to get up behind, he himself mounted to the scarlet and gold seat of honour on the box. The writer rode inside. When all were seated, the vehicle started on its first and last progress of State. The soldiers and slaves sweated and puffed as the wheels sank deeper and deeper into the swampy ground, and the "progress" was slow indeed. Slow, too, were the paces of the procession that followed us, for, doubting but fascinated, the whole menagerie was in our wake, led by an emu whose courage had already been proved by an unprovoked attack upon the Scottish piper.

It rained that night, and the next day the little wake of water in which the state coach stood was purple from the dye of the harness, and the beautiful hammercloth of scarlet and gold flapped limp and ruined in the wind. Inside, there was a pool of water on the green-brocaded seat.

Among the other European influences were sports. Inside his high-walled palaces, the cycling sultan was also taught how to play tennis and cricket.

Moulai Abdul Aziz had a unique manner of scoring at cricket . . . We used to play cricket in the palace at Fez, generally four on each side. The score was carefully kept, but no names were entered. When the game was finished, the sultan himself placed the names against the score, always, of course, putting his own in front of the largest . . . If one is an autocratic monarch one can do anything – even poach your neighbour's cricketing score.

In this anecdote, Harris admitted his cricket was not up to much. This is a bit surprising since modesty was not really his forte. At every point in his memoirs, it seems that Harris was at the very centre of all the important historical events. He would always be the one, luckily, who came to the rescue to resolve arguments just when they threatened to turn into major diplomatic incidents.

Given the confidence of the sultan, Harris tried to warn him not to spend so much, but the advice fell on deaf ears. He also told Abdelaziz to take care to look after his subjects, but with the same pitiful result.

I only once saw him annoyed, and it was with myself. We were standing on the summit of an old outer wall of the palace. Immediately beneath us, in the shadow of the wall, were a dozen or so ill-clothed, half-starved members of what was inappropriately called the Moorish army. Many of the little group were evidently suffering from fever, very prevalent in Fez in summer, and altogether they formed a pitiful sight.

I spoke, perhaps, too warmly of the neglect with which the soldiers were treated, of their stolen pay, of their abject misery, and

I failed to notice that the Sultan was not in a mood at that moment to listen to my complaint.

"It isn't my fault," he said pettishly.

"It is," I replied. "Your Majesty doesn't take the trouble to see that your orders are carried out."

The blood rushed to the sultan's face, and he drew himself up. "Remember," he said, "you are speaking to the 'Commander of the Faithfull'," referring to his most coveted title.

"I do," I replied, "remember it. It is Your Majesty who forgets that these men are 'the Faithfull.'"

He bore me no grudge for what I said, and his look of anger passed into one of sadness. For a little while he stood looking over the great plain that lay before us, then turned and said very gently, "You don't know how weary I am of being a sultan," and tears stood in his eyes.

In 1903, Harris had the misfortune of being kidnapped by the warlord, Mulai Ahmed Ben Mohammed er-Raisuli or Raisuli for short. He terrified everyone and haunted Moroccans in their sleep. He also cast a magnetic spell over Harris when they met.

Tall, remarkably handsome, with the whitest of skins, a short dark beard and moustache, and black eyes, with profile Greek rather than Semitic, and eyebrows that formed a straight line across his forehead, Mulai Ahmed er-Raisuli was a typical and ideal bandit.

Raisuli was originally descended from one of the country's most aristocratic families and was also a Shereef or direct descendant of the Prophet, but he took to a life of crime. He began with cattle rustling and grew to become a powerful rebel against the state and a thorn in the side of the Spanish, who were trying to subdue northern Morocco. Harris' kidnapping enabled this great raconteur to dine out on the adventure story for the rest of his life.

On 16 June 1903, Moroccan troops set fire to Raisuli's headquarters in Zinat, east of Tangier. Harris rode out of Tangier to find out more. The place was 'entirely deserted' as the local population had fled to the Anjera Mountains. Harris' curiosity got the better of him and he ventured 'nearer than was perhaps advisable to the scene of the morning's action.'

> We were crossing a small gully, thick with crimson-blossomed olean-ders, when suddenly I discovered that I had fallen into an ambush. Flight was impossible, and as I was unarmed, resistance was out of the question. From every side sprung out tribesmen, and in a second or two I was a prisoner, surrounded by 30 or 40 men, one and all armed with European rifles. I received no rough treatment at their hands, but was told that I was their prisoner and must proceed to Zinat . . . Messengers were sent to inform Raisuli of my capture, and in a short time I was taken to him. He was seated under some olive trees in a little gully, surrounded by his men and by the headmen of the neighbouring tribes . . . Raisuli received me pleasantly enough.

Raisuli led Harris through a crowd of several thousand hostile tribesmen and took him to his house.

> The room in which I found myself was very dark . . . When I was able to see more clearly, the first object that attracted my eyes was a body lying in the middle of the room. It was the corpse of a man who had been killed there in the morning by the troops and formed a ghastly spectacle. Stripped of all clothing and shockingly muti-lated, the body lay with extended arms. The head had been roughly hacked off, and the floor all round was swimming in blood . . . At sundown Raisuli came and some of his men brought me food, and I had a long conversation with them. Raisuli was polite, and made no secret that he intended to make use of me, though he had not yet decided in what way. He, however, kindly informed me that, should the attack of the troops be renewed, I should be immediately killed.

Harris spent nine days in captivity. He was unable to wash and went 36 hours without food. The British minister in Tangier, Sir Arthur Nicolson, conducted negotiations for his release, but Harris could not resist concluding that it was his own skill that ensured his freedom. Since Villa Harris lay only a mile or two outside of the town, local people from the Anjera tribe were often trying to cross a river on the other side of his garden in order to carry charcoal to the market in Tangier. Seeing many women and girls stuck there in the winter months, Harris would take pity on them and would offer them shelter and food in his home. His generosity paid off.

A very short time after my capture, a proposal was made from Tangier that a very considerable sum of money should be paid for my immediate release. This was discussed by the tribesmen and refused. They decided that in the case of one who had shown such hospitality to their women and children, and often to themselves, there must be no question of money – and there was none.

I used every opportunity to bring the friendly tribe of Anjera over to my side, and on the night of the ninth day my friends rose nobly to the occasion. They surrounded Raisuli's house and village with perhaps a thousand men, all armed and prepared, and demanded that I should be handed over to them, threatening that, if this were not immediately carried out, they would shoot or arrest Raisuli. It was a little coup-d'etat and it was successful.

Less fortunate than Harris were some of Raisuli's other victims. Ion Perdicaris was a wealthy American playboy of Greek extraction. He had moved to Tangier, where he built a house known as the Place of Nightingales and filled it with exotic animals. On 18 May 1904, Perdicaris was kidnapped from his other house, Aidonia, outside the city, by Raisuli's bandits. An unconvincing replica of the house has been built in the forested area, Parc Perdicaris, where families gather to have picnics. The warlord demanded a ransom of $70,000 from Moulay Abdelaziz. During his confinement Perdicaris seemed to experience some sort of early form of Stockholm syndrome.

I do not regret having been his prisoner for some time . . . He is not a bandit, not a murderer, but a patriot forced into acts of brigandage to save his native soil and his people from the yoke of tyranny.

When he heard about the kidnapping, the American president Theodore Roosevelt was furious and his Secretary of State, John Hay, described the demands as preposterous. They dispatched seven warships and several naval companies, although they had little idea of what the forces would actually do on the ground. America threatened to seize Morocco's customs buildings if it did not persuade Raisuli to release Perdicaris. Roosevelt's resolve faltered when he was advised that Perdicaris was not actually American, having forfeited his American passport for a Greek one 40 years earlier, but the US President concluded that since Raisuli too thought Perdicaris was American, it made little difference. Roosevelt tried to get Britain and France to join the USA in a combined military action to rescue Perdicaris, but the two countries refused. Instead, the two powers were covertly recruited to put pressure on the sultan to accept Raisuli's demands, which he agreed to on 21 June. Secretary Hay saw the need to save face so he issued a statement to the Republican National Convention, saying that his government 'wants Perdicaris alive or Raisuli dead.' According to all witnesses, the convention, which had been lukewarm towards Roosevelt up until then, went wild at this remark. One delegate exclaimed, 'Roosevelt and Hay know what they're doing. Our people like courage. We'll stand for anything those men do.' This famous catchphrase quickly caught on and helped Roosevelt secure his election.

Raisuli received his ransom money for Perdicaris as well as various concessions. He was appointed as the Pasha of Tangier and Governor of Jibala province and his men were released from prison, but in 1906, he was ousted from the post after allegations of corruption and cruelty to his subjects. A year later he was banished altogether as an outlaw, but not to be deterred, shortly after, Raisuli kidnapped Sir Harry 'Caid' Maclean, a British army officer serving as a military aide to the sultan's army. Maclean was eventually freed, but Britain had to pay a ransom of £20,000. It also agreed to make Raisuli a British subject, giving him immunity from prosecution by the Moroccan authorities.

In 1913, Raisuli led several Rif tribes in a bloody revolt against the Spanish and continued guerilla warfare against them for eight years. During World War I, Raisuli was reported to be in contact with German spies who wanted him to lead a rebellion against France. French troops then launched a punitive expedition into Spanish Morocco in 1915, which dispersed his followers but failed to capture the warlord himself. In September 1922, he handed himself in to the Spanish authorities, changed sides and became one of the Spanish leaders in

the Rif War against another rebel leader, Abd el-Krim. In 1925, Abd
el-Krim's supporters attacked Raisuli's palace and kidnapped the great
kidnapper. He died in captivity in April of that year, having suffered
from dropsy for a long time, but there were persistent rumours that
he was not actually dead. Even today, Raisuli is considered by some
Moroccans to be a folk hero.

Harris remained friends with Raisuli and spoke of his former captor
with respect.

> There are few countries that could produce a Raisuli . . . Yet, during
> the last few years of his career he has made himself famous, and a
> real touch of romance surrounds the brigand, who, born of an aris-
> tocratic family, had terrorised and yet in a way protected Tangier, a
> city of 40,000 inhabitants, the seat of a dozen legations. In spite of
> his celebrity, very few Europeans have ever seen him. He has seldom,
> if ever, been photographed, and never written his name in the auto-
> graph collector's album. He has been throughout, a sort of myste-
> rious personage, half-saint, half-blackguard, whom every courageous
> male tourist has volunteered to capture, and many a still more
> courageous female tourist to marry. Moulai Ahmed er-Raisuli is
> unique – and perhaps, after all, one of his kind is enough.

But, we have run a little ahead of ourselves. In 1905, while the
country was still ruled by the Sultan Moulay Abdelaziz, the First
Moroccan Crisis began. This was an international wrangle over the
status of Morocco, which has been cited as one of the causes of World
War I. In 1905, Moroccans witnessed the visit of the German Kaiser,
Wilhelm II, to Tangier. Germany was troubled by the growing encroach-
ment of France and Britain. In 1904 they had signed a Franco-British
agreement, the Entente-Cordiale. The treaty came as a blow to Abdelaziz,
who had been relying on Britain as a buffer against France. The Kaiser
landed at Tangier on 31 March 1905, declaring that he had come to
support the sovereignty of Morocco. Once again, Harris seems to have
had a front seat in the theatre of history.

> The Emperor looked nervous as he rode through the decorated
> streets to the German Legation. Immense crowds of natives, who

had been told that this visit meant the saving of independence of their country, had gathered on the open marketplace in front of the Legation, and volley after volley was fired by them as the Emperor arrived and left. Many of the guns and rifles contained bullets, one of which, in its downward course, struck and indented the leather helmet of one of the suite, but fortunately no accident occurred. I was in the room while the diplomatic corps and the native officials were presented to the Kaiser, and heard both his words to the French *Chargé d'Affaires*, Comte de Cherisy, and to the Moorish authorities. To both, he announced his intention of considering Morocco as an independent country, and of treating its sultan as an independent sovereign.

The Tangier Crisis deepened by June 1905. Germany sought a multilateral conference where the French could be called to account in front of the other European powers. The German Chancellor, Count Bernhard von Bülow, threatened war over the issue. France moved troops to the German border and Germany called up all its reserve units.

On the advice of Germany, Abdelaziz agreed to a conference, thinking that it would ensure that foreigners would no longer interfere in Morocco. The opposite was true. The summit was held in the Spanish town of Algeciras in 1906 and the sultan also gave his approval to the ensuing Act of the Algeciras.

The results of the Conference of Algeciras and of the 'Acte' which promulgated its decisions were what might have been expected. All Europe sent its delegates to the pleasant little Spanish town lying a few miles from Gibraltar.

While the special ambassadors, whose titles fill a couple of pages of print in the tiny volume that contains the 'Acte', were discussing public works, international police, the state bank, and the difference between 'fusils rayés et non-rayés' – and a host of other things – Morocco was sinking deeper and deeper into a state of anarchy.

In 1907 the French bombarded Casablanca after the massacre of European workmen by locals. Once again Harris was quickly on the scene.

I saw it a few days after the bombardment, and the scene was inde-
scribable – a confusion of dead people and horses, while the contents
of almost every house seemed to have been hurled into the streets
and destroyed. The looting was incomplete: piles of cotton goods,
cases of foodstuffs – in fact, every class of merchandise still lay
strewn about the roads. Many of the houses had been burned and
gutted. Out of dark cellars, Moors and Jews, hidden since the first
day of the bombardment, many of them wounded, were creeping,
pale and terrified. Some had to be dug out of the ruins of their
abodes. Over all this mass of destruction, horses and men had
galloped and fought. Blood was everywhere . . . It was the beginning of the French occupation of Morocco, and the final end of
centuries of cruelty, corruption, and extortion.

Abdelaziz finally threw in the towel in 1908 and announced his
abdication. His half-brother, Moulay Hafid came to the throne that
year, but his tenure only lasted until 1912, the year of the French
Protectorate. The protectorate came about partly because of a trade-off
between the British and the French. The latter agreed to stay out of
Egypt if the English confirmed their disinterest in Morocco. Jonathan
Dawson explained that London therefore gave Paris, 'a nice piece of
sand for the Gallic cockerel to peck in.'
Moulay Hafid's position was tenuous and he was besieged by the
rural tribes. So, the new sultan asked for help from the French, who
were already installed in Casablanca and who were only too keen to
help. A few weeks later the Treaty of the French Protectorate was
signed. Moulay Hafid decided he would abdicate but only on terms
that were highly advantageous to him. There then ensued a game of
cat and mouse between the sultan and the French over the terms of his
departure.

Even when everything was arranged, and the letters for the proclamation of his younger half-brother, Mulai Youssef, had been
despatched to the interior, Mulai Hafid changed his mind. On
reconsideration, he stated, he thought he wouldn't abdicate or leave
the country, as had been decided . . . Then Mulai Hafid said that
possibly he might be persuaded again to change his mind. He was;

but it cost another £40,000, which was given him in a cheque as he left the quay at Rabat for the French cruiser that was to take him on a visit to France.

It was on board this ship that a particularly amusing incident occurred. Harris, of course, was one of the passengers accompanying the sultan and able to tell the tale.

The sea was calm, the night warm, and after dinner the performance took place – singing, dancing and some juggling. One item of the show took place in the saloon, where a very attractive and skillful lady conjurer performed some most astonishing tricks. The sultan and his suite were much impressed, but their astonishment reached its climax when the charming young lady filled an apparently unlimited number of glasses with an apparently unlimited variety of drinks out of a medium-sized teapot.

As we threaded our way out of the saloon, one of the more influential of the native suite whispered in my ear, "What do you think the lady would take for the teapot?" I naturally replied that probably all the wealth of the world could not purchase so unique a vessel. My friend was disappointed . . . "It would have been," he added with a sigh, "so useful when one was travelling."

When the former sultan returned to Tangier, the old Kasbah was placed at his disposal, and he took up residence, together with his staff, wives and children who numbered around 160 in total. Once again, he argued over the terms of his abdication. 'The negotiations were being carried on by him in a spirit of grasping meanness,' Harris wrote, 'that rendered any solution impossible.' Well nearly impossible; the cavalry arrived, yet again, in the form of a certain Walter Burton Harris. 'It was at this moment, when everything seemed almost hopeless,' Harris recalled, 'that the writer was asked, independently by both sides, to intervene in the interests of peace.'

During the following weeks the principal points of the negotiations were successfully solved – the question of the pension, funds for the construction of a palace in Tangier, the retention of certain large properties in the interior, and the future of the ex-sultan's wives and children.

Like Abdelaziz before him, Hafid also had his royal menagerie to think about.

While two elephants were being brought from Fez to Tangier at the time of the abdication, one of them escaped on the road, and being an unknown beast to the villagers of the countryside, it met with many adventures. Wherever it appeared arose panic and consternation, and the whole male population turned out with such weapons as they could lay their hands on to drive away this terrible and unknown beast. The country population, however, possessed little but very primitive firearms, whose range was short, and whose bullets dropped harmlessly off the sides and back of the huge pachyderm, thereby increasing the panic. The elephant, luxuriating in the spring crops, grazed undisturbed, while from as near as they dared to approach, the outraged proprietors poured volleys against its unheeding bulk. But one day it found itself on the road again, and came rolling along into Tangier none the worse, but remarkably spotted all over with the marks of the spent bullets.

Harris found himself in the same position as Pepys, two centuries earlier, trying to sort out complicated property claims. Harris had to negotiate who would pay the sultan for the most bizarre royal possessions including lions, watches and wardrobes. Harris was again called in to broker a truce. 'By dint of great persuasion,' Harris said, 'the writer eventually brought about a settlement.' Thus, the sultan abdicated. Harris clearly had an eye for the comical and the absurd and the Moorish court provided both. 'Amongst many mechanical toys which Moulai Hafid possessed,' Harris remembered, 'was one which in its absurdity surpassed any toy I have ever seen.'

It was – or had been – a parrot, life-sized, seated on a high brass stand which contained music. Moth and rust had corrupted it, and there was little left of the gorgeous bird except a wash-leather body the shape of an inflated sausage, with two black bead eyes still more or less in place, and a crooked and paralyzed-looking beak. The legs had given way, and the cushion of a body had sunk depressedly on to the brass perch. One long red tail-feather shot out at an angle, and round its neck, and sparsely distributed over its body were the remains of other plumes, of which little but the quills remained. On either side were the foundations of what had once been its wings, consisting of mechanical appliances in wood and wire.

Every now and then, apparently for no reason, this strange toy came to life. The sausage-like body wriggled, the broken beak opened, the tail-feather shot out at a new angle, and the framework of the wings extended itself and closed again with a click; and then after a mighty effort, which gave one the impression that the ghost of a bird was going to be seasick, the whistling pipes concealed in the brass stand began to play. The music was on par with the bird – notes were missing, and the whole scale had sunk or risen into tones and demi-tones of unimaginable composition . . . It seemed as though there was a race between the bird and the pipes to reach the climax first. Both grew more and more excited, until suddenly there was a long wheeze and a longer chromatic scale from high to low, and with an appealing shake of its palsied head, the parrot collapsed once more into its state of petrified despair.

Thus the last days of pre-colonial Morocco came to an end, not with a bang, but with the whimper of a stuffed parrot.

There followed a scramble for Tangier that would result in a stalemate, in which Britain, France and Spain adopted "dog in the manger" attitudes. If they could not have complete control of the city, then neither should anyone else. 'Morocco was like an overripe plum,' wrote Tessa Codrington, 'waiting to drop into the lap of one of the European powers.' Early signs of collaboration had been witnessed when the British and French agreed to build the lighthouse at Cap Spartel, which was finished in 1864. European residents later set up a health committee to deal with the city's diseases. From such small beginnings, the International Zone would emerge. When France and Spain partitioned Morocco into French and Spanish protectorates in 1912 under the Treaty of Fes, the position of Tangier still remained unclear. Negotiations over its future dragged on, interrupted by World

War I. Britain and France finally signed the Tangier Convention in 1923 recognizing a neutral demilitarised zone of some 373 square kilometres, the International Zone, with grudging acceptance by Spain. Other nations; namely Italy, Portugal, Belgium, the Netherlands and the United States would sign up later. In accordance with the Tangier Protocol, the city was under the nominal sovereignty and jurisdiction of the sultan, but in reality it was a unique experiment in multinationalism, with a reputation for tolerance as well as cultural and religious diversity. The International Zone would last until shortly after Morocco's independence in 1956.

Villa Harris was the first of several properties that Harris acquired. As it was in a remote section of the bay, Harris bought it for a pittance and began to build on it in the 1890s. Later, Harris expanded the house, bringing craftsmen from Fes to decorate the interior. He also imported trees from France, Spain and Algeria for the garden which was populated by peacocks. But after Ba Ahmed's death in 1904, the house was attacked by bandits. Although he was brave, Harris was no fool and he moved into town, never setting foot in the villa again. He went on to build four more houses.

Up on the Old Mountain lies a sumptuous boutique hotel called Villa Josephine. Otmane and I were exploring the area one day and took a small diversion in a petit taxi to have a look around. A short drive leads you through a green trellised arch, past a fountain on a pink patio and up towards the entrance. The white two-storey building, with wrought iron verandas and French shutters, has been immaculately restored and looks like a colonial plantation house in the Caribbean. Two wooden Dalmatians eye you with disdain as you enter. The interior walls are painted turquoise and decorated with nineteenth-century French oil paintings. Further inside is a wood panelled bar and library, complete with open fires, pink velvet sofas and leather armchairs.

Villa Josephine belonged to the Lords of the Atlas and quislings of the French regime, the Glaouis. Before that, Walter Harris lived here. Its lawn, palm trees and the hydrangeas surrounding the swimming pool are constantly watered and from here you can see the Strait of Gibraltar and, in the middle distance, another house that clings to the cliffs. This is Dar el Quaa, the House of Arches, which now belongs to the Emir of Qatar. I tried to enter it once but was ejected by a security guard. It was also known as Scott House as it had been the home of Basil Scott, the former Chief Justice of Bombay. Scott's son Michael wore an eyepatch following an accident. 'He looked like Moshe Dayan,' Otmane recalled. He also used to converse with a plastic parrot attached to his shoulder. Basil's wife, Lady Gwendoline, was known for her absent-mindedness. One day she was planting bulbs in her garden when she realised she would be late for dinner. She rushed inside to get changed and stuck a daffodil bulb in her cleavage, having planted her diamond brooch in the flower bed, or so they say. 'Did people make things up?' I asked Annie Austin, who lived in Tangier in those days, 'I expect so,' she replied, 'One didn't have time to check, we just moved on to the next thing.' Lady Gwendoline herself is reputed to have said 'Never ever believe anything you hear in Tangier, and only half of what you see.' The same could perhaps be said of the life of Walter Harris.

Harris' last house, Dar Sidi Hosni in the Kasbah remained unfinished at the time of his death. It passed into the hands of the US diplomat Maxwell Blake and later, the American socialite Barbara Hutton.

As a benign snob, Walter Harris' marriage to Lady Mary Savile may have had something to do with the fact that she was a daughter of the fourth Earl of Mexborough, but things fell apart on their honeymoon and although she tried to patch things up by coming to Tangier in 1899, the marriage was never consummated and was annulled six years later.

In 1926, Harris fell in love with an American woman, Barbara Harrison, even though he was over 60 and she was 21. She was to walk out on him during a trip to the East Indies. In 1933 Harris set off for another adventure in the Far East but only got as far as Malta, where he suffered a stroke and died on 4 April. His obituary ran to 1,700 words. Tributes and condolences came in from the French Resident General, Marshal Lyautey and King George V.

As was befitting a man for whom truth might occasionally get in the way of a good story, rumours persisted for several years that Harris had not died of natural causes, but had been murdered by the French secret service.

A month after his death, Walter Harris was buried in Tangier. His funeral was attended by the sultan's representative, the Mendoub and all the diplomats of the International Zone. Shops were closed and a huge crowd of Moroccans, many of whom had made long journeys to be there, came to pay their respects, but even at the bitter end there was comedy. The ecclesiastical hierarchy at the Protestant church of St Andrew's had deliberated long and hard about whether to bury a man who had become a Catholic through marriage. In the end, they conducted a Catholic service at the port and his coffin was then carried up the hill to St Andrew's. Spanish Franciscans were however, said to have come in the dead of night to reconsecrate his grave according to their own rites.

St Andrew's Church has an English interior, although the ceiling is made of cedar, carved by craftsmen from Fes and the Lord's Prayer is scrolled in Arabic above the chancel. Outside is a lush, shaded cemetery. I found Harris' gravestone near the church entrance. On the stone was an inscription that I would be proud to have on my own.

Walter Burton Harris
born August 29th 1866
He came to Tangier in 1886
and was associated with
The Times
as correspondent in Morocco
and elsewhere
from 1887 till his death
April 4th 1933
He loved the Moorish people
and was their friend.

Jonathan Dawson told me that, to keep his 'options open,' he had reserved two burial plots for himself: one at the Catholic church and the other at St Andrew's. 'I prefer St Andrew's,' he said 'I've got a very nice plot there, not too far from Walter Harris. But I'm not ready to join the turf club just yet.'

Henri Matisse

Shall we ever see the sun in Morocco? Since Monday at three when we arrived,
until today, Saturday, it has rained continuously.

When I first started researching this book, I was unable to get inside the Grand Hotel Villa de France, because, like the Caves of Hercules and many other things in Tangier, it was closed for refurbishment. It had actually been shut since 1990, but in September 2014 it was finally reopened and a few months later I managed to have a look around. Its owner, the Iraqi businessman, Nadhmi Auchi, whose property port-folio includes the El Minzah hotel, spent 11 million dollars upgrading the Villa de France. It sits on the Avenue d'Angleterre and its front façade, painted cream with a yellow trim, gives it the air of an ornate cheesecake. I was shown around by the German manager of the two hotels, Albrecht Jerentrup, who was, as you might expect, efficient but also, as you might not expect, warm and sometimes deliciously indis-creet. From the windswept terrace we looked out on a spectacular 180-degree view that takes in the Kasbah, the Grand Socco, St Andrew's Church, the harbour, the beach and a McDonalds.

It was here in 1912, that one of the greatest painters of the twentieth century, Henri Matisse first stayed. The hotel renovation has made much of this. The entrance lobby and the bar are bedecked with Matisse reproductions, the wrought iron staircase is made from Fauvist leaf shapes and an abstract wavy line, reminiscent of his collages, serves as a ceiling frieze.

We walked up to the second floor where an arrow directed us to Room 35. Albrecht let me have a look inside. A large double mattress is encased in a mahogany bedstead and above it hang three more copies of works by the modernist painter, including one of his most famous, *Paysage Vu d'Une Fenetre* (Landscape Viewed from a Window). The room is sparse, equipped only with a wardrobe, chair, mirror and dressing table. Next to the bed is a vintage telephone, presumably for vintage conversations. On another wall hangs a reproduction of a black and white photo of Henri and his wife Amelie. They are standing in the same room in front of a bed, a traveller's trunk, an easel and the original canvas of *Paysage Vu d'Une Fenetre*. Between us, Albrecht and I managed to prise open the stiff shutters, although from time to time the sirocco wind would blow them violently shut again. The view from the window has hardly changed since *Paysage* was painted more than 100 years ago. You can still make out the green roof and white steeple of St Andrew's Church, nestling in a bed of date palms and evergreens, a tall minaret, the Kasbah on the hill and the Mediterranean beyond. Luckily, from this window you cannot see the 'Golden Arches' of McDonalds.

When the 42-year-old Matisse first set eyes on Tangier on 29 January 1912, he was full of optimism.

On a slightly rough sea, but of the purest blue, the ship glides without rocking or pitching. On the left, the horizon is lined with a few clouds; on the right by the mountains of the Spanish coast.

In this upbeat tone, Matisse wrote a letter to his daughter Marguerite in Paris, as he and Amelie approached the port. 'Splendid weather,' he added. But that purest blue was a mirage and those few clouds turned out to be more ominous than he could have ever imagined. When Matisse and Amelie landed they were hit by torrential rain. '*Ici, nous sommes dans la pluie, un déluge,*' he wrote to Marguerite two days later.

It was to continue like this for weeks. 'Shall we leave again?' Matisse said in a plaintive postcard to his friend Henri Manguin, 'what a misadventure!' and he wrote to Gertrude Stein in a similar vein.

Shall we ever see the sun in Morocco? Since Monday at three when we arrived, until today, Saturday, it has rained continuously, as in tropical countries. It's been like that for 15 days. What's to become of us? It's impossible to leave our room.

Henri and Amelie checked into their room at the Villa de France. Matisse himself says it was room number 38, although most art historians think it was number 35. We are at least talking about the same room with the same view, situated on the corner of the hotel, even if the numbers have become mixed up. At that time the Villa de France was the best hotel in Tangier, yet despite the view, the Matisses found it poky, dirty and overpriced.

Matisse had been commissioned by the Russian art collectors, Sergei Shchukin and Ivan Morozov. In November, the French artist had stayed in Moscow and was desperate to see the sun. Light was vital to painters who worked outdoors, especially Matisse, who was obsessed with colour. In Morocco, the more or less constant presence of the sun usually guaranteed stable light conditions for each painting session. Matisse was such a perfectionist that he would descend into fits of anxiety if the meteorological conditions changed.

His oldest friend, Albert Marquet, had recommended Morocco, having been there in 1911. Matisse had been seduced by Marquet's blue and white canvases of the Kasbah, with their almost abstract architectural geometry.

Shchukin did not tell Matisse what to paint, but his letters contained subtle hints that he had a preference for figures. The problem was that in a Muslim country, Matisse struggled to find people who were willing to pose for him. After several frustrating weeks he recruited a reluctant ragbag of locals including a teenage prositute, a bandit and a hotel boy, but the Russian influence seemed to seep into Matisse's paintings; the figures had the feel of icons, saints and prophets, as his biographer Hilary Spurling writes, 'each posed lightly like a flower on a flat ground of turquoise, gold and black.'

Confined to his dark room like an inmate in an asylum, Matisse painted several still life pieces. Although not rich at this time, Matisse's one luxury was to have fresh flowers delivered and his very first painting in Tangier was *Vase of Irises* in which the flowers are set against an oval dressing table mirror. The painter filled the area between their stems with black, making the arrangement of irises stand out, but also making the picture slightly haunting. Above the vase are patches of yellow and green, as well as an inexplicable blue shadow. 'Only the pale yellow and green stripes reflected in the dressing table's mirror hint at the extraordinary colours that Matisse was to discover in Tangier when the clouds finally lifted,' writes the art critic Michael Kimmelman. Perhaps Tangier was already beginning to have an effect on Matisse. *Vase of Irises* anticipates many other still lifes that the artist would paint back home in France.

Another picture in the room, *Basket of Oranges*, evokes a sense of the Morocco that existed outside the hotel. Here, the fruit compete for attention with peonies on a white silk cloth. The oranges and lemons with their black stems and green leaves still attached are arranged in a shallow basket, just as they would have been sold in the souks. In 1940, Pablo Picasso bought the painting. His lover, Françoise Gilot, was amazed when Matisse told her that it had been 'born of misery.'

When the weather cleared intermittently, Matisse depicted the view from his window. Michael Kimmelman sees *Paysage Vu d'Une Fenêtre* as a groundbreaking painting.

This is a scene parched by the sun. Like so many of Matisse's Moroccan paintings, it is covered only in the thinnest washes of pigment, as if Matisse wanted the texture of the unpainted canvas to show through so that it would add rawness to the browns and grays.

Paysage became the left hand side of a triptych with *The Casbah Gate* on the right and *On the Terrace* in the middle. Morozov would pay 8,000 francs for the picture.

Another depiction of the city is *View of the Bay of Tangier*. This was rendered extremely quickly, as if the artist was worried about a change in the weather, as can be seen in the backdrop of a grey cloudy sky, a dark stormy sea and gentle hills, green with rain. In the foreground are architectural features of the Kasbah, including the white-domed shrine of a Muslim saint which can still be seen today near the horseshoe shaped arch of Bab al-Assa. The view is slightly tilted so that the spectator feels he is hovering above the bay.

Matisse would look back on those first few weeks, held hostage in the Villa de France with a sense of dread, and 'the famous room number 38' became a grim in-joke among the Matisse family. Years later while stuck in thick fog in London and holed up in the Savoy he recalled those weeks in Tangier where they were 'stranded like lost souls.' Decades later, William Burroughs was also confined to his hotel room; not by bad weather but by drugs, yet out of this incarceration a different masterpiece would emerge.

On 12 February, the rain finally subsided. The Matisses rode out along the beach, entranced by the sun and the luminous vegetation. High up in the fields above the town the painter's paradise unfolded in the form of yellow and orange nasturtiums, purple heliotrope and blue morning glories.

Once the rain stopped, there sprang from the ground a marvel of flowering bulbs and greenery. All the hills around Tangier, which had been the colour of a lion's skin, were covered with an extraordinary green under turbulent skies as in a painting by Delacroix.

While he was showing me around the hotel, Albrecht said that about 20 years ago an art expert identified a mural that had been painted by Delacroix, but by the time this man returned to do something about it, the mural had been indelibly painted over.

Ferdinand Eugene Victor Delacroix was Matisse's biggest inspiration for visiting Morocco. 'I have found landscapes in Morocco,' Matisse wrote, 'exactly as they are described in Delacroix's paintings.' The Romantic painter had landed in Tangier almost exactly 80 years earlier. He accompanied Count Charles de Mornay, an ambassador sent by King Louis-Philippe to negotiate a treaty with the sultan shortly after the French conquered Algeria.

Delacroix also went to Morocco to escape Parisian civilization, hoping to see what he considered a more authentic, primitive culture. He would go on to produce more than 100 paintings and drawings of scenes from North Africa and added a new dimension to the contemporary interest in Orientalism. For Delacroix, Tangier and its people became subjects that he would revisit again and again until the end of his life. Delacroix was fascinated by the costumes of the indigenous people and thought that they suited his classical scenes. 'The Greeks and Romans are here at my door,' he said, 'in the Arabs who wrap themselves in a white blanket and look like Cato or Brutus.' Delacroix fell in love with Morocco. He was inspired by its brilliant light, architecture and colours. 'The picturesque is plentiful here,' he wrote in April 1832, 'At every step, one meets ready-made paintings that would bring twenty generations of painters wealth and glory.'

'Delacroix was impressed by the way Moroccans walked, their posture and their balance,' Gipi de Richemont said. We were sitting in the Café Tingis in the Petit Socco. He wore a lime green suit, topped with a scarf like whipped cream around his neck. Round spectacles perched on his nose and at his side lay an antique walking cane. Gipi is another of Tangier's great characters. He was born in Tiznit in southern Morocco, his father fought for the French colonial infantry against Rommel in Tunisia and his great-grandfather was the French consul in Tangier in 1875.

In nineteenth-century France, the women wore tight corsets and the men starched collars, but in Morocco, Delacroix saw very natural gestures. There was an ease and voluptuousness in the way they reclined on couches, so he started to draw and see people in a totally different way. All this influenced him a lot.

One day in Tangier in 1832, Delacroix and de Mornay hid in an attic and through the cracks of a shuttered window, witnessed the frenzy of a fanatical Muslim sect, the Aïssaouas. The turmoil of that event is conveyed in a vividly coloured and vigorously brushed depiction of the fanatics hurling themselves down the street. *The Fanatics of Tangier* remains one of Delacroix's most disturbing images. Another notable event was a Jewish wedding that he went to in February 1832. Like Matisse, Delacroix had difficulty finding women willing to be his subjects as Muslim women wore veils, but this was not a problem when it came to Jewish women. In 1841 he turned those sketches into the final canvas, *Jewish Wedding in Morocco*.

In February 1912, with clearer skies and a lighter heart, Matisse wrote to Manguin of the 'melting light' which was 'quite different from the Cote d'Azur.'

The vegetation has all the blazing brilliance of Normandy and such decorative force! How new everything seems, too and how difficult to do with nothing but blue, red, yellow and green.

Walter Harris introduced Matisse to another Englishman, Jack Brooks, who made his home, Villa Brooks, available to the artist. Villa Brooks does not exist any more but was located near the Intercontinental Hotel.

The property was immense, with meadows stretching as far as the eye could see. I worked in a corner planted with very tall trees which spread their foliage high and wide.

He stored some of his materials in an outhouse in the garden and settled down to paint the acanthuses every day for the next month and a half, with Amelie by his side. This time together seems to have helped their relationship and he wrote to his daughter Marguerite that Amelie was looking young again.

In Tangier, Matisse lived with the promise from Shchukin of a commission of 6,000 francs for each of the 11 canvases. The city and its Muslim culture came as a shock to Amelie though, who had hardly ever left her homeland. In the souk they trampled on carcasses, blood and sewage and although they saw camels, snake charmers and sorcerers they were also horrified by the beggars with open sores and mystified by the veiled Arab women whom the Irish painter John Lavery had described as 'surgeons masked and gowned for the operating theatre.' The European quarter did not make them feel particularly at home either, although it did remind Matisse of 'seedy, suburban Paris,' as he wrote to Gertrude Stein in March.

Matisse used the Bab al-Assa in the medina as a frame for another picture, the *Casbah Gate*. In this he foreshortened the perspective, rearranged buildings and added other elements to improve the composition. The result is a virtually abstract painting, in which a bold red diagonal stripe runs through other shapes dipped in deep blue.

Artists say that the quality of the light in Tangier is exceptional because it bounces off two seas: the Mediterranean and the Atlantic. The same has also been said of St Ives in Cornwall. The American artist, Elena Prentice, who lives in Tangier, has spoken of its 'marvels of reflected light dancing along a watery surface flickering off in all directions.' Gipi de Richemont told me that 'Living in Tangier is like being in a boat, we are surrounded by the sea and when the light of the sun hits the water, it's like a mirror. If you go inland you don't get this reflection, but you see it in the Sahara, with the sand dunes, and the mountains with the snow.' He also said that Tangier owes the clarity of its light to the wind, the Chergui, which blows in from the East.

> You know why there is an East Wind in Tangier? Because Hercule (sic) was so tired after his all his work − separating Africa and Europe − that he breathed very deeply and we are still living under the breath of Hercule! The sun is very strong because there is no mist. We have no pollution thanks to Hercule.

Just as sovereigns, politicians and military leaders prized Tangier for its strategic location, so artists valued the city for its geographic position. 'A rare point on the planet,' as Gipi called it.

By the time Matisse visited Tangier, the city was already swarming with artists, who had followed in the footsteps of Delacroix in search of the exotic. In 1889, Edgar Degas had set up his easel in the nearby Hotel Continental. It looked as though half of the modernists in Paris might descend on Tangier, asking Matisse to reserve them a room. He received postcards to that effect from Marquet, Manguin, Signac and Apollinaire, but Matisse conspicuously avoided seeing anyone too arty or bohemian because, as he said to Amelie, such people always mistook him for a madman when they inspected his paintings. The Irish painter John Lavery also stayed at the Continental from where he contemplated the changing light on the beach. Lavery asked the Scottish watercolourist James Guthrie what he made of Matisse's work. 'It may command attention, but it won't wash in the long run,' was Guthrie's reply.

'What lousy painting,' Matisse wrote home after seeing some of Lavery's works depicting the mosques, markets and moonlit alleyways of Tangier. Lavery was accompanied by the Canadian artist, James Wilson Morrice, who had also checked in at the Villa de France. Morrice encouraged other potential modernists to learn from Matisse.

Tangier's weather was proving erratic and the city was not revealing itself to be the Oriental wonder that Matisse had dreamed it would be. There were hardly any museums and the mosques were closed to Christians, as were the houses whose tiles, mosaics and woodwork remained out of reach. Apart from seeing merchants selling carpets and silks in the souk, Matisse rarely caught a glimpse of the artefacts that had inspired his visit and it was still hard to persuade Arabs to sit for him, as the locals believed that contact with a foreigner would make them unclean. John Lavery told him that the few he had persuaded to sit for him were all convinced that he had the Evil Eye. Harris had procured a couple of elderly female sitters from the local brothel, but Lavery was so disappointed with them that he sent them back.

Eventually in March, the hotel owner Mademoiselle Davin managed to find a girl willing to pose for the French master. Her name was Zorah and she was no older than 12. Matisse sat her down on the ground in a soft yellow robe against a pale blue-green wall and painted her swiftly with light touches. Her oval face is offset by the curves of her body and she sits Buddha-like with her legs tucked beneath her. Davin had told him that it would be wise to hire a separate studio so Zorah could have access to it without being seen, but even so the sittings came to an end almost immediately. On 6 April, Matisse told Amelie that Zorah's brother would probably kill her if he knew that she was posing.

At the time Morocco was deeply conservative and foreign men who took a shine to Moroccan women could regret doing so. Lavery told Matisse the story of a young, French soldier who was invited to dinner by the Pasha of Tetouan. The soldier was entranced by a girl who danced for him. The next morning the Pasha sent the subaltern a parcel containing the girl's head. Walter Harris also described severed heads impaled on the parapets of palaces. Amelie Matisse told her grandson that walking in Tangier was like being chased by a rider galloping towards her between the high white walls of a narrow street. The French novelist Pierre Loti, who visited Tangier in 1889, observed that even the ordinary conversations he heard beneath his window sounded more like people slitting each other's throats.

Loti had seen bulls sacrificed to the French ambassador as he rode from Tangier to present his credentials to the Sultan Moulay Hassan. The sultan's successors had angered the population by making concessions to France during the Scramble for Africa and that fury culminated in a revolt in 1911. Germany then sent a warship to Agadir, and Matisse, clearly worried, asked Marquet, who was in Tangier that summer, if France would go to war over Morocco. The Morocco-Congo Treaty signed on 4 November 1911 put an end to the Agadir Crisis and, from the painter's point of view, it made him feel much more comfortable about visiting Morocco. To Moroccans themselves, the treaty was a sell-out. By the time the Matisses arrived in January 1912, the sultan was in Fes being besieged by Berber tribesmen. French troops were dispatched from Casablanca and Henri and Amelie wisely decided not to visit Fes, which would have been a tough ten-day mule ride away.

Their consolation prize was a day's ride with two or three other hotel guests and Arab guides to Tetouan, which Harris had recommended for its scenery. They were mounted on flat wooden saddles, but Matisse enjoyed the journey. They left around dawn and went through a green valley of daisies and buttercups. For Matisse it was one of his most enduring memories of Morocco: 'We rode in among this sea of flowers as if no human being had ever set foot there before,' he said, 'It was a tremendous attraction, a sort of paradise found in which I was completely free, alone, at peace.' The ride had such a profound effect on Matisse that he compared it with the day his life changed forever, when he was given his first paint-box.

Back in Tangier on 28 March, Matisse returned to Villa Brooks, hoping to recreate that feeling of freedom from that valley of flowers. Matisse painted three canvases in the garden of Villa Brooks, *Acanthus*, *Periwinkles (Moroccan Garden)* and *Palm Leaf Tangier*, often referred to as the *Moroccan Garden Triptych*. In these you can see the luminous foliage of the Rif, and layers of green that Loti had said would need colours unknown to any palette. As Spurling says, 'colours that would incorporate the strange sounds, the rustlings and above all the silences of Africa, its thundery undertones, its darkness and its translucent delicacy.'

Although he spent about six weeks working on *Acanthus*, Matisse was not pleased with the result. 'I made a large canvas' he wrote 'and when it didn't satisfy me, I decided that I would bring it back the following year.' *Periwinkles (Moroccan Garden)* looks more spontaneous but a recent infrared examination revealed that he stuck to a pre-meditated composition and followed the drawing underneath rigidly.

In the first two weeks of April, Matisse had a breakthrough, like a thunderstorm that cleared the air. He was enchanted, he told Amelie, every time he returned to the Villa Brooks, remembering years later that *Palm Leaf Tangier* had come easily to him 'in a burst of spontaneous creation – like a flame.' The palm fronds seem to burst out from the middle of the canvas and are each created with a single stroke, emphasised with lines scratched into the surface with the end of a brush. The painting was finished in just a few sessions.

Periwinkles and *Palm Leaf Tangier* were among 23 paintings displayed in 1990 at the 'Matisse in Morocco' exhibition at the National Gallery of Art in Washington. In Villa Brooks, 'He found what he wanted,' said the curator Jack Cowart. 'Besides, Matisse really didn't like to travel farther than a 400-yard radius from his hotel. He always had so much baggage to move about: canvases, stretchers, paints.' Morocco, Cowart says, was the hinge between Matisse's earlier European, Fauvist style and his more powerful later work.

Satisfied that her husband had installed himself in this peaceful garden, Amelie returned to France on 31 March. Their parting in the harbour was strained and Matisse admitted to her that it was only the small talk of Madame de Beaumarchais, the wife of the French *Chargé d'Affaires*, that managed to calm him down. He also told her that he was consulting a Russian doctor who prescribed hot baths, exercise, rest and early nights, believing that his sojourn to Tetouan had exhausted him. He later told Amelie that he had achieved nothing in Tangier and only stayed on in the hope of finishing the paintings for Morozov. In his letters he admitted being hard on himself and that he got 'worked up too easily.'

Matisse spent the rest of his time in Tangier working furiously. As the Russian doctor had ordered, his work was punctuated by morning horse rides and early bed times. He saw no one apart from other guests in the hotel and Morrice. The two artists planned to take the same boat back to Europe. They also met Lavery and Harris who came to say goodbye before Matisse left. The Englishman was treated to a sneak preview of the unearthly beauty of the three works from the garden of Villa Brooks.

Matisse also made a little painting of a Muslim shrine (the Zaouia of Sidi Ahmed Bouqoudja can still be found in the Kasbah) and another of Zorah. When Zorah gave up posing, Matisse replaced her with a boy called Amido, a former worker at the Hotel Valentina. He posed so well that Matisse was able to finish Zorah Standing for Shchukin quickly, something that he had despaired of doing before. In the first of these paintings, entitled simply Amido, the model wears pink pantaloons, a green vest and a pouch. He stands gracefully with one hand on his hip, gazing through long eyelashes towards a window.

If Matisse's mood was lighter, dark clouds were gathering over Morocco. On 30 March 1912 the sultan finally signed the Treaty of Fes that turned his country into a French protectorate. Walter Harris reported on the unrest which climaxed in a battle on 7 April when the French defeated the Moroccans. On the same day in Tangier the ferry taking people to and from the mail boat capsized in the bay and all on board were killed, including the family of the Chargé d'Affaires, Beaumarchais. Upset by this tragedy and the continuing political unrest, Matisse sailed for France a week later, travelling in the same boat as Beaumarchais, who told him not to tell anyone about the accident.

On the 17 April, the day that Matisse arrived back in Paris, all hell broke loose in Fes. Moroccan soldiers mutinied and murdered 17 army instructors, the only personnel left in the old city. The killing carried on for two more days until French reinforcements arrived and stormed the gates. Those Europeans who survived were barricaded inside their homes, while those who were not, were decapitated and thrown into the river.

When Matisse learnt what was happening in Morocco he was deeply saddened. He had sought out a paradise, but now it was tainted by death, darkness and destruction. This intensified his search for purity and peace in Tangier. Marcel Sembat, a socialist politician and the husband of the Fauvist painter Georgette Agutte, published a book about Matisse based on their conversations later that year. Sembat wrote that Matisse's Moroccan paintings were driven by a craving for peace. Matisse had told him that he instinctively simplified and abstracted his work to come closer to a sense of ecstasy. As soon as Matisse returned to Paris, Marcel and Georgette bought *View of the Bay of Tangier*. Georgette was so delighted with the paintings of Zorah that she asked Matisse to paint more for them on his next trip to Morocco. Marcel and Georgette were not rich but they were shrewd enough to hang on to *View of the Bay of Tangier* and *Basket of Oranges*. These two canvases were Matisse's only works in France and remained there for nearly 30 years, until the latter was bought by Picasso.

Sembat and Agutte became friends of the Matisse family and would visit them at their house outside Paris. There, in the spring and summer of 1912, Matisse finished an enormous canvas called *Conversation*. The lush luminosity of the garden was inspired by Tangier and the expanse of blue was like the Moroccan sky. Discussing this years later with his son-in-law, Matisse said that a good painting should have the power to generate light. *Conversation* looks a bit like a David Hockney painting, as the flat backgrounds make the figures appear to float in unrelated space. There is even an uncanny similarity between *Conversation* and Hockney's *Mr and Mrs Clark and Percy* painted 60 years later, as the figures adopt the same poses by a window.

Matisse returned alone to Tangier at the end of September 1912, spurred on by his Russian benefactors. Shchukin had commissioned him to paint another figure and Morozov had asked for two landscapes. Back in the same room at the Villa de France, Matisse picked up from where he left off, with a routine of work and horse riding. He would explore the old town, make sketches in the mornings and paint in the afternoons. He would spend his evenings writing to his family, providing daily updates to Amelie, and postcards to his son Jean, who like his father, was prone to bouts of melancholy. In one letter to his daughter Marguerite, he said, 'You ask what I do all day here alone in Tangier that stops me writing to you for a week, but, my sweet, I'm working.'

Things were picking up. The hills above Tangier were burnt dry by the sun and Matisse was sleeping well. 'I'm nothing like I was this time last year,' he wrote to Amelie, 'luckily, otherwise I wouldn't stay a week.' The clarity of the light also pleased him and this time Amido acted as a companion, guide and procurer of models.

One of these was Fatma, an Arab-African who was not afraid to be painted unveiled. While Zorah had been submissive, Fatma was brusque, abrupt and abrasive. Matisse came across her 'stretched out like a panther, a mulatto in Moroccan costume that showed off the slender, supple elegance of her young body.' Matisse decided to paint her outdoors on a roof terrace. In a long thin canvas he painted her in a pink, purple and turquoise kaftan, whilst in a smaller picture, she sits with her legs crossed against a blue backdrop, in a red and orange blouse. Fatma knew her value to the painter and threatened to stop modelling for him if he did not pay her more. 'It is not enough,' is a common refrain that Westerners hear from Moroccans. Matisse became exasperated by her behaviour and unhappy with the long narrow canvas, at one point turning it to face the wall. 'I brought it home and haven't the courage to turn it round for fear of disappointment,' he wrote. The brilliance of the paintings however, seemed to recreate the frisson caused by their arguments.

There was no sign of Zorah on this second trip but with the help of Amido, Matisse tracked her down in a brothel whose occupants were not allowed to work outside the building. Matisse then arranged for Zorah to pose on its roof terrace. She would shuttle back and forth between these painting sessions upstairs and her work downstairs. After the brief time she spent attending to her client, Matisse would again paint Zorah in the sunlight, eating *petit beurre* biscuits and looking flushed. The paintings of her sitting between a goldfish bowl and a pair of slippers seem to have an iconic purity to them that makes the viewer oblivious to the fact that she is a prostitute. In another image, Matisse placed the portrait of a tribesman from the Rif on a flat background of ochre, blue and green, giving it a simplicity that concentrates the eye on the model, like a photographic portrait in which the background is deliberately out of focus. The modernity of these images is, according to Hilary Spurling, still startling today. The portraits have highly expressive faces, but very little in the way of additional features. Hands and feet for example, are rendered with just a few brushstrokes.

By October, Matisse was on a roll and it was clear that he would not be returning home by November as originally planned. By this time, Amelie was lonely and depressed so she left Paris for Tangier on 20 November with the Fauvist painter Charles Camoin, a friend who had recently broken up with his lover. 'Charming, courageous and full of faith in her husband's work,' was how Camoin described Amelie. The latter's mood improved as she found herself back in the company of painters and their work. In Tangier, she quickly adjusted to the rhythms of the artists' routines. She would walk in the old town with them searching for motifs and join them after work for games of dominoes or trips to the cinema. Family legend had it that Amelie would even escort her husband on visits to see Zorah, which caused commotion in the brothel, where the girls had no idea how to deal with a Frenchman who had also brought his wife.

Amelie trusted her husband and was not there to check up on him, knowing that he did not mix business with pleasure. 'Don't imagine there is anything madly exciting going on here, apart from work,' he wrote to her soon after he arrived. On entering the brothel, Matisse reminded Camoin that they were there in a 'strictly professional capacity, like doctors.' Despite the occasional bawdy banter with his friends, Matisse was in fact a sober innocent abroad. 'In bed every night by ten,' he wrote to Marquet.

Matisse took Camoin, who was ten years his junior, under his wing, once taking him to hospital in Tangier when he contracted diphtheria. The two painters were joined by Morrice, who returned in December. The three of them kept each other company, comparing their work; Morrice would drink rum at breakfast and be inebriated by lunchtime. Small boys would run down the alleyways after him shouting 'whisky!' and Matisse would accompany him to cafés, where the Canadian would drink as many glasses of spirits as the Frenchman did of mineral water. Matisse described Morrice as 'always on the wing, like a migrating bird with nowhere to touch down.' He thought both Camoin and Morrice, like many of the writers, artists and musicians who would follow in their footsteps over the next hundred years were always looking for an external stimulus to inspire their creativity.

For their part, Morrice and Camoin were a little disappointed by Matisse's straightlaced sobriety, but Matisse accessed his inner self through travel, not substances. When in January the rains began to fall again, Matisse hired a photographer's studio in the heart of the medina with huge windows that looked over the bay, so that all three artists could work indoors. In a rare touch of arrogance he wrote to Manguin that from here he could deliver a masterpiece 'with an orange, three carrots and a rag.'

Morocco helped Matisse to push the limits of his exploration of structure via colour, but his experimentation and abstraction left his companions far behind. Camoin tried to experiment, but doing so pushed him over the edge. He would write to his mentor describing a mounting sense of panic, ending in a frenzied destruction of 80 canvases. Both lesser artists still admired Matisse and were grateful for his help, admitting they would have struggled without it. 'Matisse had a totally new vision of colour, like Delacroix,' Gipi de Richemont informed me in our interview in the Petit Socco.

Moroccans and Africans have a sense of colour that is much more daring. They dared to put colours together that normally no painter or designer would put together. The Africans, maybe because of the light, have different perceptions of colour. For example, they might mix a Persian pink with a very dry green – just like this woman walking past us! And they might add a very violent orange, and a line of white and it works. Also these colours go very well with their darker skin. Black people can wear any colour they want.

Sitting one day in a café in the Kasbah, Matisse could not help being reminded of Delacroix again. He thought he recognised the background to *The Capture of Constantinople by the Crusaders* and when Matisse drew the same landscape he inserted a horseman as a nod to his predecessor. For both men, travel to an exotic land was a fresh way of seeing; enabling them to cleanse their vision. As William Blake said, 'if the doors of perception were cleansed everything would appear to man as it is, Infinite,' and, as Picasso would say, 'art washes away from the soul the dust of everyday life.' For many later artists in Tangier, cleansing the doors of perception was achieved through mind-altering substances.

A few weeks after arriving in Tangier for this second visit, Matisse decided to work on two large panels for Shchukin. These two paintings would be more ambitious and strange than those he had brought back from his first trip and both began life as café scenes. *The Moroccans* began as a quick sketch of a group sitting on the terrace of a café. The other, *Moroccan Café*, emerged from sketches made in a second establishment; a whitewashed building covered in trellises of blue and purple flowers. It had one tiny square room, with a window looking out over the bay and 12 birdcages hanging from the ceiling. This building can be seen through the archway of *The Casbah Gate*. Matisse had found it by accident after following the sound of a violin as he was walking back to his hotel. He even took the violin from its owner and began to play, 'I played well,' he told Amelie modestly 'I gave them some nice sounds.' The Frenchman was made welcome there and would regularly return in the evenings. 'It's a quiet café, full of serious people,' he told his wife. Today's equivalent would be the unassuming café next to the museum in the Kasbah, *Les Fils de Detroit*. Here, in a room as narrow as a train carriage, a few elderly men strum Andalusian lutes and play drums, while a small clientele drink mint tea and smoke kif, slumped against Berber rugs. Art historians remain unsure whether the original setting for *Moroccan Café* was in fact the Café Maure near the Kasbah Museum, or the Café Baba by Bab al-Assa.

Matisse sketched rapidly. He drew reclining or squatting figures, playing cards and smoking hashish. In *Moroccan Café*, six djellaba-clad men appear in front of a grey-green background. The two figures in the foreground are bent curiously over a goldfish bowl and a flower in a vase. They have their own lackadaisical rhythm, almost like smoke emerging slowly from a pipe or hubble-bubble. They were also influenced by the posture and disposition of the figures in Delacroix's *Jewish Wedding in Morocco*.

The café sketches show the arcade, wallpaper, decorations, glasses of mint tea, hashish pipes and slippers, but when it came to the final painting, Matisse stripped all the details out, including the faces of his sitters. The arcade is still there, acting as a frame within a frame, but the birdcages are invisible. 'Matisse took care not to paint the cages,' wrote Marcel Sembat, 'but a little of the sweetness of the birdsong passed into his picture.' Spurling thinks that in Moroccan Café, Matisse had 'reached a pitch of abstract purity and intensity unprecedented at that point in the West.' 'Matisse,' she says 'had broken through to a new visual level of reality where few of his contemporaries could follow him.'

When I started really looking at the picture, it instilled in me a sense of peace amid a period of panic and dissatisfaction with the writing process. Matisse had told Sembat that he was seeking to convey a feeling of meditation, 'that's what struck me: those great devils who remain for hours lost in contemplation of a flower and some goldfish.' Years later, William Burroughs would similarly write that a junkie could spend eight hours looking at the end of his shoe. The painting seems to sum up the café lifestyle that struck me when I first went to live in Morocco. In dimly lit bars that line the pavements of Moroccan cities, men sit, doing very little, making their coffees stretch for hours.

In the middle of February 1913, Henri and Amelie left Tangier again. Matisse's works went on show in a Paris gallery for just six days in April and from then on were destined for their Russian owners. 'Soon your pictures won't ever be seen again except in Moscow,' Amelie had written to Henri, but Sembat still believed that they had left an indelible mark on the minds of gallery visitors: 'no one who saw them will ever forget that show,' he wrote. Moroccan Café had failed to sell at the Bernheim-Jeune gallery in Paris and ended up in a small, private dressing room in Sergei Shchukin's house, where he would spend at least an hour a day looking at it, such was the contemplative effect it had on him. Shchukin was one of the few people who had really believed in Matisse and was prepared to follow him into the future. Others were too scared.

Some of Matisse's works went on show in February 1913 at the New York Armory Show. 'Ugly, coarse, narrow and revolting in their inhumanity,' was how they were reviewed in the New York Times. Matisse or 'Henry Hairmattress' as the protesting students in New York and Chicago called him, was considered to be the ringleader for this gross display of lewdness. The students went on to stage a mock trial accusing the said Hairmattress of treason, as the Americans could not cope with this wave of modern art from Europe.

In Germany, Matisse was hailed as a genius, but there was less interest in France where he was pilloried for not being avant-garde enough. Picasso, however, never underestimated Matisse. The two put their previous rivalry behind them because, as Spurling writes, 'Picasso was anxious to distance himself from his crowd of followers; Matisse had taken steps to ensure he had none.'

Although he never returned to Morocco, Matisse continued to work on paintings that had been sketched, conceived in or inspired by Tangier. Among them was *Bathers by a River*, which he had originally set as a scene on a Moroccan beach, but which would turn into something much darker. He started work on it again at home in the summer of 1913, but it would be three more years before he finished. The painting has been likened to some of Picasso's raging nudes, and the darkness of the times showed in the huge canvas. 'He transposed his Moroccan bathing beach into a monumental image of grief and stoicism,' Spurling writes, 'he drew on ancient myths of the passage from light to dark.' *Bathers by a River* was sold to the Art Institute of Chicago in 1953, a year before Matisse died. At the time, he confided in the director of the Institute that he considered it to be one of the five most pivotal paintings of his life. In 1990, one of the curators, Catherine Bock, said, 'this work could only have been painted in 1916, at the moment when the enormity of World War I was finally realised.'

Memories of Tangier lingered for a long time and seeped into Matisse's other paintings. In December 1915 he embarked upon a large and ambitious work based on ideas that had come to him while writing to Amelie from Tangier. It was another café scene in which figures lounge under a striped umbrella. In February 1916 he wrote to Camoin.

I have been totally unsettled in my mind for a month, with a picture of Morocco that I am working on at the moment, it's the terrace of the little café of the Casbah that you know well. I hope to get myself out of it, but what troubles. I'm not in the trenches, but I seem to be there all the same.

It was worth the trouble. In *The Moroccans*, which he began in Tangier but finished in the summer of 1916, representation parts company with reality – watermelons look like robed Arabs and flowers have turned into an umbrella, the ramparts of the Kasbah are rearranged into flat blocks and discs, and the humans have dematerialised completely. With its abstract shapes, *The Moroccans* looks more like a Picasso and it is light years ahead of its time. Tangier's darkness and light are also present in this painting. The blackness serves as a depiction of shadow and the intensity of the sun that can produce such darkness 'It is the beginning of my expression with colour, with blacks and their contrasts,' Matisse said of it in 1951.

His painting of the long-suffering Amelie, *Portrait of Madame Matisse*, 1913, was inspired by his Moroccan figure paintings. The painting has a haunting, other worldly, melancholic beauty to it. It took more than a hundred sittings and when she finally saw the finished work, Amelie wept.

Matisse's brief sojourn in Morocco also had a profound effect on him in more general terms. 'Before 1912, Matisse's work is under the sign of a savage god,' writes Pierre Schneider in the introduction to *Matisse in Morocco*, 'after that date, it was born under the sign of a tender god who manifested himself in Tangier.'

This change of register coincides with another transformation, brought about by the Moroccan spring that had impressed Matisse so deeply: the growing importance of the vegetal reign as the supreme reference. What one might call the botanization of his art . . . Tangier had fulfilled Matisse's dream of coalescing abstraction and reality.

'Although Matisse spent only a few months in Morocco,' writes Michael Kimmelman, 'his experiences remained vividly with him for the rest of his long life.'

To see, for example, the paintings he completed in Nice during the Twenties, with their odalisques and their dizzying arrangements of carpets and wallpaper is to see Morocco transplanted to the Riviera. And to see the cutouts of Matisse's last years, with their brilliant floral concoctions, is to see the spirit of Morocco still alive in the artist's imagination.

Is it perhaps too much to see similarities between Matisse's cutouts and the cut-ups of two later residents of Tangier, William Burroughs and Brion Gysin?

The memories of Matisse's time in Tangier continue to live on in the psyches of other artists. The Californian abstract expressionist Richard Diebenkorn said he was influenced by the 'haunting colours and rhythmic patterns' of Matisse's Moroccan paintings. 'It's almost as though Diebenkorn did what Matisse would have done if he'd kept painting,' said Janet Bishop, who curated an exhibition comparing the two artists in 2017. The Chilean hyperrealist painter Claudio Bravo moved to Tangier in 1973, like Matisse to contemplate the light and create 'symphonies of colour.' Others who have been inspired by Matisse include the American watercolourist Elena Prentice, the Spanish artist Antonio Fuentes (who was born in the city in 1905 and became known as the 'Toulouse-Lautrec of Tangier'), the Moroccan painters Mohammed ben Ali R'bati and Tarik Banzi, as well as the Anglo-Irish painter Francis Bacon.

SEVEN

Paul Bowles

If I said that Tangier struck me as a dream city, I should mean it in the strict sense. Its topography was rich in prototypical dream scenes, squares built on sloping terrain so that they looked like ballet sets designed in false perspective, as well as the classical dream equipment of tunnels, ramparts, ruins, dungeons and cliffs

I arranged to see Josh Shoemake, a writer who taught at the American School in Tangier in the 1990s. We met in the Petit Socco and walked up the Rue des Siaghines to the Grand Socco. From there, we ambled past St Andrew's Church, and the Villa de France via the Avenue d'Angleterre. As an American and an Englishmen we could equally appropriately have taken the parallel street, the Rue San Francisco. 'That's the Villa Miramonte,' Josh said as he pointed out a yellow building with brown roof tiles, tucked behind high walls, 'the rumour was that the Moroccan secret service, the DST, used to torture people in the basement. You could hear the screams as you walked by.'

We strolled past a weird, undulating cream and red edifice that was once the American Embassy, turned a corner and found ourselves facing the Immeuble Itesa on the Rue Imam Kastalani. It was an ugly, grey, oblong block built by Italians in the 1950s and would not have looked out of place in Bucharest or Pyongyang. The front was clad in square concrete slabs, interspersed with sinister looking ventilation grids and a central section of balconies. The roof supported television aerials, satellite dishes, cables and wires making it look like a centre for surveillance. On the ground floor were several desultory shops: a pizzeria, a computer game store with graffiti sprayed on its awning and a hardware outlet selling gas canisters, kitchen appliances and crisps.

The Immeuble Itesa was where Paul Bowles lived for many years. He stayed on the fourth floor and communicated with his wife Jane, who was in the apartment beneath him via a plastic purple toy telephone. The lift rarely functioned, so many visitors made their pilgrimage to see their literary guru on the hill, via the staircase. In her biography of Bowles, Millicent Dillon recalls that the building was 'surrounded by empty fields, littered here and there with small mounds of rubble.' Bowles enjoyed it there.

In the nine years during which I had a headquarters at the Immeuble Itesa I had grown fond of the place. There was no particular reason to like it, save that it was visually neutral, and the bedrooms had a wide view of the leafier quarters of Tangier, with thousands of houses in the distance and a strip of sea. But I also liked the nights. Sometimes there were the cries of frogs and owls, and sometimes there were only crickets and the sporadic, distant barking of dogs.

As Bowles was losing his eyesight in his later years, Josh would go to his apartment every Thursday to read to him for an hour. Josh recalled that the novelist enjoyed listening to stories by Bret Easton Ellis and Flannery O'Connor, whose works were quite violent. Josh spoke of Bowles' dark humour.

He was always a complete gentleman. There would be people showing up all the time, almost in queues and he never turned anyone away. He was extremely polite. But he did play his little games. One day I went to his place to have tea. Bowles' manservant, Abdelwahid, would come home at four o'clock to fix him tea and this time Abdelwahid was late. Bowles was distressed. "He always comes back at four. What's going on?" he shouted. I was 23 and an idiot. So I said, "I'll make you tea." I went to the kitchen. I had no idea how to make tea, so I made him this pale lukewarm muck by putting tea leaves into a kettle and then pouring it back and forth through napkins. He winced when he drank it. At that moment, Adelwahid arrives and he's absolutely furious. He flips out, hates me. There's screaming; a whole scene and Bowles is just lying there in bed smiling. Obviously I'd been set up.

Bowles and Abdelwahid were not averse to such practical jokes. Millicent Dillon says that in the 1970s, Bowles was frequently visited by an American woman called Valeska, who developed an obsession with him. On one occasion Abdelwahid went to pick her up from the airport. When she asked how Paul was, Abdelwahid 'with great sadness, told her that Paul was dead. Valeska began to scream and cry.' When they reached the apartment, Paul was coming down in the lift and bumped into Valeska on the ground floor. The strangest part was that Valeska had wanted to bring her camera to photograph his corpse.

Embedded in the medina is the American Legation Museum. To find it, I walked down Zankat America until I spotted an American eagle on a wall. I rang the doorbell and a smiling Moroccan security guard welcomed me into the sprawling complex that, for 140 years, had housed American diplomats. The museum's director, Gerald Loftus, a softly spoken man with glasses and a grey beard, showed me around. He explained that the property was the first diplomatic mission ever acquired by the United States in 1821, and its only historic landmark outside of America. Much of the museum is devoted to the history of Tangier. In glass cabinets are documents relating to 'the Perdicaris Incident.' These included a poster of the 1970s Hollywood film *The Wind and the Lion* starring Sean Connery. The movie was loosely based on the kidnapping except that the victim was a female character, Eden Perdicaris, played by Candice Bergen. Among the more contemporary memorabilia were photographs of King Hassan II and Ronald Reagan at the White House.

Gerald also showed me a diorama with 600 small figurines that recreated the Battle of the Three Kings, when the Moors routed the Portuguese in 1578. 'The level of detail here is astounding,' he said, 'each one of these soldiers is made from its own mould. They're all different. It's not mass production.' The scene was made for the American millionaire, Malcolm Forbes, who bought the Palais Mendoub, on Rue Mohammed Tazi on the Marshan, in 1970, specifically to house his collection of toy soldiers. He had more than 110,000 of them. In the mid-1980s, a scene from the James Bond film *The Living Daylights* was shot here. 'The arch villain can be seen playing war games,' Gerald explained, 'setting off explosions among the toy soldiers.'

In 1989, Forbes spent 2.5 million dollars celebrating his seventieth birthday at the Mendoub. He invited 800 of the world's rich and famous, including Elizabeth Taylor, Henry Kissinger, King Constantine II of Greece, Gianni Agnelli, Robert Trump, Rupert Murdoch and Robert Maxwell, most of whom he had flown in on a specially chartered Concorde.

'Malcolm Forbes? Oh he was a complete ham,' Charles Sevigny told me.

He really was too much. I saw his houses in New York, Normandy and here in Tangier and in every place you went, he used to have these tables with hundreds of photographs – hundreds – and every single one of them was of Malcolm Forbes. Next to him might be famous people like the Prince of Wales or President Carter – looking as they always look – but then you saw Malcolm Forbes himself, standing there with a big grin.

Six months after 'that party' Malcolm Forbes died of a heart attack. The Palais Mendoub was sold to the Moroccan government and is used occasionally to impress foreign dignitaries.

Another section of the American Legation Museum, beyond a shaded central courtyard, is devoted entirely to the life of Paul Bowles. Its walls are cream and the ceilings are green. A central glass cabinet houses books, magazine articles, a musical score, spectacles, postcards and floppy disks. To one side are three leather suitcases stacked on top of each other like a wedding cake, with a blue-green Olivetti typewriter perched at the summit. On the wall behind are various photos of the writer posing with a cigarette holder. The room has been extended further to include a Paul Bowles Wing, which displays more portaits, paintings, sketches and a poster for *The Sheltering Sky*.

An alcove off the main room is devoted to his collection of Moroccan folk music. 'In 1959 he was chosen by the Rockefeller Foundation to do a recording project for the US Library of Congress,' explained Loftus. 'He wrote about it at length, so we've interspersed his photos with some of his writings. It was very challenging, but in the end he had recorded some 250 selections and 72 hours of music.' Beneath a photo of musicians performing at a religious festival or *moussem*, is a passage from *Their Heads Are Green*, which explains some of these challenges.

> There was a slight altercation at the moment of payment, because in spite of the agreement by which the men were not to discharge their rifles, they had not been able to resist participating, so that at separate points in the music they fired them off, all eight of them, and simultaneously. At the end, they presented a bill for 24 cartridges.

A map on the wall shows several trips that Bowles had made on this musical exploration of Morocco. Loftus said that Bowles travelled in a Volkswagen Beetle carrying reel-to-reel tape recorders. Above another cabinet of his books, sits an old radio. This emits digital extracts of the music, held in the Library of Congress in Washington, D.C., as well as the ghostly, disembodied voice of Bowles travelling across time and reading eerily from his short stories, such as 'He of the Assembly' from *A Hundred Camels in the Courtyard*.

> He of the Assembly was sitting in the same part of the café. He was listening to the wind in the telephone wires. The sky was almost empty of daytime light. "The eye wants to sleep," he thought, "but the head is no mattress."

By the time I had finished looking around, Gerald Loftus had already excused himself as he had other commitments and I found myself alone and thoroughly lost in the museum. Unable to find the main entrance again, in a panic I pushed a door with an emergency exit sign and almost fell onto the street outside. The security guard, who had been all smiles when I first arrived, heard the commotion, ran up to this door that was never used and berated me for my poor protocol.

Paul Frederic Bowles was a precocious child. Born in 1910, he wrote his first story at the age of three and his mother, Rena, read him the tales of Edgar Allan Poe when he was four. It was an early sign of Bowles' dark psyche and macabre imagination, which would be explored in

The Sheltering Sky and *Let it Come Down*. His father, Claude, resented him so much that when Paul was just six-weeks-old, he stripped him naked, placed him in a wicker basket and opened the window. When his grandmother was woken by the baby's cries, she found him covered in snow and was convinced Claude had tried to kill him. Claude was later staggered when he found the two-year-old reading aloud from the labels of cereal boxes. He was convinced that Rena must have tutored the boy to make him look more intelligent than he was. This pattern of scepticism in his son's talents continued for much of Claude's life. 'I vowed to devote my life,' Bowles wrote, 'to his destruction.' Paul spent most of his time playing on his own indoors in the family's house in Jamaica, New York, much to the annoyance of his father, who loved the outdoors. Bowles' autobiography, *Without Stopping*, conveys this sense of loneliness.

> I spent my days playing by myself in the house, except for the occasional hour when I was turned out into the backyard. It was a large, flat, plot of grass shut in by a very high wooden fence. There was no way of seeing anything beyond the yard. However, on one side there were nine windows, looking out on me like nine eyes, and from any one of them could come a sudden shout of disapproval. If I stood still and watched the clock that was always placed in the window so I would know the hour was up, I heard taps on a third-storey window and saw my mother making gestures exhorting me to move around and play. But if I began to gallop around the yard, my father would call from the second storey: "Calm down, young man!"

'At the age of five,' Bowles wrote, 'I had never yet spoken to another child or seen children playing together.'

When Bowles later moved to Tangier, in 1947, he was not only escaping the prison of a repressive and conservative America, but his own upbringing. 'Any life,' he said, 'would be preferable to returning to live with my parents.'

At school, he felt he was so much more advanced than the other children, he refused to take part in group activities and handed in assignments written backwards. He first heard about Tangier from an anthropologist, Katherine Cowen, 12 years his senior, whom he liked immediately. By this time Bowles had already enrolled at the University of Virginia, because that is where Edgar Allan Poe had gone, but he aborted his studies and fled to Paris at the age of 18. He was drawn there after coming across a Paris-based Surrealist literary magazine called Transition.

It was in Paris that Bowles would rub shoulders with André Gide, Jean Cocteau, Ernest Hemingway, Ezra Pound, Gertrude Stein and Alice B. Toklas. Perhaps it was this exposure to the avant-garde in Paris, and later Berlin where he spent the afternoons in the *Café des Westens* with Christopher Isherwood and Stephen Spender, that would make him want to recreate a similar scene in Tangier. Stein adopted the young Bowles as a sort of mascot and he considered her his mentor, 'a sort of very loving grandmother, very warm and motherly, and lots of bosom.'

> I existed primarily for Gertrude Stein as a sociological exhibit; for her
> I was the first example of my kind. I provided her initial encounter
> with a species then rare, now the commonest of contemporary
> phenomena, the American suburban child with its unrelenting
> spleen . . . After a week or so, Gertrude Stein pronounced her verdict:
> I was the most spoiled, insensitive, and self-indulgent young man she
> had ever seen . . . "If you were typical, it would be the end of our
> civilization," she told me, "You're a manufactured savage."

Bowles would later say that he had always been attracted to crazy people like Stein, whose writing made no sense, but it was Stein who urged him to go to Tangier and stay in the Hotel Villa de France. He travelled there in 1931 with his music teacher, the American composer Aaron Copland, and his first sight of North Africa had a huge impact.

> On the second day I went on deck at dawn, saw the rugged line of
> mountains of Algeria ahead, and felt great excitement. It was as if
> some interior mechanism had been set in motion by the sight of the
> approaching land . . . As I stood in the wind looking at the moun-
> tains ahead, I felt a stirring of the engine within, and it was as if I
> were drawing close to the solution of an as-yet-unposed problem.

He later admitted to another biographer, Virginia Spencer Carr, that he was really talking about the stirrings of sexual emotions he experienced when he was with Copland.

By the time Bowles and Copland arrived, Tangier was truly international. In 1923, France had agreed to share it with her allies from World War I: Britain, Spain, Italy, Portugal, Belgium, the Netherlands and later Sweden. So began the city's 'Gilded Age', governed by a committee of European powers, as Bowles noted in *Without Stopping*.

The city was self-sufficient and clean, a doll's metropolis whose social and economic life long ago had been frozen in an enforced perpetual status quo by the international administration and its efficient police. There was no crime; no one yet thought of not respecting the European, whose presence was considered an asset to the community.

Tangier was governed by consuls from eight European nations and had three official languages: French, Spanish and Arabic. It was a hub of unregulated free enterprise. Anyone with a valid passport could become a citizen. It was a free port with no import duties or income tax. Gold could be bought over the counter. Anyone with a storefront and letterhead could open a bank and anyone with a fistful of cash could become a moneychanger. In 1952, *The New Yorker* magazine said that at the time there were 85 banks and 42 brothels in Tangier. Searching for Nazi gold and eager to trace the ill-gotten gains of war criminals, the USA put pressure on Switzerland to divulge its hidden bank accounts. Nervous European clients then moved their money and gold out of Switzerland and into Tangier where banking secrecy still remained. The city was the capital of permissiveness and smuggling was a respectable profession. Guns came in and drugs went out. It was said that CD number plates on cars did not mean *Corps Diplomatique* but *Contrebandier Distingué*.

When the two Americans landed, they met a friend of Stein's, a Dutch painter called Kristians Tonny. At one point, Tonny drew Copland to one side and asked if Bowles was 'slightly off his head.' As the Villa de France was full, Bowles found a run-down house on the Old Mountain, about three kilometres out of town, without running water.

A piano was delivered on the back of a donkey that balked at the entrance and dropped its load. 'We have an African piano that sounds like hell,' Copland wrote to Stein. Bowles was more positive; the house was 'swell, with palms and olives waving in the second-storey windows,' he wrote, 'and a view towards the mountains far away south; the town itself is too beautiful for words.'

Two years later he travelled in the Algerian desert where he met George Turner, who would be the role model for Tunner in *The Sheltering Sky*. On his return to Tangier he rented another house near the top of the cliffs on the Marshan. It too, had a stunning view of the city but again, no running water.

Back in New York, Bowles achieved success as a composer but pined for Tangier. 'I tried to drown my melancholy in work,' he said, 'but I was obsessed by memories of the air and light of North Africa.'

In the winter of 1936, Bowles met Jane Auer. He was introduced to her by Erika Mann, the daughter of Thomas Mann and the wife of W.H. Auden. He was immediately attracted to Jane's red hair, pointed nose and slight limp, although she did not initially have the same feelings for him. 'Like Paul,' Millicent Dillon writes, 'Jane was an only child who lived in great part through her imagination.' They married in 1938 and travelled to Central America together. 'It appears to me now,' Dillon adds, 'that when Paul and Jane arrived at that geographic border on their first trip together, each came to an edge within; he to the edge of his most intense excitement, she to the edge of terror.' Mohamed Choukri felt that Jane spent most of her life in fear.

> She had to anaesthetize herself with alcohol and sleeping pills just to get to sleep, or when she wanted to take the elevator . . . As for tunnels, she was afraid they would never come to an end. Jane was equally scared of fire, dogs, crocodiles and seaweed.

In Latin America, Bowles wrote one of his first essays, about a parrot. Like the Sultan Moulay Hafid with his mechanical stuffed bird, Paul and Jane loved parrots. They later bought one, calling him Budupple. In Antigua, Budupple ate his way out of a cage and escaped via an avocado tree. 'We never saw him again,' Bowles lamented. Jane created a fictional character called Bupple Hergesheimer who thought he was a parrot and they would act out a game in which Paul was Bupple and Jane was Bupple's governess, who would hold out her hand for him or order him into his cage as he squawked.

Before their marriage, Paul and Jane had agreed that they should each be free to sleep with others of either sex. Noting that their sex life had tailed off, Mohamed Choukri remarked: 'they each took refuge in their homosexuality, while continuing to live close to and apart from each other simultaneously.'

In 1939 Paul and Jane joined the Communist Party, although they disowned it later as they worried it would get them into trouble with the authorities. That same year, Bowles wrote his first short story. It was set in Tangier and called 'Tea on the Mountain'.

Jane was to have a novel published first: *Two Serious Ladies*, in 1943. 'I never would have written anything,' Bowles told Dillon, 'if I hadn't gone over the manuscript of *Two Serious Ladies* carefully, making corrections in spelling and punctuation. It was the excitement of participating in that that got me interested in writing.' One of his first stories was 'A Distant Episode', published in 1947, in which a professor allows himself to be led into the desert at night. This 'monstrous letting go' as Bowles later called it, exposes the professor to horrific violence at the hands of his captors. He has his tongue cut out and is forced to sing and dance in a coat made entirely of tin cans. This haunting tale is at once a precursor to both *The Sheltering Sky* and *Let it Come Down*. Perhaps this was Stein's 'manufactured savage.'

In his introduction to Bowles' *Collected Stories*, Gore Vidal ranked them as 'among the best ever written by an American.' 'The floor to this ramshackle civilization that we have built cannot bear much longer our weight,' wrote Vidal, 'It was Bowles' genius to suggest the horrors which lie beneath that floor as fragile, in its way, as the sky that shelters us from a devouring vastness.' 'Paul Bowles opened the world of Hip,' wrote Norman Mailer, 'He let in the murder, the drugs, the incest, the death of the Square . . . the call of the orgy, the end of civilization.' Jay McInerney said Bowles associated Morocco 'with the anarchic forces of the unconscious', whilst Millicent Dillon talks of 'a universal internal darkness' at the heart of Bowles' writings and Choukri noted that Bowles inflicted cruelty on his literary creations.

Bowles hasn't lacked the courage to create protagonists whom he would then torture mercilessly. He wallowed in the torment of his characters in order to avenge what he had suffered in his childhood. This rescued him from insanity: to find solace he put others in Hell.

Bowles travelled again to Tangier in 1947 and decided, even before he set off, that he would settle there.

One balmy night in May, asleep in my quiet bedroom, I had a dream . . . In the late afternoon sunlight I walked slowly through complex and tunnelled streets. As I reviewed it, lying there, sorry to have left the place behind, I realised with a jolt that the magic city really existed. It was Tangier. My heart accelerated, and memories of other courtyards and stairways flooded in, still fresh from sixteen years before. The Tangier to which I wandered in my dream was the Tangier of 1931 . . . It did not take me long to come to the conclusion that Tangier must be the place I wanted to be more than anywhere else.

But there was one small problem.

I began to collect my things. Soon, I realized that my passport was seriously missing . . . It was nowhere to be seen. We searched feverishly; the car was due to arrive in a half hour . . . We continued to look for it everywhere. Just before the car came, I unearthed it, buried beneath a neat pile of Jane's underwear in the back of a bureau drawer. It was a mystery. Jane claimed to know nothing about it. We looked at her accusingly. She laughed. "You know I don't want you to go."

As he made plans to go to Tangier, Bowles signed a contract for a novel with Doubleday.

North Africa had long since acquired a legendary aura for me; the fact that I had decided to go back there made the place more actual and revived hundreds of small, forgotten scenes which welled up into my consciousness of their own accord. I got on a Fifth Avenue bus one day to go uptown. By the time we had arrived at Madison Square, I knew what would be in the novel and what I would call it.

He remembered a popular song before World War I called 'Down Among the Sheltering Palms'. He said it was the strange word 'sheltering' that had fascinated him and since his novel would be set in the Sahara where there was only the sky, the book would be called *The Sheltering Sky*. The main characters, Port and Kit Moresby, would be based on Paul and Jane.

On his arrival in Tangier, Bowles wrote simply: 'Then we landed, and Morocco took over.'

In 1947, Tangier was recovering from its wartime years, which consisted of international espionage. Jean Genet called it 'the capital of treason.' During World War II the strategically desirable city had been buzzing with German spies who liked to stay in the Rif Hotel, down by the corniche. It was said that the barman at the Rif spied for the Americans and was on permanent standby to poison the Germans' cocktails. Among the various Nazi agents was Otto Skorzeny, who had worked for the Gestapo, once kidnapped Mussolini and set up an operation supplying weapons in Tangier. Skorzeny also moved Nazi gold to neutral countries during the last year of the conflict.

The *Abwehr*, the German military intelligence service, occupied a villa on the Rue de la Falaise. Here, they had an infrared device code-named Bodden that monitored Allied shipping in the Strait. This in turn, was monitored by the British spy and later traitor, Kim Philby. The villa was blown up by the British (who along with the Americans, preferred to stay at the Minzah) in 1943 under an operation with the not very cryptic codename, Falaise. A previous bomb plot was bungled in 1942, when a parcel concealed at the docks exploded and killed 15 people, ten of whom were Moroccans. A year later, a trade attaché at the British Consulate, James Ponsonby, pretended to be a special operations officer in financial trouble, prompting him to sell classified papers to the Germans. These were actually part of a deception campaign to mislead the Axis forces about the Allied landings in Italy.

Rachel Muyal, a Jewish lady who was born in Tangier in 1933, told me that from a big house near the Café Hafa, an American called

Gordon Browne, watched out for German ships through his binoculars. He was working for the Office of Strategic Services (OSS, the precursor to the CIA). Rachel said that Jewish families lived in constant fear and there were rumours that staff at the German Consulate, installed at that time in the Palais Mendoub, were constructing gas chambers. Four years after the Spanish occupied Tangier in 1940, General Franco ordered all German diplomats out of the International Zone.

From his arrival onwards, there was always a sense that Bowles would not initiate things, but just let them happen. This applied to his travel plans and his writing. As a child, his mother had taught him how to meditate and clear his mind. He seemed to use the same principle in his writing and rely on a Joycean stream of consciousness. His first novel, 'would write itself, once I had established the characters and spilled them out onto the North African scene.'

Although a talented writer in her own right, Jane was plagued by insecurity. 'You have more of a career after writing a few short stories, than I have after writing an entire novel,' she wrote from New York.

In September 1947, Bowles relocated from his hotel on the beach to the Old Mountain. 'Here, I was able to have a small two-room cottage with a fireplace and an exceptionally beautiful view,' he wrote, 'I bought an Amazon parrot that giggled.'

Struggling with the scene in The Sheltering Sky where Port dies, Bowles took a hashish cake; majoun, climbed up the mountain and lay on a slab of rock. 'The transition is rather sudden, like gusts of wind along the vertebrae, and an upward sweep into the clouds,' he wrote. He completed the death scene by handing 'the job over to the unconscious. It is certain that the majoun provided a solution totally unlike whatever I should have found without it.' The death of Port Moresby is one of the most memorable parts of the novel.

A black star appears, a point of darkness in the night sky's clarity. Point of darkness and gateway to repose. Reach out, pierce the fine fabric of the sheltering sky, take repose.

If you find yourself in the Kasbah, try walking along the Place du Mechoir towards the sea, then take a right turn under Bab Haha and follow the street as it morphs into Place Amrah. Here, in a narrow alley, Bowles moved for a second time in 1947. It was a small building with a communal latrine. Much to her annoyance, Bowles bought his more modest house in the Kasbah without consulting Jane, as Dillon recalls.

Paul and I were walking through the medina. We passed by the house where the English diarist Samuel Pepys had lived and came to the Place Amrah, where Paul pointed out the house he had once owned. He told me he bought it in 1947, soon after his arrival in Tangier, for five hundred dollars.

Later that year, Bowles travelled through the Algerian desert, taking his Amazonian companion. 'I don't know how my parrot survived,' Bowles said, 'but he did. I regretted that he didn't have the vocabulary to tell me about it.'

In January 1948, Jane finally arrived in Tangier. Bowles introduced her to a local girl, Cherifa. He recalled that 'Jane had fallen passionately in love with Cherifa, who played harder to get than anyone else she had courted.'

They both attempted to finish their novels together. *Without Stopping* gives an insight into how Jane struggled with the writing process. Each morning they ate breakfast in bed in Jane's room; then Bowles retired to his, but left the door open so that they could talk. At one point, Jane called out, 'Bupple! What's a cantilever, exactly?' or 'Can you say a bridge has buttresses?' He said the first thing that came to mind, but after several days, realised she was still trying to build her bridge.

I got up and went into her room. "Why do you have to construct the damned thing?" I demanded. "Why can't you just say it was there and let it go at that?" She shook her head. "If I don't know how it was built, I can't see it."

In May 1948, at a hotel in Fes, Bowles finished *The Sheltering Sky*. While Jane was obsessed with Cherifa, Bowles had fallen for a 16-year-old Moroccan boy, Ahmed Yacoubi. Bowles said that he was attracted by Yacoubi's primitive qualities and did not want him to ever lose them.

Later that year, Paul returned to New York to write music for Tennessee
Williams. This time, it was Jane who wrote glowingly from Tangier.

> The view of the Arab town from my window is a source of endless
> pleasure to me. I cannot stop looking and it is perhaps the first time
> in my life that I have felt joyous as a result of a purely visual experi-
> ence. I am just beginning to try to work now.

In December, Bowles convinced Tennessee Williams and his
companion, Frank Merlo to accompany him to Tangier. They took
with them the playwright's new maroon convertible. On the voyage
across the Atlantic, Bowles worked on a story, which he called 'The
Delicate Prey' and gave it to Tennessee Williams to read. 'It is a
wonderful story,' Williams remarked, 'but if you publish it, you're
mad.' 'It wasn't the Arabs I was afraid of in Tangier,' Williams confessed
to a friend, 'it was Paul Bowles, whose chilling stories filled me with
horror.' Bowles however, did not think that Williams was comfortable
in Tangier. 'He was violently perturbed by the Moslem scene, and
couldn't leave fast enough,' Bowles wrote.

In 1949, after travelling together in the Sahara, Jane and Paul returned
to Tangier, where they were sucked into a whirl of social activities
mainly orchestrated by David Herbert, the second son of the Earl of
Pembroke who had settled there in 1947. Among the couple's friends
were Cecil Beaton, Truman Capote and Gore Vidal. In one of Beaton's
photos, Jane stands on a boulder at Merkala Beach with David Herbert,
whose head is wrapped in a towel. Vidal found the squalor repugnant.
Jack Dunphy, who arrived with Truman Capote, remembered being
greeted by Jane, Paul and Gore Vidal 'looking like vultures awaiting
the wash-up after a hurricane'. Dunphy said he despised Herbert's attitude towards the locals, whom he treated as if they were his servants.

Paul's American publisher Doubleday, rejected *The Sheltering Sky* on
the basis that it was not a novel, but, under different publishers, this
non-novel rapidly climbed up the bestseller list. 'A series of remarkable episodes [which] though increasingly macabre and pointless,
still retain some kind of hallucinatory logic,' said *The Times Literary
Supplement*. A review in *The Commonweal* said Bowles had 'met the French

existentialists on their own ground and held them to a draw.' In 1949, Paul Bowles was at the peak of his literary powers and sensed that he was living through Tangier's heyday. Life would never be so good.

The summer proved the apogee of postwar prosperity in the International Zone. Immediately afterward, the cracks in the façade began to appear, and they constantly grew wider, until the entire edifice collapsed in the riots of 1952.

As Bowles set sail on board a freighter bound for Ceylon in November 1949, the inspiration for his second novel *Let it Come Down* came to him.

The night we sailed through the Strait of Gibraltar, I stood on deck staring longingly into the dark on the southern side of the ship. A rush of nostalgia for Tangier had seized me. I went inside and got into my berth. Then I began to write something which I hoped might prove the nucleus of a novel about Tangier. The first scene was on the cliffs, opposite the point we were passing at that moment.

He felt he had to write enough of *Let it Come Down* on board the ship before he landed in an unfamiliar place, otherwise he would lose it. He continued writing in Ceylon, sitting at an upright piano which one day sounded out of tune.

A large snake was rising vertically out of the piano's open top, its black tongue flickering in my direction . . . In my world, to have a ten-foot serpent come out of the piano and disappear into the ceiling was an extraordinary event, but my hosts appeared only mildly surprised.

In 1950, when Bowles was back in Morocco, his short stories were published under the title *The Delicate Prey*. He wrote to his mother in October that he was surprised she liked them so much, as he had intended to make them as gruesome as possible. Another admirer was

Millicent Dillon, who praised the quality of the prose: 'I read and reread his fiction, noting again the elegance and precision of his language, the brilliance of his narratives . . . the tales involving violence and cruelty caused me unease.'

On the corner of the Boulevard Pasteur and Rue de la Liberté lies the Gran Café de Paris. Inside, against a bland backdrop of wood panelling, beige linoleum flooring and brown banquettes, middle-aged Moroccan men in brown leather jackets and square-toed shoes sit and stare into the middle distance, nursing their *nous nous* coffees for hours. Outside, dotted along its polygonal walls, like flies around a lampshade, marginally younger men sit and stare at mobile phones. If there is anywhere in Tangier that reminds you both of the past and that the party is well and truly over, it is the Café de Paris. The ghosts of Jean Genet and Samuel Beckett are long gone. The café enjoyed a brief renaissance as a setting in *The Bourne Ultimatum*. In the 2007 movie, Matt Damon and his pursuer are seen pushing past local people. These were not extras. Tangier was so crowded and the flow of the people so hard to control, that the actors actually had to barge through the crowd. After *Bourne*, the Café de Paris settled down again, like the Moroccan men, into a state of comfortable semi-boredom. 'This evening I was having a beer at the Café de Paris,' wrote John Hopkins in his diary on 12 September 1962, 'when a line of camels, ridden by lean, hawklike men in black turbans and blue robes ambled by.' They were on their way to one of Barbara Hutton's parties in the Kasbah. 'Life was very good at that time,' Bowles told Mohamed Choukri. 'You could listen to the sounds of the cicadas in the eucalyptus trees while sitting on the terrace of the Café de Paris. Today though, you won't hear anything but the deafening noise of traffic.'

At the end of *Without Stopping*, Bowles says he became a resident of Tangier by accident.

I did not choose to live in Tangier permanently; it happened. My visit was meant to be of short duration; after that I would move on, and keep moving onward indefinitely. I grew lazy and put off departure. Then a day came when I realized with a shock that not only did the world have many more people in it than it had had only a short time before, but also that the hotels were less good, travel less comfortable, and places in general much less beautiful. After that when I went somewhere else I immediately longed to be back in Tangier . . . In defense of the city I can say that so far it has been touched by fewer of the negative aspects of contemporary civilization than most cities of its size. More important than that, I relish the idea that in the night, all around me in my sleep, sorcery is burrowing its invisible tunnels in every direction, from thousands of senders to thousands of unsuspecting recipients. Spells are being cast, poison is running its course; souls are being dispossessed of parasitic pseudo-consciousness that lurks in the unguarded recesses of the mind. There is drumming out there most nights. It never awakens me; I hear the drums and incorporate them into my dreams, like the nightly cries of the muezzins.

Bowles was notoriously careful with money. Jane complained that he wrote letters to her on poor quality paper. 'People call him frugal,' Choukri said, 'but in fact he's tight fisted.' Yet, in 1951, Bowles went against his natural inclinations and splashed out on a new Jaguar convertible. He employed a chauffeur, Mohammed Temsamany and they drove into the Sahara with Ahmed Yacoubi and the Canadian artist Brion Gysin. That year, he wrote to a friend that his driver was attacked by a djinn while driving in Fes. It had seized the steering wheel, jerked it from his hand as he shifted gears, and caused the car to crash into a bridge. Given this brush with death, Bowles wondered if he should really call his travel piece for a magazine: 'No More Djinns.'

Let it Come Down was published in Britain and America in 1952. In December, Ahmed Yacoubi moved from Fes to Tangier with a large portfolio of his paintings. Bowles arranged for an exhibition of his work in New York and Yacoubi stayed with Libby Holman, a rich, eccentric, former lover of Jane's.

Ahmed chose to stay at Treetops (Holman's mansion) with Libby, who told me upon our return that they had become sexually involved, and that she was in love with him.

Feeling used and abused by Yacoubi, Bowles returned to Tangier alone in May 1953, but by June, Yacoubi was back in Morocco. Holman had ended the affair after her adopted seven-year-old son Timmy told her that Yacoubi had pushed him into the swimming pool and tried to choke him. Timmy also said that Yacoubi had come to his bedroom one night and 'played with his pee-pee.' 'What actually happened was not entirely clear,' wrote Holman's biographer Jon Bradshaw, 'Ahmed was subsequently expelled from Treetops and Timmy was despatched to a psychiatrist.'

As he again made his way to Tangier, Bowles felt that the city was becoming more dangerous.

> I was in a hurry to see what Morocco would be like now that the terrorists had started their campaign against the French; behind my curiosity lurked the fear that the country would cease to be inhabitable for foreigners under the new circumstances. My fears seemed well grounded; there was an element of distinct unfriendliness abroad in the streets of Tangier. I had the impression that everyone was waiting for a signal to be given, and that when it came, all hell would break loose.
>
> As the trouble increased, the French became more difficult and querulous. They were specifically anti-American in their behavior, because they believed the arms that the Moroccans used against them came from the American bases. There were demonstrations by Moroccans in the streets of Tangier nearly every day; the shopkeepers were kept busy rolling the steel shutters of their shop fronts down and up, as the sound of the mob came and went.

In 1955 Bowles finished his third novel *The Spider's House*, which was set in Fes prior to independence. He wrote most of it in the imperial city and when he returned to Tangier he thought it resembled a ghost town. 'It is now impossible to go to French Morocco and drive around,' he wrote to his mother, 'so we have only the Spanish Zone to visit if you come now. Everything is prohibited since the Sultan was exiled.'

As the political temperature rose, Bowles felt increasingly unsafe in the Kasbah; 'a strictly Moslem neighbourhood,' he wrote. So he took a lease on two flats with adjoining terraces on the top floor of the Edificio San Francisco, a nine-storey building near the centre of town.

There was a sense that Tangier was becoming a city under siege. 'We still come and go in the streets,' he wrote, 'and no one molests us. But the possibility of being attacked is uppermost in every non-Moslem's mind.' Bowles' friend, Christopher Wanklyn, was stabbed while walking in the early hours in the Kasbah.

Having finished a magazine article entitled 'Parrots I have Known', Bowles found it ironic that he was actually presented with another parrot, a young African grey. Normally the African greys are considered good talkers, but this one, whom he named Seth, was like a Trappist monk. Until Seth's arrival, Cotorrito, the Amazon parrot had ruled the roost and talked constantly, but when the intruder came Cotorrito was so enraged that he also refused to talk. 'He adores parrots,' wrote Choukri, 'and from them he's borrowed the virtue of circumspection. He talks to them, and it may be that they're the only ones who know his secrets.'

In 1957, Jane suffered a stroke. 'I did not know it,' Bowles wrote later, 'but the good years were over.' She was admitted to a hospital in England where she had electric shock treatment. When she was well enough they both returned to Tangier, where they discovered that in their absence, hundreds of Europeans had been arrested and deported.

In 1959 Bowles was embarrassed to find that a piece had been written in the London Magazine about him smoking kif. A new anti-drug law had been introduced after independence. 'I wonder why they bothered to pass it,' Bowles wrote, 'Without having ruled off at least a third of the Moroccan territory for concentration camps. How otherwise can they accommodate the seven or eight million who will have to be incarcerated?'

Bowles even considered leaving the country in 1961 because of the new legislation, as he had no intention of giving up hashish. 'Kif-Weeks fly by, seasons change, the sun shines, one works and writes letters, people come and go, and one remains in just the same position that one was in a good while ago,' he wrote in a letter that December. Remembering a North African proverb, 'a pipe of kif before breakfast gives a man the strength of a hundred camels in the courtyard,' Bowles wrote four short stories about the power of taking hashish and called them *A Hundred Camels in the Courtyard*. In the preface he said the drug was a passageway to enlightenment.

For some time, Tangier had been on the brink of losing its charter, so money could no longer move freely in and out of the city. The French and Spanish residents departed in droves, but most of the English and Americans decided to stay on. Writing became Bowles' way of getting by and what happened to him or others became material for his fiction. Jane's cat Dubz died after falling from a balcony. 'The tale seemed just right for my kif volume,' Bowles recalled. In a 'Friend of the World', the main character Salam moves into a Jewish sector where he finds his beloved kitten Mimi dead one day. Salam avenges Mimi's death through black magic. Similarly, when Bowles' Amazon parrot died for no apparent reason, he was convinced that Cherifa was behind it and Jane found packets containing nail clippings, pubic hair and dried blood under her bed.

Those who wrote about Bowles' life found him frustratingly elusive. One such writer, Christopher Sawyer-Laucanno, called his biography, *An Invisible Spectator* and Millicent Dillon describes him as becoming 'transparent, opaque, and transparent again.'

> In our conversations he had the remarkable capacity to be forcefully present in his own right and yet to be almost transparent to my gaze at the same time . . . the more I questioned him, the less, it often seemed, I knew . . . It seemed to me that his withholding was a process akin to his method of telling a story, where what is revealed is revealed only at the necessary moment.

Annie Austin lived in Tangier in 1979 as a guest of David Herbert, going from one soirée to the next. 'There was this garden party,' she told me, 'Bowles just sat under a tree and watched everybody.'

> You would often see him observing. He was very reserved. He had to know who you were before he had a conversation with you and he had to be convinced you'd be able to have a decent conversation about something. He was very kind and charming, but he didn't open up very easily to people he didn't know. I suppose he was making notes.

One party that Bowles observed was given by the Swiss aristocrat, Louise de Meuron. For Bowles, the most enduring image was the entrance of an outrageous, English faux aristocrat, David Edge.

He appeared at just the right moment, completely naked and painted silver, borne by a team of Moroccans who were also painted silver. He looked like the Caterpillar from *Alice in Wonderland*.

Millicent Dillon spent months with Bowles in 1992, only to find to her dismay that he had also promised to work with another biographer, Virginia Spencer Carr.

I have already been through uprush of anger, downrush of hurt, chastisement of myself for thinking I have the right to either anger or hurt. After all, I tell myself, he doesn't belong to you; he doesn't belong to anybody. If he wants to have two, five, a hundred biographers, it's up to him.

Bowles' success prompted a pilgrimage of admirers who invaded Tangier to smoke kif in the Sixties. 'Everyday one sees more beards and filthy blue jeans,' he wrote in late 1961, 'the girls look like escapees from lunatic asylums, with white lipstick and black smeared around their eyes, and matted hair hanging around their shoulders. The leaders of the 'movement' have moved their headquarters here.'

'Tangier in the 1960s was more than a city,' says the American writer, Paula Wolfert, 'it was a state of mind, a place people came to reinvent themselves and to live out their most eccentric fantasies. The phone book listed several "countesses" and "barons" who were actually courtesans and butcher boys. The phone company didn't care. The phones didn't work anyway.' Famously, Bowles was not fond of telephones (apart from the toy one he used to speak to Jane). When his fellow American novelist Jay McInerny visited him in 1985, he had not had a phone for 16 years. 'Who can be bothered?' he said, 'You'll be working, or else you're in the bathtub, and the phone rings. You answer and a voice says "Allo, Mohammed?"'

Mohamed Choukri also remembered the endless stream of visitors to the Itesa, where Bowles 'had entrenched himself there like the Sphinx.'

Through his writing, travels and unconventional lifestyle, Bowles played a significant role in hippie culture, although he strenuously denies having any connection with the Beat Generation. All the same, he welcomed many beatniks into his home, where he would converse with them at great length, despite the large amounts of his time they took up . . . It reached the point where they would leave their bags at the entrance of his small apartment, languidly saying: "Hey man, we've come to see you." Eventually he grew tired of them.

Among the more welcome guests were John Hopkins and Joe McPhillips, who first came to the city in 1962. They had graduated from Princeton, travelled around South America and ended up working at the American School of Tangier. Hopkins stayed for 17 years and McPhillips for the rest of his life. 'We'd eaten the Lotus and we weren't going home,' Hopkins told me. In The Tangier Diaries, he gives this description of Jane and Paul.

Dinner with the Bowleses in Jane's apartment. The spontaneous affection and sense of fun they share make them seem more like brother and sister than man and wife. Their intimacy is more fraternal than sexual . . . It was like being in New York except for Cherifa, who rattled on in Arabic in a gruff mannish voice and laughed uproariously at her own jokes. A rough, alien presence, who acted as though she owned the place. Jane, a fragile figure like a priceless vase that has been knocked to the floor. The pieces have been glued back together, but crudely and the cracks show . . . In the evening we ate with our fingers, listened to music, and took in the stars – kiffed-up stars that revolved, changed colours, and winked on and off.

'I used to go to Paul's after midnight,' Hopkins said, 'I'd give a tip to the guy at the door and up you go. It was fantastic.' There are more details of these visits in The Tangier Diaries.

We go up on the roof to look at the stars, listen to music, talk. Paul is an attentive host during these late night sessions and deftly anticipates the effects of the weed he loves to smoke. When you get the munchies, he produces a box of cookies or a bowl of fruit. When the pipe makes you so thirsty your throat begins to feel like the inside of a tin cup, he serves Lapsang Souchong with lemon and sugar. When there's a gap, something missing – and you're too spaced out to know what it is – he lights a joss stick dipped in some magic ointment brought back from the Orient.

'He was very sociable,' Hopkins said in our interview, 'it was open house at his apartment. He had all these people sitting at his feet, waiting for the great man to open his mouth. He had the biggest tolerance for fools.' When the hordes of tourists finally became too much that summer, Bowles rented a small house in Asilah. Here, he began recording and transcribing several tales by a young, illiterate Moroccan called Larbi Layachi, whom he discovered working in a café on Merkala Beach. The stories evolved into *A Life Full of Holes* under the pen name of Driss ben Hamed Charhadi. Describing the process of transcribing the tales, Bowles recalled that it was as if Layachi had memorised the entire text and rehearsed the speaking of it for weeks.

From 1967 onwards, Jane's health continued to decline and she was in and out of psychiatric hospitals. Later, to everyone's surprise she checked herself and Cherifa into the Hotel Atlas in the centre of town. When John Hopkins asked Paul how Jane was, he told him she spent most of her time in the Parade Bar, 'handing out money and drinks to every lush in Tangier.'

The Parade Bar, on the Avenue Prince Heritier, no longer exists, having been usurped by a large new building, yet it is still part of Tangerine folklore. Before he died, I was fortunate enough to meet Joe Abensur, whose family owned the Pariente Bank, just off the Petit Socco. Joe knew Bill Chase and Jay Haselwood, who owned the Parade. In his memoirs, Joe recalled how they asked him to appear in a film there.

My role consisted of looking tough, walking out one door, lighting up a cigarette, and going out another door. I did it so well that apparently I did not need a re-take, and I did not end up on the cutting room floor.

However, two months later, one of the clients of the bank told me that he went to see an X-rated film on 42nd Street in New York called *White Slavery*, and guess who walked in and out of the doors of a bar in the film?

Meanwhile, Jane continued to deteriorate. Bowles wrote that one of their friends, Victor Kraft, had 'been to see Jane and had communicated with her by putting his finger between her teeth, and having her bite once for yes and twice for no.'

Jane Bowles died on 4 May 1973. Her obituary in the *New York Times* included a reference to the rarity of her book, *Two Serious Ladies*, adding that when the publisher, Peter Owen, wanted to reprint the novel in 1970, not even Jane could supply him with a copy. 'It is hoped she will be recognised for what she is,' *The Times* said, 'one of the finest modern writers of fiction in any language.' Tennessee Williams concurred, 'I am not alone in regarding Jane as the finest writer of the century in English prose-fiction.'

Devastated by her death, Bowles wrote, 'there is nothing to keep me here, save habit, but I shall probably stay on until outer circumstances force me to leave.' 'When Jane died,' Dillon writes, 'he realised that it was only through her that he had been living. Then, after her death, he felt he was not truly alive.' Bowles told Dillon of his profound sadness.

She had begun to die sixteen years earlier, and I'd given up hope of seeing her herself, as she had been. Earlier, we had given each other our work to read. She was a confidante. Since then, there is not anyone to write for. It was a terrible thing to have happened.

Nearly two years after she died, Hopkins and McPhillips made a pilgrimage to her grave, but had trouble finding it in the cemetery near Malaga. 'In the end, one of the gardeners led us to it,' Hopkins wrote, 'there were no tiles; there wasn't even a cross. Only a stick with a number on it: 453-F. We stood around and stared at it for a while, clutching our flowers . . . It had become the refuse dump of broken flower pots and bottles and dead stalks cast aside by the assiduous ladies in black.'

Mouth of the Caves of Hercules, where the demigod is said to have rested before his eleventh labour.

The Bay of Tangier from above.

Phoenician tombs at *Gharsa Ghanam* on the Marshan. Nearly 100 ancient graves were discovered in archaeological digs that began in 1910.

Roman ruins at Lixus. It is the second most important Roman site in Morocco, after Volubilis.

'Sertorius and the Example of the Horses,' after Hans Holbein the Younger, c1540.

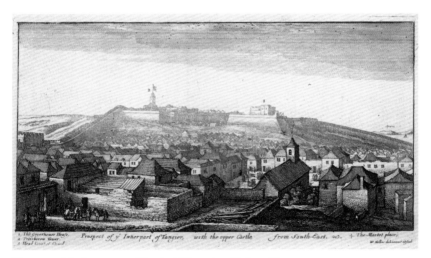

'Prospect of the inner part of Tangier,' Wenceslaus Hollar, 1669.

The Tomb of Ibn Battuta. The mausoleum is notoriously difficult to find in Tangier's medina.

The Kasbah, near Bab al-Assa.

Fig tree in Dar Zero, Kasbah.

Villa Harris.

Villa Josephine. In the distance is Dar el Quaa, or the House of Arches, which now belongs to the Emir of Qatar.

Window in room 35, Hotel Villa de France.

'Paysage Vu d'Une Fenêtre,' Henri Matisse 1912.

Paul Bowles photographed outside Tangier.

The Immeuble Itesa. 'It was an ugly, grey, oblong block built by Italians in the 1950s and would not have looked out of place in Bucharest or Pyongyang.'

Inside the Continental Hotel. 'On the first floor landing, a long-case clock stood sentinel, chiming away hours and half-hours which never seemed to pass.'

The Petit Socco. 'The meeting place and switchboard of Tangier.'

(From left to right) Peter Orlovsky, William Burroughs, Allen Ginsberg, Alan Ansen, Paul Bowles, Gregory Corso and Ian Sommerville in the garden of the Villa Muniria, 1961.

Gran Café de Paris. 'The ghosts of Jean Genet and Samuel Beckett are long gone.'

Brion Gysin in a hospital bed after his motorbike accident riding pillion on John Hopkins' 'White Nile' in July 1969.

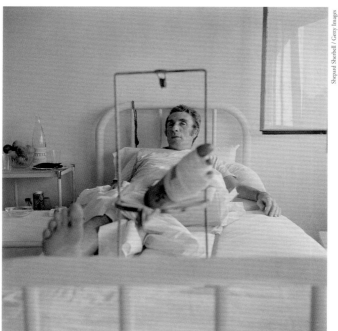

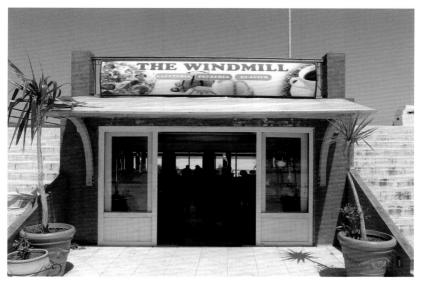

The Windmill on Tangier's Corniche. A favourite haunt of Kenneth Williams and Joe Orton.

Mohamed Mrabet in his apartment, surrounded by some of his artwork.

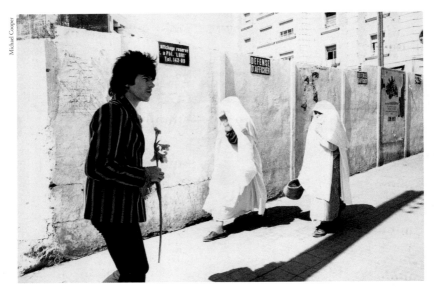

Keith Richards in Tangier, 1967.

Brian, Anita and Keith in Marrakech 1967. Michael Cooper's photograph was, according to Richards, 'a chilling image in retrospect, the last picture of Anita and Brian and me together. It has a tension about it that still radiates.'

Marianne Faithfull, Mick Jagger, Robert Fraser, Brian Jones, Achmed and Anita Pallenberg inside Achmed's shop. Keith Richards said of it: 'You could stay there all day, all night; you could live there. And always Radio Cairo, with static always off the tuning.'

Michael Cooper

The mouth of Boujeloud's cave, in Joujouka, looking out towards the Atlantic. The cave is 'as cool as a fridge and as quiet as noise-cancelling headphones.'

In the 1980s and 1990s, the flow of visiting journalists increased, as they sought interviews with the now legendary American writer at his apartment in the *Itesa*, as Dillon recalls.

Although he had always had a cult following in the underground press, now he frequently mentioned being besieged by biographers, journalists, and moviemakers from the mainstream world. He protested the disruption of his life; yet it was clear that he enjoyed the attention being showered upon him.

In 1984, Bowles underwent surgery for prostate cancer and after this he was meticulous about his health. David Herbert remembered in his autobiography, *Second Son* that this went back some time.

I once had a headache and asked Janie if she had any aspirin. "No but look in Paul's medicine cabinet," she said. I did and took two. The following day, Paul said; "Janie, did you take two aspirins out of the bottle?" "No, but David did." "Oh, that's all right. I just wondered because the last time I took one out there were 73 left in the bottle, and now there are only 71."

The Hotel Continental is seemingly bent like a piece of cardboard to follow the shape of the shoreline. It is built on the sea walls of *Dar Baroud* ('the House of Gunpowder') and from the terrace, palm trees frame a panoramic view of the harbour. Here, you can sip mint tea and breathe in the whiff of fish, seaweed and diesel. A plaque at the entrance explains that the Continental was founded in 1870 and is a national heritage monument. In the preface to *By Royal Appointment: A History of the Continental Hotel*, its owner Mohammed Souissi, describes his establishment as 'a survivor from an age when good service, comfort, integrity, excellent cuisine and discretion mattered more than elevators, in-house discos or saunas.' In the foreword, Terence MacCarthy, who described Tangier as the 'University of Perversity,' recalled his first visit there 25 years earlier.

The Continental had once been a 'Grand' hotel in the real sense of that word, an elegant fusion of Arabesque influences and high

Edwardian tastes, a veritable fin de siècle palace of comfort and ease. A grand piano, doubtless long out of tune, dominated the hallway, and the walls were hung with the lances of the long defunct members of the Pig-sticking Tangier Tent Club. On the first floor landing, a long-case clock stood sentinel, chiming away hours and half-hours which never seemed to pass.

Not much had changed when I went. By the side of the reception stands a Bakelite switchboard, with a sign saying 'look but don't touch.' On the other side, an Edwardian grandfather clock guards the stairway and the Arabesque influences can be seen in Moorish arches over-zealously plastered with zellij. On one wall is a drawing of Hassan II with a smart black suit and disproportionately large lips. On the others are black and white photographs, providing snapshots of Tangier's history: Kaiser Wilhelm arriving at the port in 1905, King Mohammed V calling for independence in 1947, and Habib Bourguiba's motorcade crawling up the Boulevard Pasteur ten years later.

There is also a sepia portrait of Bernardo Bertolucci in a Panama hat. In May 1987, the movie director first came to the Continental to start work on The Sheltering Sky and two years after that Bowles was involved in the filming, playing himself. 'Bertolucci now thinks I should appear in certain scenes in the film,' Bowles wrote in Days: A Tangier Diary, 'I don't know exactly why.' At the hotel's in-house shop, the modestly titled 'Jimmy's World Famous Bazaar,' I spoke to its owner Mohammed Jami (aka Jimmy). He remembered John Malkovich, Debra Winger and Campbell Scott performing their scenes in the Continental. I asked him how long he has been here. 'Forty-eight years,' he said, 'but I am not counting. You have the watches; we have the time.'

'Will you order me some petit dejeuner?' Winger says to Scott in a bedroom of the Continental, 'I'd like some of their awful coffee and plaster croissants!' Bowles was underwhelmed by the film and rated it on a par with the croissants, 'the less said about it the better,' he wrote. Although he admitted that it helped bring him and his book out of 'distinguished obscurity.' Bertolucci said the movie explored the dark side of human nature. 'I wanted to show the poison that creeps into relationships, no matter how close they seem to be,' he told the New

York Times. By the time the film came out in 1990, Bowles was finding the political situation in Morocco unpredictable.

> I remember being fined upon claiming a package sent to me that contained only a jar of jam, but the postal authority declared that it was an insult to Morocco since there was "perfectly good jam made here." It made no difference that I had not ordered it, and that it was not my fault someone had seen fit to send it to me, but they were inflexible. Their response was that I should not have been consorting with people who believed Morocco to be an under-developed country. They've been burning the American flag publicly, and the streets are empty of tourists.

In 1994, Bowles flew to Atlanta for further cancer surgery. He told Dillon he 'no longer felt connected with anything'; and that he had lived his life 'vicariously and didn't know it.'

One morning Otmane and I walked along the Route de Boubana. We passed a Carrefour supermarket to our right and two subterranean nightclubs on the other side of the road. The first was *The Loft Club*, northern Morocco's largest disco. A poster promised a night under the guidance of a rotund DJ called Hassan Bond, who wore dark sunglasses and a matching black t-shirt with the words: 'Keep Calm I'm Hassan Bond.' The second was *Mille et Une Nuits*, which offered the prospect of a *Cabaret Oriental* with a scantily clad nymph by the name of Anissa. 'I have something to show you,' Otmane said mysteriously. Sadly, it was not a rendezvous with Mr Bond nor Anissa, but something even more bizarre and somewhere not frequented by tourists or middle-aged men from the Gulf. We walked unsteadily down a steep slope of dust and loose pebbles. I slipped and landed on my buttocks, but pretended to look unflustered. We then hopped over a narrow stream and waded through wispy grass. Here, under the shade of cork and eucalyptus trees, was a patch of scrubland with many tiny abandoned grave-stones. This was Tangier's pet cemetery and it was here that Paul Bowles had told Virginia Spencer Carr he wanted to be buried.

> Naturally, since I would be an interloper, my interment in the pet graveyard would have to be carried out surreptitiously, presumably

late at night before anyone realized what was happening. Officially, no person can be interred there . . . I do rather relish the thought of lying anonymously amidst the Fidos and Rexes.

'Kuki' said one tombstone from 1907, 'you will remain in our hearts forever.' Similar sentiments were expressed on the graves of Hugo, Coco, Danton, Chica, Saki, Tomy, Jicky and Cheaky, although ironically Lucky's headstone had been stolen and an improvised message had been scratched on the granite where a plaque had once been. It was a strange, otherworldly tribute to the faithful companions of colonialists. This canine charnel house must have left the locals bewildered and bemused. 'Entrée interdite' said a superfluous message on the stone blocks that had once supported the entrance gate. Like the marble slabs, the gate too had long gone. 'The site is not protected,' sighed Otmane, 'and one day it will disappear.' Perhaps, one night in the future, the successors of Hassan Bond and Anissa, together with a new generation of sybarites and Lotus-eaters, will dance on the graves of dogs.

On 18 November 1999, Paul Bowles died in the Italian Hospital in Tangier at the age of 88. 'He was a sweet old boy,' remembered Jonathan Dawson, 'I knew him at the fag end of his life. My friend, James Chandler, was dying in the room next door to him in the Italian Hospital and Paul's driver was selling a place at the door to people who wanted to come and watch him croak. The day he did actually croak, Chandler moved into Bowles' bed because he thought the bedroom was better. That's so Tangier, isn't it?'

Bowles' body was taken, not to the pet cemetery, but to Casablanca from where it was shipped to America. His ashes were interred beside his mother at Lakemont Cemetery in New York. Virginia Spencer Carr read a poem at the funeral and later recalled how Joe McPhillips had also planned to give a reading, but only remembered as he was leaving the cemetery. 'Ah here's the passage,' he announced to friends as they made their way to the airport. It was the lines from The Sheltering Sky in which Port dies.

A black star appears, a point of darkness in the night sky's clarity. Point of darkness and gateway to repose. Reach out, pierce the fine fabric of the sheltering sky, take repose.

EIGHT

William Burroughs

Tanger is the prognostic pulse of the world, like a dream extending from past into the future, a frontier between dream and reality

When I arrived in Tangier in 2014, one of the first things I wanted to do was to find the Villa Muniria, but there was something about the odd shape of the road behind the Rembrandt Hotel where I was staying that fooled me. I would walk down towards the seafront and keep missing the Muniria. One night I stayed up for hours, checking my map of the city and looking out of the bedroom window, but it did not add up. Even Google Maps seemed to betray me. About two days later it dawned on me that I had been gazing in the wrong direction. I had miscalculated the configuration of the Rembrandt and the Muniria lay at another angle altogether, about 200 yards from my window. Although slightly obscured by another building, it had been in front of my nose the whole time.

To get there, I simply had to turn right out of the reception lobby and take the first right, the Rue Jabha Watania, which runs alongside the Rembrandt and descends slowly to the sea. I walked past yet another salon de coiffeur (Tangier, it seems, is not a city of literary ghosts, but a city of hairdressers), a Spanish restaurant and a tapas bar on my left, while the Elysium Spa (aka massage parlour) on the other side warned 'hommes' not to come during 'les heures des femmes.' Just as you approach the appropriately named Maison des Caprices, you take a right down some steps into a narrow side street which smells of urine and screams of danger. 'The alleyway can be a bit dodgy at times, we had a guy follow us and start masturbating,' wrote someone on TripAdvisor. 'I'm not surprised,' Gerald Loftus told me later, 'it's a place where you want to appear not to be lost. You want to look as if you know where you're going because several people I know have been mugged in that area.' I walked on down Rue Magellan, clutching my rucksack to my chest, wary of muggers and masturbators, alongside a building that, in some parallel universe, reminded me of London's National Theatre, except that it was yellow, empty and faced not a river but a wall of graffiti. In 2009, Sara and Hicham had expressed their love for each other on the wall, while Rachid and Lina wrote simply 'Let's Go!' On the right, I saw a Volkswagen camper van patrolled by mangy miniature cats, followed by a completely derelict space, which is all that remains of the Hotel Ibn Battuta and looks like a car park overgrown with weeds or the aftermath of a nuclear bomb. Facing this empty space, heralded by signs in red letters, is the Muniria, a simple white block with blue windowsills and a castellated roof terrace. It was in room nine, of 'Villa Delirium' as it was nicknamed, that William Seward Burroughs wrote one of the twentieth century's most shocking and groundbreaking novels, Naked Lunch.

I rang the doorbell. A young Moroccan opened the door and listed the prices of the rooms. He said I could look around, but that room number nine, downstairs, was out of bounds.

'It's closed.'

'Why's that?'

'It's private. It belongs to the family now.'

'I see . . . but could you open it anyway?'

'No, my uncle has gone away . . . for a long time . . . with the key.'

The terrace was spartan, decked only with washing lines. Beyond was a palm tree, a view of the marina and the Mediterranean. I peered beneath the blue shutters into rooms seven and eight. They had bare light bulbs, simple beds and solitary radiators. The corridors were desolate with a patch of mould on the walls. A black and white portrait of Burroughs in trademark fedora and dark sunglasses stared enigmatically at visitors between the leaves of a rubber plant. The bathroom was bleak, like the inside of a sanatorium, with endless white tiles, exposed yellowed pipes and a mirror that hung at an odd angle, about to fall into the sink. The toilet looked like the end of the world.

I ventured downstairs to the family quarters where the young man's mother was watching television. Her name was Rabia and she showed me around. We stood in front of room nine. It was locked. As at the Caves of Hercules and Dar Zero, a lot of my research seemed to involve trying to get inside places, to unlock the secrets of the city.

'It's not possible to see inside?'

'Well, the thing is . . . it's a bit messy.'

'That's ok. But you have the key?'

'Yes of course, wait a minute.'

Rabia came back and opened the door to room number nine. It was a family bedroom with an unmade bed, an old radio and dark wooden wardrobes. Photos of her relatives hung from pale peach walls illuminated by a tiny light bulb that dangled from a ceiling rose.

She said Burroughs lived in room nine, while Ginsberg and Kerouac rented rooms four and five on the floor above. Occasionally Bowles would use room seven. Visitors came to stay from all over the world. About 20 years ago she said, a famous Spanish singer, who had been at the Minzah, liked the look of room seven so much that she checked out of her more luxurious accommodation. Warning me to beware of a bulldog, Rabia opened a gate to let me into the garden, where a photo of Burroughs and his friends was taken in 1961.

Beneath the Muniria, lay the Tanger Inn. Its walls were blue and red. A lantern and a drape were suspended from the ceiling. There was a piano and a bar stocked with dusty bottles of spirits. The walls were decorated with photos of Burroughs *et al*, as well as a dartboard. It was very dark. The inn was a hangout for writers and was run by Peter Tuckwell and John Sutcliffe, who sold copies of his own novel from behind the bar. Tuckwell told a friend of mine that Burroughs was, 'a strange man, looked like an undertaker.' Nowadays it is open until 1.30 a.m. but Rabia assured me that guests on the top floor would not be disturbed by the music. A review in *Lonely Planet* said it was 'jumping with the cool folk of Tangier . . . not like the other bars in town which are full of prostitutes.'

William Burroughs was born in 1914 to a wealthy family in Missouri and was the grandson of William Seward Burroughs I, the inventor of the Burroughs Adding Machine. In 1932 he studied English at Harvard and later went to medical school in Vienna. After being turned down for military service, he dropped out and became afflicted with the drug addiction that affected the rest of his life. In New York in 1943 he befriended Allen Ginsberg and Jack Kerouac. Together, they would become the leaders of the countercultural movement, the Beat Generation.

Burroughs had one child, Billy, with his second wife Joan Vollmer. She died in Mexico City in 1951. Burroughs was playing a game of William Tell and tried to shoot a glass tumbler perched on her head. He missed the glass and killed her. Burroughs was convicted of manslaughter and Vollmer's death cast a lifelong shadow over his writings.

In 1953, Burroughs was at a loose end. When Ginsberg refused his romantic advances, Burroughs went to Rome to meet W.H. Auden's secretary, Alan Ansen, on a holiday financed by his parents. Burroughs found Rome and Ansen boring though, and inspired by the fiction of Paul Bowles, he headed to Tangier. 'Leaving Monday for Tangiers via Gibraltar,' Burroughs wrote to Ginsberg on 2 January 1954, 'Will arrive with $50 to last me until Feb 1.'

Burroughs tried to settle into life in Tangier. It was a sunny place for shady people and should have suited him to a tee. 'A sun-bleached, sybaritic outpost set against the verdant hills of North Africa,' was how Michelle Green described it in *The Dream at the End of the World*. Compared to Tangier, Robert Ruark wrote in 1950, 'Sodom was a church picnic and Gomorrah a convention of Girl Scouts.' The place contained 'more thieves, black marketeers, spies, thugs, phonies, beachcombers, expatriates, degenerates, characters, operators, bandits, bums, tramps, politicians and charlatans,' than anywhere else he had ever been. Burroughs was quickly disillusioned, as he told Ginsberg in a letter on 26 January.

> I like Tangiers less all the time. No writers' colony here or they keep theirselves hid some place. Everybody has both feet in your business; like some character I never see before says: "Your friend Ali is in the Socco Chico. Please give me one peseta." And the payoff is I never get to lay Ali . . . What's all this old Moslem culture shit? They are just a gabby, gossipy simple-minded, lazy crew of citizens.

Burroughs first found a room near the Socco Chico on Calle de los Arcos owned by 'Dutch Tony' who made a living fixing up Moroccan boys with his foreign tenants. He features in a letter from Burroughs to Kerouac on 22 April 1954.

> Tony, the old Dutchman who runs this whore house I live in, keeps casting me reproachful glances in the hall and saying: "Ach thirteen years and never before I haff such a thing in my house. And since two weeks are here in Tangiers two good English gentlemens I know since long times. With them I could make good business except my house is so watched at." However I am still his star boarder and he hesitates to evict me.

Mohamed Choukri described Burroughs' first few weeks.

> When William Burroughs arrived in Tangier he greeted Tanjawi society, both the Moroccans and the expatriates, with hostility. The former he saw as intellectual inferiors and swindlers, while the latter were ostentatious, boastful of their comfortable financial situations that allowed them to frequent all the best restaurants and bars. Everyone avoided him. Burroughs lived in isolation.

Despite being a drug addict, the 'Invisible Man' had considerable strength of character. He decided to live a certain way and persevered where others might have given up. He also had a dark side, recalling that his nannies had brought him up on black magic and that he had been 'receptive ground' for them. The belief in the occult never left him. One of his biographers, Ted Morgan, says the reality of the spirit world was the most important element in Burroughs' life. In Tangier, magic was part of everyday existence. In the city's souks, medicine men sold their wares arranged on anatomical charts on the ground.

Burroughs immediately caught the special character of the city, what Morgan calls 'its quality of exemption,' that is exemption from laws, morals, constraint and interference of any kind.

The Petit Socco is one of my favourite places in Tangier. You can sit outside Café Central or Café Tingis and sense that little has changed since the days of Bowles and Burroughs, or even Walter Harris, who frequented the Café Central's predecessor Sotiry's, in the 1880s. Set on a gentle incline, from these cafés the Petit Socco, Zocco Chico or Souk Dakhel has a pleasing diagonal perspective. With its art deco façades, wrought-iron balconies and yellow awnings, it feels more like a stage set. David Stotter, an expert on stamps and postal history, told me that in this tiny square were the British, French, Spanish and German post offices, all competing for business and a testament to the peculiarities of the International Zone. 'The sound of clerks stamping letters echoed into the night,' he said. Otmane said that in the 1930s the Zocco Chico was frequented by Spanish spies who kept an eye on suspected communists and enemies of General Franco. He also said that opposite the Café Central was a part of the medina known as Quartier Beni Yeder that had a famous brothel. Burroughs spent a lot of time hanging out at the Café Central in the Socco Chico, which Morgan describes as the 'meeting place and switchboard of Tangier.' Here, you could find a boy as well as gaze on a parade of lost souls, the stranded exiles who washed up like pebbles on a beach. Mohamed Choukri used to sleep on the floor of the Café Rakassa in the Socco. This is another of his descriptions of Burroughs in those days:

> He could be seen in the Petit Socco, sitting in a café, leaning against a wall, or walking around . . . There was always something severe about his bearing. Anyone who saw him then would get the impression that he was a spy surreptitiously gathering information, the collar of his overcoat perpetually raised, his fedora tilted slightly downwards on his forehead, his gaze steady, one hand clutching the front of his coat, the other in his pocket.

Burroughs was an outsider and was even marginalised in Tangier, the city of outsiders. 'Cast adrift in the midst of the International Zone's polyglot culture,' writes Michelle Green, 'tortured souls like Burroughs fell prey to searing loneliness and a wrenching sense of dislocation.' He was not invited to parties by the likes of David Herbert. Instead, he made friends with those who were as unfortunate as him. There was 'Calamity Kate', Eric Gifford, who worked for the *Tangier Gazette* and took care of his elderly mother. Gifford was spectacularly unlucky. He had lost money in a bee-keeping venture in the Caribbean and was later held in a detention centre in Spain. There was also Paul Lund, who turned to crime for fun and over the years became an expert on the insides of English prisons. His father told him to be a blackguard somewhere else, so he went to Tangier where he started smuggling cigarettes. Even more corrupt than Lund was the Australian journalist George Greaves, who was suspected of spying for the Moroccan police.

The one person Burroughs really wanted to meet was Bowles. The established author was everything Burroughs hoped to be. The first meeting between them did not go well, as Burroughs wrote in a letter to Kerouac on 18 August 1954.

> The one time I met Paul Bowles he evinced no cordiality. Since then he has made no effort to follow up the acquaintance . . . He invites the dreariest queens in Tangiers to tea, but has never invited me, which seeing how small the town is, amounts to a deliberate affront. Perhaps he has some idea that trouble might result from knowing anyone associated with narcotics.

To Bowles, Burroughs was a thin, grey man who looked as if he was coming in and out of focus. Perhaps it was the drugs? Burroughs wondered if Bowles was engaged in some sort of illegal currency deals.

The younger man played down his disappointment. In another letter to Kerouac on 3 September, he seemed to almost enjoy being an outcast.

> I am not so all fired anxious to meet Bowles . . . I wanted to meet what there was here to meet. But they seem to have scented my being different and excluded me.

Burroughs' humour is apparent in a letter to Ginsberg on 9 February 1954; a humour that cannot be disentangled from an insensitivity to Arab culture.

> This town is left over from a boom. Hotels and bars empty. Vast, pink stucco apartment houses falling apart, not even finished. In a few years Arab families will move in with goats and chickens . . . This town seems to have several dimensions. I have experienced a

series of Kafkian incidents . . . For example: I go to bed with an Arab in European clothes. Several days later in the rain (and loaded on hash. You eat it here with hot tea), I meet an Arab in native dress, and we repair to a Turkish bath. Now I am almost (but not quite) sure it is the same Arab. In any case I have not seen no.1 again. When I walk down the street, Arabs I never see before greet me in a manner suggesting unspeakable familiarity (in past or future?). I told one of these Arabs, "Look, I don't like you and I don't know you. Scram." He just laughed and said, "I see you later, Mister." And I did in fact go to bed with him later, or at least I think it was the same one. It's like I been to bed with three Arabs since arrival, but I wonder if it isn't the same character in different clothes, and every time better behaved, cheaper, more respectful . . . I really don't know for sure. Next time I'll notch one of his ears.

The fact that Burroughs had not heard from Ginsberg for four months hurt him deeply. By the time he wrote to Kerouac on 4 May, he was desperate: 'I don't know what I would do if anything happened to Allen.' His drug addiction was getting worse too. He could not work, write or take an interest in anything.

I lived in one room in the Native Quarter of Tangier. I had not taken a bath in a year nor changed my clothes or removed them, except to stick a needle every hour in the fibrous grey wooden flesh of terminal addiction. I never cleaned or dusted the room. Empty ampule boxes and garbage piled up to the ceiling. Light and water had been long since turned off for non-payment. I did absolutely nothing. I could look at the end of my shoe for eight hours.

But, in February things began to pick up. He met Kiki, an 18-year-old Spanish boy, who came to see him everyday. Burroughs enjoyed lolling about, smoking pot and having sex with Kiki, but the latter's intellectual limitations only added to the American's loneliness. Burroughs felt he had no one to talk to and his solitude increased his drug intake. Over the counter, he bought a synthetic, heroin-like German drug, Eukodol, which he described in a letter to Ginsberg, on 7 April 1954.

Trying to write a novel. Attempt to organize material is more painful than anything I ever experienced. Shooting every four hours. Some semi-synthetic stuff called Eukodol. God knows what kind of habit I am getting. When I kick this habit I expect fuses will blow out of my brain from overcharge and black sooty blood will run out eyes, ears and nose and staggering around the room acting out routines like Roman Emperor in a bloody sheet.

Recent research suggests Hitler was addicted to Eukodol. After the war, having discovered that its side effects included euphoria, the manufacturers of Eukodol stopped making it. There were, however, plenty of supplies still left in Tangier, which Burroughs proceeded to exhaust. As Ted Morgan writes, 'the days slid by, strung on a syringe with a long thread of blood.' Burroughs would stay in his room with the shutters closed, but he was determined to quit and offered Eric Gifford 50 dollars to help him. Gifford was to keep Burroughs' clothes so that he could not go out, bring him food and dole out a decreasing amount of drugs for ten days, but on the second day Burroughs took another lodger's clothes and snuck out to buy more drugs. Gifford found out, confiscated the ampoules, took Burroughs' money and locked the door.

Slowly, Burroughs began to cut down on junk, but went down with a fever and would sleep for 20 hours a day. He described his condition in a letter to Ginsberg on 3 July.

I am really ill. Pain and swelling in the joints . . . So here I am sick and broke. Hope to God I don't get laid up here. I want to get out of Tangiers . . . This place drags me like a sea anchor.

Kiki nursed him through his illness. Sometimes, Burroughs felt that he loved Kiki, but the Spaniard was his second choice – he was still in love with Ginsberg. He went back to the United States later that year but things did not work out with the poet. Burroughs returned to Tangier in November 1954, feeling that staying any longer in America, 'the air-conditioned nightmare,' as Henry Miller described it, would have driven him insane. 'It would literally kill me to live in the US,' he wrote to Ginsberg on 13 December, 'It's like I can't breathe, especially in suburban communities.'

Palm Beach is a real horror. No slums, no dirt, no poverty. God what a fate to live there! No wonder men die young . . . The US simply does not provide sustenance for a man. He gets fat, and his vitality drains away, and he dies from spiritual malnutrition . . . So I am counting my blessings in Tangiers.

As his second year in Tangier began, Burroughs concentrated on trying to write but found it excruciating. Convinced he had no talent, he would sit for hours staring at a blank page. He would try to write a novel, but knew it would be unpublishable. But in a twist of fate, his letters to Ginsberg would become the material for this elusive work. They became the 'routines,' his vignettes featuring parodies of characters in the city and grotesque science fiction elements such as 'talking arseholes.' 'Suppose you knew the power to start an atomic war lay in the hands of a few scientists who were bent on destroying the world?' Burroughs wrote to Ginsberg on 12 January 1955, 'That is the terrifying question posed by this searching novel.'

"The book grabs you by the throat," says the distinguished critic, L. Marland." It leaps in bed with you, and performs unmentionable acts. Then it thrusts a long cold needle deep into your spine" . . . I can work in all my routines, all the material I have written so far on Tangier that is scattered through a hundred letters to you.

'For about eight years in Tangier I was writing sporadically and a lot of this material was in the letters to Allen Ginsberg.' Burroughs recalled later, 'I was surprised reading back over them, how much of Naked Lunch is in those letters.'

He also began to realise that Tangier could serve as the novel's backdrop. Tangier was a construct of the imagination more than any real geographical location. It was a metaphor for somewhere at the end of the world, a dead-end place of limbo and a reconstruction of the world on a micro-level. Burroughs called the early drafts Interzone but, at Jack Kerouac's suggestion, it would become Naked Lunch. The title referred to 'a frozen moment when everyone sees what is on the end of every fork.'

'He wasn't sure what he was writing about,' Morgan says, 'but he began to see that it had to do with larval forms, transitions, emergent telepathic faculties, attempts to control and stifle new forms. He knew that the routine was his special form – it was unpredictable.' To write with any consistency or coherence though, Burroughs had to rid himself of his addiction. In May, he checked into a clinic on the Marshan to see a Dr Apfel, who, like other Tangier personalities, became the inspiration for a character in *Naked Lunch*, Dr Benway. At the clinic Burroughs took barbiturates and other drugs and lost 30 pounds, but by July 1955, he was hooked again.

By this time, Bowles had returned from Ceylon and invited the younger man to tea. It was a great success. Bowles appreciated Burroughs' storytelling and humour. In contrast to Bowles, Burroughs had made no effort to adapt to Moroccan ways. As Morgan writes, 'he remained as American as the general store in a one-horse town.'

In September Burroughs checked himself into the Jewish Hospital. The cure was dolophine every four hours. It gave him bizarre ideas. He was writing, but he had no control over what he wrote. 'I am trying,' he told Ginsberg on 20 October, 'to create something that has a life of its own, that can put me in real danger.'

'The Italian school is just opposite, and I stand for hours watching the boys with my 8-power field glasses,' he wrote to Kerouac and Ginsberg three days later.

Curious feeling of projecting myself, like I was standing over there with the boys, invisible earthbound ghost, torn with disembodied lust. They wear shorts, and I can see the goose pimples on their legs in the chill of the morning . . . Yesterday I took a walk on the outskirts of town. Environs of the Zone are wildly beautiful. Low hills with great variety of trees, flowering vines and shrubs, great, red sandstone cliffs topped with curiously stylised, Japanese-looking pine trees, fall to the sea. What a place for a house on top of those cliffs! I used to complain I lacked material to write about. Mother of God! Now I'm swamped with material . . . beginning to dig Arab kicks. It takes time. You must let them seep into you.

At the start of 1956, Burroughs took stock of the situation. The last two years had been a blur of drugs. All attempts to kick his habit had failed. 'Last night,' he wrote in *Naked Lunch*, 'I woke up with someone squeezing my hand. It was my other hand.'

Burroughs heard of a doctor in London who treated addicts, so he went to visit John Yerbury Dent who had developed a treatment involving apomorphine. The doctor had first tried it on alcoholics, and then on heroin addicts. Burroughs' initial shot of apomorphine made him vomit for two minutes; it was then reduced and given to him every two hours, day and night for six days. The entire treatment lasted 14 days. For four days and nights, Burroughs could not sleep. Dr Dent would come to see Burroughs at 2 a.m. and they would talk for a long time about the Mayans. Dent discharged the writer with tubes of apomorphine for emergencies. This turned out to be the most successful cure Burroughs had ever taken and he remained clean for several years.

In September 1956, Burroughs returned to Tangier and was glad to be back. The city was the only place he could think of where he did not want to be somewhere else. The beauty of the town lay in its changing combinations. There was always something that would surprise you. 'There is no town like Tanger town,' he wrote to Ginsberg on 16 September, 'the place relaxes me so, I am subject to dissolve. I can spend three hours looking at the bay with my mouth open.'

By now, there was a lot of political agitation in Morocco. Demonstrators called for the return of the exiled King Mohammed V. There were riots in the French zone, and in August they spread to Tangier. Its international status was no protection from the surge in nationalism. Burroughs saw women rushing their babies indoors and people running through the streets giving the three-fingered salute (for Allah, the King, and Morocco). He described the situation in a letter to Ginsberg on 29 October 1956.

This town really has the jihad jitters – jihad means the wholesale slaughter by every Moslem of every unbeliever. Yesterday I am sitting in the Socco and suddenly people start running and all the shop-keepers are slamming down the steel shutters of their shops – I plan to market an automatic shop closer whereby you press a button

and your shutter falls like a guillotine . . . So at that point about 30
little children carrying the Moroccan flag through the Socco . . . A
few days ago we had a general strike. Everything closed, restaurants, drug stores, no cars allowed on the street. About this time,
such a racket breaks out like I never hear and I can see thousands of
Arabs marching down the Boulevard yelling . . . The chaos in
Morocco is beautiful. Arab hipsters are developing in Casablanca,
and a vast underworld. The police drive around in jeeps machine-
gunning each other.

In September 1956, the French promised to give Morocco independence, and in November the king made a triumphant return. One of
his first pronouncements was that he would abolish Tangier's international status and it would become a Moroccan city like any other. For
foreigners, this was like sounding the siren to abandon ship. Overnight,
hundreds of homes and businesses posted 'FOR SALE' signs. Forty
tonnes of gold in Tangier vaults were transferred to Geneva and the
golf club lost members so fast, there were more caddies than golfers.

Up in the Kasbah, off Rue Amrah, is a narrow entrance to another
whitewashed building with an inconspicuous sign saying 'Sidi Hosni.'
We could not see inside the house, but later found an online Sotheby's
brochure (price on application) revealing a complex of Alhambra-style
courtyards, gardens and a swimming pool. Michelle Green describes it
as: 'A mazelike fifteen room folly that had been created by joining no
fewer than five Moroccan houses.' In 1946 it was bought by Barbara
Hutton, the Woolworths heiress, who offered twice as much as General
Franco had and then proceeded to throw ridiculous parties there. She
once imported 30 camels from the Sahara to form a guard of honour
for her guests and had the narrow side streets of the Kasbah widened
to accommodate her Rolls Royce.

Frank W. Woolworth started life poor but ended up one of America's
richest tycoons. His granddaughter, Barbara Hutton, reversed that
trajectory. Frank W worked every day of his 66 years and, when he
died, left the equivalent of a billion dollars in his will. His family, and
particularly Barbara, blew it all. She was the daughter of FW.'s daughter
Edna who committed suicide and whose body was discovered by

Barbara. At the age of seven, she inherited what today would amount to approximately a third of a billion dollars. While the Woolworth's workers toiled for ten hours a day on paltry wages, Barbara went shopping. She was the richest girl in the world, but also the original 'Poor Little Rich Girl.' She went shopping for husbands and in the end collected seven. In between, she had various lovers; including Howard Hughes and Porfirio Rubirosa. Hutton longed to be from the aristocracy and among her spouses were counts, princes and a baron. Her most famous husband was Cary Grant. When they married, they were nicknamed 'Cash 'n' Cary.' When they split up four years later, Grant gave this assessment of her.

Barbara surrounded herself with a consortium of fawning parasites – European titles, broken-down Hollywood types, a maharajah or two, a sheikh, the military, several English peers and a few tennis bums. If one more phoney earl had entered the house, I'd have suffocated.

'She was very difficult,' Charles Sevigny recalled, 'They wrote a lot of things about her which are not true, and some that are. She was not a happy person. It was her own fault.' Before buying Sidi Hosni, Hutton had spent the equivalent of £20 million on a house in Regent's Park, now the residence of the US ambassador to Britain. She then squandered around half that amount on jewels that had belonged to Napoleon. She was very generous. No one who ever bumped into Hutton walked away poorer, apart from the Woolworth's shop workers.

By the time she bought Sidi Hosni in Tangier, Barbara's tenuous grip on reality was beginning to loosen. Seemingly incapable of being satisfied, sexually or otherwise, the 'Queen of the Medina' suffered from depression and indulged in alcohol and drug abuse. Her daily diet consisted of cigarettes, 20 bottles of Coca-Cola mixed with vodka, intravenous megavitamin shots along with amphetamines, a cocktail of codeine, valium and morphine. Most of these were supplied by her last husband, a Vietnamese chemist. She bought him a title and she died a pauper.

The great event of the moment, said Bowles in 1956, was Barbara Hutton's party for 200 guests at Sidi Hosni. It was the biggest party since the war and invitations were sold on the black market for 20,000 francs. But Burroughs was not invited. Most of the gatecrashers did not get past the bouncers. One woman, a banker's wife, went into hysterics and had to be dragged off. Others, who had arrived in evening dress, had to leave on foot through the dirty streets of the Kasbah, lined with locals who had come to observe the goings on. Bowles was startled to see how strongly people felt about such things. After all, it was only a party. 'In a drawing room stood a throne from India,' Morgan writes, 'insured for a million dollars and encrusted with thousands of pearls, rubies, sapphires, and emeralds, upon which the hostess received her guests.' On her head rested a tiara that had once belonged to Catherine the Great. There was a jazz orchestra on the terrace, Gypsies performing on a patio, a Moroccan orchestra in another room and a concert pianist on an inner balcony. Each guest had been insured against accident or loss. The flat roofs of adjacent houses were crowded with the curious. The party went on until nine the next morning.

Oblivious to the party of the decade, Burroughs took a room in the Muniria.

Me and Dave [Woolman] have found us the original anything goes joint. Run by 2 retired junky whores from Saigon. On the ground floor will be Dave, myself, and Eric . . . Anyhoo we three occupy the ground floor with our rooms opening on the garden and have a private entrance: "You can be free here, you understand?" the old whore says to me, digging me in the ribs. The houseboy is a Spanish queer, good-looking in a depraved sort of way.

As part of his recovery Burroughs threw himself into a new form of addiction, exercise. He did abdominal crunches and rowed in the bay. Off junk, he was writing daily. 'After his exercise and rowing,' Morgan writes, 'he would get started around noon and work until evening, with no central plan, just writing along. He felt the power coming in. In Tangier, the other dimension was always breaking through. Compared to this, what he had written so far was just kids' stuff.'

The man who lived next door (Don Cotton) said he could hear Burroughs' wild laughter along with the typing. Every other day he took hashish cake and the rest of the time smoked a lot of weed, which stimulated the associative process and the flow of images. The book was beginning to take shape. When Bowles visited him in the Muniria, the floor was covered with hundreds of loose pages. Many of which had sole and heel marks on them. They were covered with rat droppings and bits of cheese sandwiches, as Burroughs ate at the same table at which he typed. 'What is all this?' asked Bowles. 'That's what I'm working on,' Burroughs replied. 'Do you make copies before you throw it on the floor?' 'Nope.' 'Then how are you going to read it?' 'Oh, I figure it'll be legible.'

Burroughs built an orgone energy box in the garden of the Muniria and tried to sell it to Bowles. 'Just sit in it and you'll feel different when you come out,' Burroughs said. The box reminded Bowles of a dog kennel, but so as not to offend Burroughs, he sat in it. The night was cold and Bowles did feel different when he came out; he was shivering.

When they were not at the Muniria, Bowles and Burroughs would meet at Porte's, one of Tangier's most famous cafés, as Barry Miles recounts.

They would sometimes meet in a café such as Mme Porte's *Salon de Thé*, in the Rue du Statut, around the corner from the Place de France, an establishment renowned for its pastries. In the morning, men outnumbered women, but in the afternoon it was the reverse. It was used as a headquarters by Abdelkhalek Torres, the popular Moroccan nationalist leader, who appeared at 10:00 a.m. with his faithful acolytes, and many other local and foreign politicians and journalists gathered there. Bill would have observed many of the nationalist leaders here, whom he parodied mercilessly in *Naked Lunch*.

'Mme Porte's was wonderful,' Annie Austin told me, 'Everybody went there.'

It was THE place to go. Alec Waugh was there every morning having his coffee. And then at six o'clock everybody would swap their tea and cakes for these marvellous long, green, cocktail glasses full of Martini. We would roll out later absolutely pissed. Tangier was very gay then, but it was very discreet. People did whatever they did behind the scenes, but outwardly they were having tea at Mme Porte's.

But behind the scenes, beyond the art deco door of Porte's, other, darker, things had been going on. For decades, Tanjawis boycotted the café because they suspected that Mme Porte and her husband had been Nazi collaborators. The same was said of Lily, who ran the Parade Bar and the French novelist Paul Morand, who lived on Rue Shakespeare on the Marshan.

Meanwhile, back in Interzone, Burroughs received a letter from Kerouac, telling him that Ginsberg had now become famous on the back of one poem, Howl. Kerouac was not far behind either, having signed a contract for On The Road, which would be published in October 1957. Kerouac promised that he would visit Burroughs in Tangier and left New York in February 1957. He awoke one morning to set eyes on the Strait of Gibraltar, 'where rough rocks groaning vegetate.' Burroughs was waiting for him at the dock, looking healthy and tanned. Burroughs got him a room at the Muniria. Kerouac saw the mess in his friend's room and volunteered to type the pages up, but the material gave him nightmares. 'Why are all these young boys being hanged in limestone caves?' asked Kerouac.

Don't ask me, I get these messages from other planets. I'm apparently some kind of agent from another planet, but I haven't got my orders clearly decoded yet. I'm shifting out of my educated Middle-west background once and for all. It's a matter of catharsis, where I say the most horrible things I can think of.

Kerouac was convinced that in the Muniria, that crucible of creativity, Burroughs was creating a hugely significant work.

He was so deeply into it that it was scary. Now his conversation was in routines, he was assuming different roles and identities. It all kept pouring out of him in mad monologues. He kept saying he was going to erupt in some unspeakable atrocity, such as waving his ding-dong at an embassy party, or slaughtering an Arab boy to see what his insides looked like. On paper, he was unleashing his word hoard, and his message was all scatological, homosexual, super violent madness.

Allen Ginsberg and his boyfriend Peter Orlovsky were due to follow Kerouac to Tangier. One night at the Muniria, Burroughs broke down in tears, admitting to Kerouac that he had been in love with Ginsberg for years.

After a month in Tangier, Kerouac had had enough. He moaned incessantly about the Moroccans, their food and their lack of hygiene. Things came to a head when an old African man sold Kerouac some dodgy hash in the Petit Socco. Kerouac smoked it and then came down with severe diarrhoea. 'It was as if his bowels were telling him it was time to go,' Morgan writes. On 5 April, the author of On The Road was on a boat, bound for Marseilles.

The day before that, Ginsberg and Orlovsky arrived. Orlovsky managed to pay for the trip after having had his disability benefit increased. He had told psychiatrists that people were shadows.

Burroughs also found them rooms at the Muniria, where his friends turned it into an *ad hoc* publishing house, working around the clock in shifts, typing and arranging scraps of paper. Alan Ansen came over from Venice to help with the editing process, as he had done for Auden. 'He worked,' said Ginsberg, 'like a great professional pedantic scholar with an unruly library full of dignified ancient manuscripts.' '[Burrough's] apartment was like a writer's factory,' Hopkins explained, 'There was a big table with scraps of paper all over it. There was static on the radio. They were doing cut-ups like mad.' Over two months, they integrated, cut and typed. They worked flat out on this mad mosaic of Burroughs' fantasies over the last three years, until they finally produced a finished 200 page manuscript. If his life were a film, this scene would be one of those sped up montages set to stirring music.

Burroughs had not seen Ginsberg since their relationship had ended in 1953 and he resented the man who had replaced him. He thought Peter Orlovsky was mad. Ansen did not like him either, calling him a 'freeloading bitch posing as an assistant *mahatma*.' Embarrassingly,

Orlovsky would stop and talk to strangers in the street. Finally, Burroughs decided he could no longer stand the sight of him, so he avoided all conversation, except one time, when he ate *majoun* and threatened Orlovsky with a machete.

With the exception of the Orlovsky question, it was a hardworking, but carefree time. When they finished writing, they would sit and drink on the terrace of the Muniria and watch the sun go down. Ginsberg asked if he could meet Bowles. The latter was away in Ceylon, so he phoned Jane, introducing himself as 'Allen Ginsberg, the bop poet.' Jane had just suffered a stroke. She did not know what to make of Ginsberg and had never heard the word 'bop.' When he asked her if she believed in God, she thought for a moment before speaking: 'I'm certainly not going to discuss it on the telephone.'

Later however, the two of them got on well. Ginsberg found Jane shy but smart. In May, Paul returned to Tangier and invited them all over, playing Indian music and smoking kif, although Ginsberg was to find Bowles slightly remote.

In early June, Ginsberg, Orlovsky and Ansen left for Spain leaving Burroughs alone again. Burroughs left to visit his friend Kells Elvins in Copenhagen, but he disliked it. 'All these people with their cradle-to-grave welfare state and socialist limbo were so unhappy,' writes Morgan, 'compared to the Spanish and Moroccans in Tangier, who had nothing.'

Suicide was almost unknown in Morocco, but in Scandinavia it was endemic. The dead-level sanity and bone dullness of the Danes appalled him. It was a police state without police, populated by robots completely conditioned by the state.

The description reminds me of a conversation I had with the Tangier writer Lotfi Akolay. 'I went to Switzerland once,' he told me, 'it was so boring. When the traffic lights turned red, all the cars stopped to let the pedestrians cross. In Tangier, life is less predictable. I never know whether I will cross the road alive.'

When Burroughs returned to Tangier in September, he heard that Kiki had left for Spain in 1956. He was later stabbed to death in a row over a girl.

By now, Burroughs found that he was merely a conduit for a novel that was almost writing itself. It was coming out of him faster than he could transcribe it. One curious by-product of this period of intensive work was the feeling that through his writing, he had solved the dilemma of his homosexuality. 'Have reached point where I don't seem to want boys any more,' he wrote, 'must have some cunt.'

The total absorption of the writer in his work created a parallel between the violence in the book and the day-to-day life of its author, who began to see himself as surrounded by dangers. He believed that a virus was spreading through Tangier and that it had already struck some of his friends. At this point, Burroughs was sick of the city and everyone in it. He had to get out, and in mid-January 1958 he ended his three year stay in the Interzone and left for Paris.

In 1961, Burroughs returned from Paris to Tangier and stayed for the summer. He was joined at the Muniria by Ian Sommerville and Michael Portman (a dissolute aristocrat) and later, Ginsberg, Orlovsky, Gregory Corso, Alan Ansen and Timothy Leary. He also returned to Tangier in 1964, staying first at the Hotel Atlas and then at an apartment on Rue Delacroix, and visited for a few months from May 1967.

The view from Christopher Gibbs' garden is probably the best in Tangier. If you climb up onto the roof terrace you take in a spectacular panorama that includes Gibraltar, Cape Malabata and Jebel Musa. His house, El Foulk, is sealed off from the rest of the city by a soft barrier of cedars and date palms, so that you might forget that Tangier actually exists.

This earthly paradise has hardly changed from the days of Henri Matisse, although Gibbs has added his own touches. He has implanted a tadelakt hammam and an oblong swimming pool, guarded by the stone busts of two French Cyrano de Bergerac-style soldiers. Gibbs, an antiques dealer and the originator of 'shabby chic,' first came to Tangier in 1958, and stayed at the Rembrandt Hotel. He brought the colours of Morocco to a grey London, thus helping to define the 'Swinging Sixties.' Previously, El Foulk had belonged to Marguerite McBey. She had been married to the Scottish artist James McBey, but before that, in 1920s

Paris, she had been Oskar Kokoschka's lover. Lower down the hill is a cottage occupied by Gibbs' partner, Peter Hinwood, an interior decorator and antiques dealer, who starred as Rocky, Dr Frank N Furter's creation, in *The Rocky Horror Picture Show*.

The garden, deliberately slightly wild and unkempt, is dotted with Roman columns and animal sculptures that seem permanently poised to leap out at you. Gibbs told the *New York Times* that he had adjusted to the pace of life in Morocco: 'There is a Muslim rhythm here,' he said. Inside one building is a large seventeenth-century canvas by Luca Giordano depicting Hercules fighting Antaeus, but it looks more like two naked men having sex. The interior of the main house is decorated with paintings by Marguerite McBey, Charles Robertson and maps by Wenceslaus Hollar. 'Someone stole these from me,' Gibbs explained, 'but they turned up five years later in the British Museum.' In the bathroom was a black and white photo of Gibbs, the painter Nicolette Meeres and William Burroughs. It was taken inside the Ibn Battuta bar on the beach at the height of summer. Gibbs and Meeres are wearing swimming costumes, Burroughs a dark suit, tie and fedora.

Gibbs told me a story about an expat in Tangier who was assumed to be an aristocrat from Dumfries, but was subsequently unmasked as a hairdresser from Essex. 'This is one of my favourite items,' he said, showing me a passport photo of a smiling young Moroccan in a jacket and tie. Moustapha spoke no English, but once came knocking on Gibbs' door asking for work. Burroughs had apparently passed the man on to Gibbs. On the back of the photo in small, spindly blue handwriting were the following words:

> Moustapha Ben Driss (photo) has <u>no recommendation</u> from me.
> He is dishonest, unreliable, lazy and sloppy.
> William S. Burroughs

'Funniest man I ever knew,' John Hopkins said to me, 'he had this laconic delivery. He used to sit in the Parade Bar facing the wall with his back to everyone else. He was a lonely, ascetic figure in a dark suit. I would take my drink, go down and talk to him for half an hour. He was terribly funny.'

In 1997, William Burroughs died at his home in Lawrence, Kansas, after suffering a heart attack. He was 83. It is remarkable that he had not died earlier.

Burroughs was to have an enormous influence on modern writers, artists and musicians, including David Bowie, Brian Eno, Ian Curtis, Tom Waits, Kurt Cobain, Roger Waters, Patti Smith, Laurie Anderson and Lou Reed, all of whom considered him a countercultural icon. 'Without William there is nothing,' wrote Reed.

Everything would have stayed the same. The genius to move things beyond – to improve the subject – requires strength. Without Burroughs modern lit would be a drama without a page, a sonnet without a song and a bone without gristle. Burroughs alone made us pay attention to the realities of contemporary life and gave us the energy to explore the psyche without a filter. Without Burroughs there is nothing.

NINE

Brion Gysin

*I reached out through space for the notebook on my night-table to mark some-
thing down and I never got there*

Gold letters welcome visitors to the Hotel Rembrandt in a jaunty
typeset above its entrance that reminded me of Lindt chocolate. To one
side, blocks of electric letters are stacked vertically on top of each
other like a scrabble word; but not all of them light up at night. Perhaps
eventually, like the ill-fated Sunshine Deserts in *The Fall and Rise of Reginald
Perrin*, they will all go, one by one. The Rembrandt used to be owned
by one of Tangier's wealthy Jewish families, the Pintos. After World
War II, one of the Pintos decided to drive around West Germany in a
Rolls Royce, in a sort of two-fingered gesture of defiance to the Germans.
Among the first visitors to the Rembrandt was the Tunisian independence hero, Habib Bourguiba, who stayed here in 1951. His stay is
commemorated by a plaque above the brown marble columns at the
entrance. Around this time Rom Landau opens his *Portrait of Tangier* with
a brief description.

Now the Rembrandt is the newest, smartest, and presumably most
expensive hotel in Tangier. You would hardly associate it with the
city's pre-history, or expect a learned society to hold its meetings in
such sybaritic surroundings. Yet, one evening after dinner I found
myself in the elegant drawing room of the Rembrandt, attending a
monthly meeting of the newly-founded Archaeological Society of
Tangier. There were drinks and cocktails in profusion, and nothing

suggested the musty academic air that we usually associate with a group of archaeologists.

When I checked into the Rembrandt in 2014, it was not the most expensive, newest or smartest hotel in Tangier. The reception smelt of musty ashtrays and the staff were grumpy. It reminded me of the Hotel Bristol in Geneva in *Tintin and the Red Sea Sharks*. There were 50 shades of brown: reddish brown columns, a dark brown horseshoe shaped reception desk, a sort of peachy brown, like a 1970s crème caramel, mottled brown marble table tops, cherry brown leather sofas and beige bed frames inside the rooms. In the lobby a group of tourists was arguing about whether a mysterious sixth person would join them. 'We don't want to miss our flight for someone who may not exist,' one of them remarked acidly. Staggering past pot plants and candlesticks supported by warrior figurines, an aged porter took my luggage to the lifts. Beyond the elevator shaft and to the left is the breakfast and dining room, the Restaurant La Veranda, encased in glass like a museum exhibit with a view of a cold swimming pool. To the right is the bar area, but the barman, bar stools, drinks and guilty guests are hidden out of sight on the other side of the wall, as if the reception area housed a false bookcase or a partition that turns around to reveal the panel of celebrities on *Blankety-Blank* or the opening of *Trumpton*. Is this the Janus face of Tangier, the town that is called both The White City and El *Kelba*, which means 'the bitch'? The permanently drawn curtains also sealed the guests off from the outside world. That evening, a few furtive Moroccans in brown jackets drank brown beer and, perched at the end of the bar, a prostitute smoked and smiled at me with dark brown dead eyes.

My room had no view of the sea, just a tiny window looking at the wall of another street a few metres away. It felt like a prison. I immediately changed to another room but the carpet still smelt of stale cigarettes and after just a few days I felt I was either going mad or had turned into William Burroughs.

It was in the Rembrandt in January 1954 that Burroughs first met Brion Gysin, who was exhibiting his paintings of the Sahara there. Writing in *Brion Gysin Let The Mice In* nearly 20 years later, Gysin recorded that first meeting.

He wheeled in, arms and legs flailing, talking a mile a minute. We found he looked very Occidental, more Private Eye and Inspector Lee: he trailed long vines of Bannisteria Caapi from the Upper Amazon after him and old Mexican bullfight posters fluttered out from under his long trench coast instead of a shirt. An odd blue light often flashed around under the brim of his hat.

If you wrote a novel about Tangier you would be hard pressed to create a character as intriguing as the tragic genius Brion Gysin. As Josh Shoemake writes in *Tangier: A Literary Guide for Travellers*:

He was a man destined for greatness, a man universally agreed to be the most brilliant anyone had ever met, but luck would always conspire against him, and a name that could have been celebrated is now known only through others who were more famous, and on whom he had a profound effect.

John Clifford Brian Gysin was born in England on 19 January 1916. As John Geiger recounts in *Nothing is True – Everything is Permitted*, there was always something different about him.

There was never any question that Brion Gysin was a remarkable child. As he wrote of his birth, no sooner had the phlegm been cleared from his breathing tract than he screamed out ungratefully: "Wrong address! Wrong Address! There's been a mistake in the mail. Send me back."

What Gysin did was spend his life in search of the right address. He became a reckless sophisticate seeking sensation and the intellectual adventure of what he termed "the magician's role." He sought to transcend his traumatic experiences by living on the run from a life of complacency and predictability.

His father died at the battle of the Somme when he was just eight months old and his mother brought him up in Canada. At 16 he left home and was recruited by the Canadian government as an intelligence officer because of his linguistic skills, but, as Geiger writes, he soon outgrew Canada.

When Gysin first applied for a passport in Edmonton – being, as he put it, "thoroughly ashamed at ever having been found in such a place" – he wrote his name out so badly on the forms that the "a" in Brian was mistaken by an official for an "o": Brion. He seized on the new spelling, recognizing it as French, and hence "really hip."

In 1933 Gysin travelled to Switzerland, where according to Geiger:

What Brion remembered best from the visit was reading *Ulysses* by flashlight under the bedcovers in the first days of 1933. He was disappointed that, in the circumstances, and contrary to attempts at censorship, the book "didn't make me jerk off."

The following year he moved to Paris, which Geiger says, 'was a city of possibilities for a young man predisposed to a creative life. The ghosts of the 1920s still haunted its cafés . . .' One of these was a literary café called the Select.

The Select turned into a sick *Cage aux Folles* . . . Queers and mad queens from all over Europe poured in, making entrances, throwing fits, making scenes, cackling like macaws . . . I stayed on too late one night and soon found myself in some pretty weird company, up to my ass. Once caught up in this sordid scene, I came out.

In Paris, Gysin joined the Surrealist Group and met Salvador Dali and Pablo Picasso. A year later he had his first exhibition with Max Ernst, Picasso, de Chirico, Dali, Marcel Duchamp, Rene Magritte, Man Ray and Yves Tanguy. On the day of the preview however, he was expelled from the group by André Breton, who ordered Gysin's pictures to be taken down. Gysin was only 19 years old and Geiger suggests this expulsion had a profound effect on him.

It seemed to condemn him to a life of disappointed expectation with regard to his career. Years later, he blamed other failures on the Breton incident. It gave rise to conspiracy theories about the powerful interests who seek control of the art world.

In 1938, in a café on the Left Bank, Gysin met Jane Bowles who later introduced him to her husband. 'Bowles,' writes Geiger, 'was intrigued by Gysin, who he decided was not like anyone he had met.' One night the three of them went to see a performance of Stravinsky (the Dumbarton Oaks Concerto). Bowles was very irritated by the woman sitting next to him who never stopped talking and fingering her emeralds. It was only Gysin who recognised the woman as Coco Chanel.

When Gysin moved to New York in 1940 he took up writing and spent a lot of time with Bowles. In 1944 he was drafted into the US army, but disliked it and made 'an elegant switch of country' and signed up for the Canadian forces. In his appraisal a commanding officer noted: 'this soldier has led a very unusual and unorthodox life.'

After the war Gysin returned to Paris, but already, there was a sense of a life unfulfilled.

He alternated between being a serious and gifted young man and a restless gadabout. In half a lifetime he had accomplished many things, but by any conventional measure he had also accomplished very little. He was a scholar without necessary academic credentials; he was a promising painter who had not exhibited in over a decade; he was a writer whose attempts to get published had met with little success, leaving him in deep chagrined despair. For all his intellectual sophistication, personal flamboyance, eminent acquaintances, Gysin had failed to divine a career for himself. At 34 he was ready for something to happen.

In 1950 Bowles told Gysin that Tangier could provide him with an antidote to his depression and invited him there. The Canadian recalled their arrival.

Almost simultaneously we were taken from all sides. Pirates in wild Moroccan tatters . . . swarmed up, yelling and howling and grabbing at our baggage and ourselves as if we were all under arrest.

Brion Gysin arrived in Tangier in 1950 and spent most of the next 25 years there. 'A wild west of the spirit,' was how Gysin summed up Morocco in his first full-length novel, The Process, a hallucinatory work set in the Sahara. Bowles was right. Gysin's love of the exotic and attraction to the strange made Tangier the perfect location. In his journals he described it as, 'a colonial world, colonial life . . . Pre-hippy, pre-anything like that, a real holdover from a past, kind of an invisible jelly, you were living in and breathing the past.'

Tangier had the capacity to trap people like insects in that invisible jelly. As Truman Capote later wrote, 'Tangier is a basin that holds you, a timeless place; the days slide by less noticed than foam in a waterfall; this, I imagine, is the way time passes in a monastery, unobtrusive and on slippered feet.'

Gysin stayed on one floor of Bowles' house in the Kasbah, as Bowles recalled.

The house in the Medina was finished at last and equipped to be lived in . . . About a week later Brion arrived. The house was pocket-sized but with several storeys. Brion lived on the second floor, and I on the fourth, in the tower, which I had built on top of the original structure. Each of us could go in and out without coming near the other's quarters.

Bowles found Gysin endlessly entertaining. 'Brion knew the strangest people,' he said, 'they smelled him out. That was a reason to admire him. When he was around crazy people he was slightly crazier himself; he seemed to be raving part of the time.'

'He was mesmerizing,' John Hopkins said. The American writer said he saw more of Gysin than anyone else in those days.

I felt I was sitting at the master's feet. He was a fantastic raconteur, but he smoked way too much pot. He never had any money. He could make literary and artistic connections you wouldn't have dreamt possible. They made perfect sense, after you'd had a few pipes.

Bowles' friend Mohamed Hamri also acted as a portal for Gysin to delve, like *Alice Through the Looking Glass* into this exotic world. Gysin admired Bowles, but noticed his notoriously frugal nature. It was Gysin who told Bowles that he could afford the convertible Jaguar and in 1951 they travelled around the country, driven by Mohammed

Temsamany. They went to Fes, Marrakech and ventured into the desert, where the younger man was inspired by the emptiness and the dunes. 'The desert burns forever on the back of my lowered lids. For one haunted moment, I bathe again in the Great Sea of Solitude,' he wrote in The Process, and in Soft Need 17, Gysin observed: 'Sometimes at night in the desert under the full moon all the dunes seem to turn into blue snow.' Bowles enjoyed being with the other writer, whom he described as 'an ideal travelling companion, more observant and articulate than I, with an awareness that was always present in full force.'

That same year, Bowles took Gysin to Sidi Kacem where they listened to Sufi music at a moussem. The sounds of the Master Musicians of Joujouka were unlike anything he had ever heard and he told the American he wanted to listen to them every day of his life. Hamri, who came from the village, took Gysin there. When he told the villagers what he had told Bowles, one of them replied, 'Sit. Sit. This house is your house. Sit the rest of your life.' Gysin became the first foreigner to witness the festival of Boujeloud in Joujouka, and was profoundly affected by it.

One day I was walking along the Marshan on my way back from the Café Hafa. On the Rue Assad Ibn Alfourat I spotted an inviting door of the deepest blue, like a Matisse painting, which turned out to be the entrance to an art gallery. I stepped inside and struck up a conversation with the assistant. Nour Eddine Merini said he was descended from members of the thirteenth-century Merenid dynasty, but the authorities in Tangier were jealous of his ancestry and he 'had to keep it hidden.' He offered me a furtive beer and began to reveal more about himself. His grandfather had lived to the age of 126 (was this Nour Eddine or the beer talking?) and had known Raisuli. Nour Eddine said that he had visited Bowles in his later years and that the American was fond of a French biscuit called Baba Oroum. I asked him if he knew where the Palais Menehbi Palace was, which I had been trying to locate for ages. 'Oh yes, it's just a few doors along,' said Nour Eddine. I thanked him, walked out and further down the road, I found a grey wooden door encased in an arch, embedded in a thick white wall that was decked with a tangle of electric cables. The building itself is closed to the public.

The Palais Menebhi was built in 1904 by Mehdi el Menebhi, Sultan Abdelaziz's minister of war. After the sultan's abdication, Mehdi fled (some said he took the ministry's funds with him) and sought the protection of the British. In *Stars in the Firmament*, David Woolman says that Mehdi's love of British ways included a passion for tennis.

Mehdi el Menebhi was a tennis buff who played a vigorous game on his own palace court. The other players could scarcely have been more colourful. Who else but that bouncing jack of all trades, Walter Harris, was one. Then there was the sinister Thami el Glaoui, scion of the family who controlled the all-powerful Glaoua tribe in the mountains around Marrakech, Spanish Minister to Morocco Merry del Val, who insisted on playing in a fencing costume, the British Legation's second secretary, Frank Rattigan, who became the father of Terence, one of Britain's finest modern playwrights and one of Menebhi's black slaves, Frooghi, actually the best player of the lot. The host always played in a flowing *djellaba*!

Mehdi died in 1941 and the family began to lose both their money and their interest in tennis. In December 1954, they rented out a narrow wing of their palace to Brion Gysin, who opened The 1001 Nights restaurant with Hamri as chef. There is another building in the Kasbah, that claims to be the original site of the restaurant and caters to tourists under this false assumption. Gysin hired the Master Musicians of Joujouka to perform alongside acrobats, dancing boys and fire-eaters. The musicians played for an international clientele that included Christopher Isherwood, Cecil Beaton and William Burroughs.

The 1001 Nights was the fashionable restaurant. With its dazzling local food, musicians and dancing boys, it marked the pinnacle of expat life in the city. The sounds of Joujouka were, according to the *Tangier Gazette*, 'familiar to 20 sultans, but rarely heard by Europeans.' The 1001 Nights prospered only briefly, but there was nothing like it before or since. 'It was well named,' Gysin recalled, 'for some unforeseen, complex, cataclysmic catastrophe occurred every night.' The decor was Moroccan: banquettes, wooden tables surfaced with tiles and brass lanterns with coloured panels. The menu was burned into a wooden tablet, the precursor to an iPad. On the walls hung Gysin's watercolours of the desert, influenced by childhood memories of the

Canadian prairies. Bowles said Gysin's depictions of the dunes were 'the only painting true to the Sahara.'

Initially Burroughs was as underwhelmed by Gysin at the restaurant as the latter had been by Burroughs at the Rembrandt. When the American went in, he found a tall, broad shouldered man with 'thick sandy hair and the ruddy, narrow-eyed face of a Swiss mountaineer, cold and imperious.' The two did not hit it off. Burroughs considered Gysin mad, paranoid and without a good word to say about anyone. As for the dancing boys, Burroughs was equally unimpressed, 'all with ferret face and narrow shoulders and bad teeth, looking rather like a bowling team from Newark.'

But in his diaries, Isherwood, who went there in 1955 was entranced by his dining experience and, in particular, the dancing boys.

> Their negligent grace, their vague yet exact gestures, their delicately mocking salutes when you gave them money . . . Their hip movements and flirtatious play with their scarves is exquisitely campy and yet essentially masculine: this is in no sense a drag show.

Gysin's culinary expertise also featured in Alice B. Toklas' cookbook in the form of a recipe for hashish fudge. 'It should be eaten with care,' the instructions warned, 'two pieces are quite sufficient.' The publishers mistakenly credited the recipe to a 'Brian Gysen' and the American edition of the book omitted the recipe altogether on legal advice.

Substantially less than one thousand and one nights later, in the summer of 1956, Gysin closed the restaurant as uncertainty gripped Tangier after independence. Never a great businessman, Gysin regretted not having charged more. 'We didn't come here for a bargain,' lamented some tycoons from Texas, 'You've spoiled our fun.' Gysin briefly reopened it in 1957, but the establishment failed again and the following year the 1001 Nights closed forever.

In 1958, Gysin returned to Paris, taking lodgings in a flophouse located at 9 Rue Gît-le-Coeur, that would become known as the Beat Hotel. The next four years there proved to be the most creative of his life. By the time they met again in Paris, Gysin and Burroughs were friends. They would spend hours discussing concepts such as control and consciousness. In a letter to Ginsberg on 10 October 1958, Burroughs wrote:

Brion Gysin living next door. He used to run The 1001 Nights in
Tangier. He has undergone similar conversion to mine and doing
GREAT painting. I mean great in the old sense, not jive talk great.
I know great work when I see it in any medium. I see in his painting
the psychic landscape of my own work. He is doing in painting
what I try to do in writing. He regards his painting as a hole in the
texture of the so-called 'reality.' Needless to say no dealer will touch
his work.

'Listening to Brion talk,' was, according to Ted Morgan, 'a little like
watching a man covered with elaborate Japanese tattoos. You might
wonder what the point of it all was, but it was hard to take your eyes
away.' Burroughs was also drawn into Gysin's fascination with arcane
subjects such as the Assassins, the followers of the eleventh-century
Persian mystic Hassan i Sabbah and the Canadian drew parallels between
the Assassins and the CIA. Gysin also helped edit Naked Lunch. 'Gysin's
influence grew,' writes Geiger, 'eventually he seemed to speak for
Burroughs, almost as if by ventriloquism.'

Working on a drawing in the hotel, Gysin discovered a new technique by accident.

William Burroughs and I first went into techniques of writing,
together, back in room No. 15 of the Beat Hotel during the cold
Paris spring of 1958 . . . Burroughs was more intent on Scotch-
taping his photos together into one great continuum on the wall,
where scenes faded and slipped into one another, than occupied
with editing the monster manuscript . . . While cutting a mount
for a drawing in room No. 15, I sliced through a pile of newspapers with my Stanley blade and thought of what I had said to
Burroughs some six months earlier about the necessity for turning
painters' techniques directly into writing. I picked up the raw
words and began to piece together texts that later appeared as
"First Cut-Ups."

By slicing up newspaper pages with a razor blade, Gysin came up
with wonderfully absurd sentences.

Asked whether he had had a fair trial he looks inevitable and publishes: 'My sex was an advantage.'

Her father, a well-known Artist until a bundle of his accented brush-work blew up in the sky, said 'We can't do that yet.'

To protect this art the right way, clout first Woman and believers in their look of things. Fourteen-year-old boy has many of her belongings.

Swiss boys were absolutely free from producers of outboard spiritual homes.

Burroughs recalled the moment when he returned to the Beat Hotel in September 1959: 'I found Brion Gysin holding scissors, bits of newspaper, *Life, Time,* spread out on a table; he read me the cut-ups that later appeared in *Minutes to Go.*'

Gysin had presented his friend with a way of circumventing control. They would also help the development of writing, which he told Burroughs was 'fifty years behind painting.' For Burroughs this was a life changing moment, 'You've got something big here, Brion,' he said.

While Gysin tried the cut-up technique in *The Process,* Burroughs did the same in *Naked Lunch,* slicing up phrases and words to create new sentences. Scenes were slotted together with little care for narrative and the experiment dramatically changed the landscape of American literature. It allowed Burroughs to introduce an element of chance into writing and, as Shoemake says, 'destroy the old contrivances of plot and character.'

The idea spread to other Beat poets including Gregory Corso and Harold Norse, who, in his memoirs recollected:

We believed we had a new vision and method to express a new dimension of consciousness, cutting words from their manipulative power over beliefs and actions, thereby undermining thought control by disrupting the traditional use of language, destroying social and religious prejudices and false teachings.

'In the beginning was the word,' Gysin told the writer Robert Palmer in 1972, 'Everything seems to be wrong with what was produced from those beginnings, so let's rub out the word and start afresh.' In a 1966 interview, Burroughs explained that Gysin was the originator of the cut-up technique.

A friend, Brion Gysin, an American poet and painter, who has lived in Europe for 30 years, was, as far as I know, the first to create cut-ups. His cut-up poem, 'Minutes to Go', was broadcast by the BBC and later published in a pamphlet. I was in Paris in the summer of 1960; this was after the publication there of *Naked Lunch*. I became interested in the possibilities of this technique, and I began experimenting myself. Of course, when you think of it, *The Waste Land* was the first great cut-up collage . . . Dos Passos used the same idea in 'The Camera Eye' sequences in the USA. I felt I had been working toward the same goal; thus, it was a major revelation to me when I actually saw it being done.

It was a cut-up phrase, based on a book about Hassan i Sabbah, that produced a slogan that Burroughs and Gysin would both use: 'Nothing is true – everything is permitted.' Burroughs began to apply the technique to the words of his friends in order to predict the future and divine their true intentions. 'If you cut into the present, the future leaks out,' he said. He even cut up an article written by John Paul Getty to produce the line: 'It is a bad thing to sue your father.' A year after this, one of Getty's sons actually sued him. In 1963, another Burroughs cut-up described '1,000 mile per hour wind here, storms . . . crackling sounds . . . dry and brittle as dead leaves.' Many years later, scientists said they had found high winds on Mars. Burroughs was becoming prophetic. Burroughs would, as Geiger writes, in the end get the credit for cut-ups.

Burroughs did his best to ensure Gysin received his due, invariably referring to "The Cut-Up Method of Brion Gysin." Yet cut-ups . . . ultimately came to be seen as Burroughs' innovation.

Gysin wrote a script for a film version of *Naked Lunch*, which was never produced. The pair collaborated on a large manuscript called *The Third Mind*, but it was not published.

Interviewed for *The Guardian* in 1997, Burroughs explained that Gysin was 'the only man that I've ever respected in my life.' Bowles was not convinced. 'Anyone who came under Brion's influence,' he said, 'fell ten years behind in his career.'

In Paris, Gysin and Burroughs met Ian Sommerville, a Cambridge University maths student, who would help them apply the cut-up method to sound and photography. Gysin used his Uher reel-to-reel to record noises, such as a pistol firing and then spliced them up in different orders. The three of them presented their experiments with tapes and projections in London. Barry Miles, who organised one such performance, called it:

> A concept of total theatre intended to create a giant tear in conventional reality by attacking the word and confusing the senses with cut up images, both visual and audio, creating anxiety and bewilderment in the audience who could no longer be sure what was real and what was not.

At sunset on 21 December 1958, Gysin was travelling by bus in the South of France. As it threaded its way along tree-lined roads, he closed his eyes. His journal recounts what happened next.

> An overwhelming flood of intensely bright patterns in supernatural colors exploded behind my eyelids: a multidimensional kaleidoscope whirling out through space.

A little over a year later, Gysin wrote to Sommerville asking how he could replicate the experience. At the time, Sommerville was studying the effects of stroboscopic light and so the two of them began on Gysin's next improbable project, what would later be described as 'the first art object to be seen with the eyes closed.' The flicker device used alpha waves to produce a change of consciousness. A cylinder with vertical slits and a light inside was placed on a record player. When looking through the slits, you could experience kaleidoscopic hallucinations. There was some science to this too. A light that flashed between eight to thirteen cycles per second had been shown to cause people to see colour patterns. Sommerville had discovered that the speed of the turntable (78 rpm) was the optimal speed and constructed a prototype. Gysin painted calligraphic symbols inside it and called it the Dream Machine. It was first exhibited in Paris in 1962 and, convinced he would make a fortune, he touted the Dream Machine to the Philips Corporation. Philips sent an executive to Paris to conduct a feasibility study on the machine, but it was rejected 'after the businessman slipped on dog excrement in a hallway of the Beat Hotel.' In August 1963, Gysin returned to Tangier with Burroughs. Shoemake takes up the story.

A wealthy American traveller named Leila Hadley heard a student in a Tangier café referring to the machine as a new sort of drug and became intrigued. She arranged a meeting for Gysin with Columbia Records in New York City, but Gysin blew the interview by advocating another obviously hare-brained scheme: records could soon be played not with needles, but with an 'electronic eye' that would read the 'disc'. He left New York disheartened, and although throughout his life he would continue to push the Dream Machine . . . he decided to focus his energies over the next few years on his novel, The Process.

The Process has been hailed as a countercultural classic. He completed it in 1969, but, in true Gysin style, it never achieved commercial success. While The Times Literary Supplement called it 'a tedious, pretentious and lengthy experimental white elephant of a book,' Robert Palmer hailed it 'a classic of twentieth-century modernism,' and like Gysin himself, 'an entertainment, an education, and an enigma.' Palmer had fond memories of his encounters with Gysin in Tangier.

From my hotel window, I hear the dogs – Tangier is known for having more, and louder, dogs than any other city – barking across the distances . . . Brion Gysin – painter, poet, visionary . . . taught me to listen to the dogs when I lived here in the early seventies. He claimed he had cracked the dogs' code and used to provide a running translation: "Everything okay there? Enough food? People good?" And from miles away in the suburbs the response would come back: "Good food here, but people beat us." "Out here we're hungry."

Another novel, *The Third Mind* was eventually published in 1978 but fared no better. 'It's quite fun,' declared *The New Statesman*, 'if you have absolutely nothing else to do.'

In between failed literary endeavours and harebrained schemes, Gysin was also interested in exploring the doors of perception. In 1961, he experimented with novel narcotics supplied by Timothy Leary, who was studying the effects of hallucinogens at Harvard University. Gysin tried some of the first shipment of pills (psilocybin, a compound of more than 200 mushrooms) that the good doctor had earmarked for Burroughs in Tangier. The Canadian artist took five of these and drew three sketches. When he showed the drawings to a French psychiatrist, the man described them as 'different.'

A few days later another package arrived for Burroughs, containing 24 pink pills. 'I've taken 23 of these,' Gysin wrote, 'if anything happens to me, cable Harvard for instructions.' It was four times the maximum recommended dose. Gysin went on a massive 36-hour acid trip feeling 'three great bursts of calligraphy between long migrations of time travel and quite a few eerie moments.' 'I reached out through space,' he later wrote in *The Process*, 'for the notebook on my night-table to mark something down and I never got there.' In July 1961, Leary visited Burroughs, Allen Ginsberg and Gregory Corso in Tangier. In his autobiography *High Priest*, Leary noted that everyone enjoyed the pills, except Burroughs, who was curled up, like a foetus, against a wall. When asked how he was doing, he replied, 'I would like to sound a word of warning. I'm not feeling too well.'

When in 1964, his ailing mother told Gysin that she was losing her marbles, the artist replied that he had 'been trying to accomplish that all my life.' By 1965, the collaboration between Gysin and Burroughs had run its course. Gysin, who was living in the Immeuble Itesa next to Paul and Jane, was resentful of failure, feeling that Burroughs had abandoned him to a penniless fate. 'I made every mistake in the book,' he said in an interview in 1984, 'you should never do two things. You should hammer one nail all your life, and I didn't do that; I hammered a lot of nails like a xylophone.' In his diaries he wrote of 'a life of adventure, leading nowhere.'

The litany of disasters continued. In March 1969, an earthquake struck Tangier. 'He was working at 3 a.m. when it hit,' writes Geiger 'and was astonished at how rubbery the whole building became during the tremor . . . Gysin spent the night sleeping in a car on the street, and remained jumpy for days.'

In July, returning from a restaurant near the Caves of Hercules, Gysin was injured in a freak motorbike accident. The bike was driven by John Hopkins, as the latter recalls in *The Tangier Diaries*.

We were about to hop aboard the bike when Brion whispered that he had just spotted Princess Ruspoli [a French writer] getting out of a car in front of the restaurant. This woman inspires a kind of dread in Brion. He calls her a witch and avoided her on the stairs when she came to visit Jane Bowles, whose flat was next door to his when he lived at Immeuble Itesa.

The weather had changed while we were in the restaurant. Instead of the gentle *poniente* pushing from behind, we drove into the teeth of the *levante*. The gusting wind buffeted the White Nile [Hopkins' bike] and I had to grip the handlebars with all my strength to keep the machine from being blown off the road.

We were zipping along the airport road opposite the textile factory when an ancient truck appeared over the rise ahead . . . When the truck passed, there was a loud click. I felt nothing; there had been no jolt or shock of contact; the BMW purred on through the cool night like the Titanic after it had grazed the iceberg.

"Brion!" I shouted. "Are you all right?"

His reply: "I think I just lost my left foot."

Gysin had to have surgery and lost a toe. He blamed it on the evil eye of the Princess Ruspoli. Later treatment included injections in his spine, which had the curious effect of enlarging his testicles. In 1969, Ted Morgan visited the accident-prone Gysin, who had been poisoned by the gas heater in his bathroom. Morgan found him lying on the bed, frail and pale but deliriously euphoric. 'It was marvellous,' he told Morgan. 'Colours of magenta and violet. I saw frosted shapes when I closed my eyes. I was floating out.'

Despite all these disasters, Gysin and Burroughs' cut-up technique was to have a profound influence. Barry Miles notes that the cut-up tapes influenced the Beatles; Paul McCartney used fragments of radio broadcasts and animal sounds on *Sgt. Pepper's Lonely Hearts Club Band*. Iggy Pop later came to Gysin for advice and David Bowie started cutting up his lyrics in 1973. U2's Bono credited cut-ups with helping him explore the vestiges of the past. 'You cut up the past to find the future,' the Irishman said. 'His cut-up writing style was massively influential to the direction of my own work,' said R.E.M.'s Michael Stipe, 'It provided room for the unconscious to seep through and overwhelm the ordinary.' Keith Haring described Gysin as an 'incredible genius', but remarked that he was quite proud of his cult status: 'In a way, his purity and "otherness" was preserved and almost exalted by being the outsider . . . It seemed to me that Brion had done everything and somehow come out on top, but not knowing which end the top was on.'

In 1982, Gysin wrote to Burroughs citing a long list of ailments and complaining that he had neither money nor friends.

On 13 July 1986, Brion Gysin died of a heart attack. His nurse, who found him, said that he appeared to have been reaching with his right arm towards the phone when he died. An obituary by Palmer said Gysin, 'threw off the sort of ideas that ordinary artists would parlay into a lifetime career, great clumps of ideas, as casually as a locomotive throws off sparks.' 'He has played starring roles in the great spiritual movies of our times,' wrote Timothy Leary. Burroughs dedicated his last novel, *The Western Lands*, to his friend. As Shoemake records, after Gysin's death, his ashes were flown back to Tangier.

On 19 January 1987, his birthday, a circle of his friends including Paul Bowles, Mohamed Hamri, Mohamed Choukri, Joe McPhillips and Marguerite McBey stood up on the cliffs [by the Caves of Hercules] and scattered his ashes to the wind. Naturally, since Gysin was involved, the ceremony was by no means an unqualified success. The wind held his dust out over the Atlantic for a moment and then whipped it back into the faces of his friends, a fitting end for a man who had never sailed smoothly through the world.

TEN

Francis Bacon

By that time, he was drinking three bottles of whisky a day, which nobody can take. In the end I think his pancreas simply exploded

The first time I saw Otmane, we met in the Minzah and drew up a plan for a walking tour of Tangier. We would start, he said, with the Mendoubia Gardens. It was here on 9 April 1947, that Mohammed V delivered a speech calling for independence to crowds in the Grand Socco; subsequently renamed Place 9 Avril 1947.

We set off for the Socco, but took a left towards St Andrew's Church. As we walked along Rue Amerique du Sud, Otmane pointed to a nondescript grey stone façade below a white colonial terrace complete with wrought iron railings, satellite dishes and air-conditioning units. 'That used to be Dean's Bar.' Apart from an old sign for '33' Export beer, there was no indication that the bar was still functioning. A plaque on the wall that used to mark the venue had been stolen.

The movie *Casablanca* was actually based on Tangier, but its makers went with the former name as it had a better ring to it. Rumour has it that Rick's Bar in the film was actually inspired by Dean's. Others say it was the Caid's bar in the Minzah and still others believe it was the bar of a now defunct movie theatre. The Cinema Vox in the Petit Socco opened in 1935 and was Africa's biggest cinema, with 2,000 seats and a retractable roof. Writing in *The Guardian*, the journalist Paul Fairclough said, 'the theatre's wartime bar heaved with spies, refugees and under-world hoods.'

Many traditional Arab stories start with the words: 'it was and it was not so.' The same could be said of Joseph Dean. He was a man of mixed race and a mysterious past. He was thought to be a spy for the British, Germans or French depending on whom you believed, as he would tell one story about himself to one customer and a different tale to the next. The writer Rupert Croft-Cooke was adamant that Dean's 'mother had been a Ramsgate lodging-house-keeper and his father a West Indian passing through Kent,' while David Herbert was convinced that Dean's mother was the French wife of a Hastings businessman, who, on a trip with her husband to Egypt, had a fling with her local guide and gave birth to a dark-skinned baby. Robin Maugham, Somerset Maugham's nephew, claimed that Dean was actually a London gigolo who, after World War I had been involved in a notorious scandal including the death of a Gaiety Girl at Brilliant Chang's opium den in Limehouse in the East End – it was said that a shady man from Notting Hill called Don Kimfull, had supplied the beautiful young actress, Billie Carleton with cocaine and then disappeared. It became the first big drug scandal of the twentieth century and, because of the Chinese connection, it sparked a media frenzy about the 'Yellow Peril.' The trail for Billie's drug supplier went cold and then, some say, many years later, Don Kimfull turned up in Tangier, calling himself Joseph Dean.

By the 1930s Dean was the head barman at the Minzah and held court there before setting up his own establishment in 1937 at 2 Rue Amerique du Sud, opposite the British Legation. He tended to his clients' every need and would have put today's office multi-taskers to shame, as Croft-Cooke explained in *The Tangerine House*.

In one morning you may hear him send a party to Tetouan complete with visas and a taxi obtained by his shrewd advice, arrange for an English resident to be taken to hospital and operated upon, put in touch with one another a man who wants to make a gift of roses to his wife and an enthusiastic rose-grower with a momentary surplus, explain the way to the Kasbah and name the only shop in Tangier at which you can purchase Angostura bitters.

Another regular from those days, Mo, described Dean as, 'the kind of guy who wore a tie without a shirt.' When he eventually passed away, more than 100 people attended his funeral. In his will, he left his paltry savings to the pharmacist who supplied him with drugs. He lies buried, presumably in a shirt, only a few hundred yards away from his bar, in a corner of St Andrews' churchyard. On a cracked headstone, partly covered in ivy are the words: 'Dean. Died February 1963. Missed by All and Sundry.'

Croft-Cooke suggested that the affection that the clientele held for their barman may have had less to do with reality than with mythology. 'I think it was that believers in Tangier as an exotic city felt there ought to be an exotic bar-owner in it,' he wrote, 'and picked on this coloured chatterer of dubious origins to fill the role.'

The bar, like Dean, became something of a legend. It is said that at one time, when pipes began to spring a mysterious leak from beneath the floor, workmen dug it up to find a concealed basement below which housed nothing except the skeleton of a centuries old camel.

Dean's was a magnet for the city's flotsam and jetsam: 'smugglers, fugitives from justice,' wrote Robert Ruark, 'and people who were being paid by other people to stay out of England.' Robin Maugham also listed some of the disreputable types who stumbled in.

Bogus barons and furtive bankers, the tipsy journalists and sober Jewish businessmen, the young diplomats and glamorous spies, the slender French and Moroccan girls, the English self-styled colonels and their friends, the foreign agents.

Dean's was a small dive with a big guest list. Ian Fleming, who wrote Diamonds Are Forever at the Minzah, would pop down, but mainly for a triple vodka and tonic rather than the company of others whom he described as 'nothing but pansies.' Another patron was Errol Flynn, whom Joe Abensur recalled in his memoirs.

I had always thought of Errol Flynn as the good-looking swordsman jumping from ship to ship, ready to go into battle, or else as Robin Hood. When I met him in 1956 he was about 51-52, had a fat belly, a pock-marked nose, an arm in a sling . . . really not the dazzling star. We used to have drinks on his yacht at about 8pm, but by that time he was already drunk, so his wife would leave him on the yacht and come out for drinks with us – he would wake up a few hours later and be furious that no one was home.

Other regulars at Dean's included Ava Gardner, Marlene Dietrich, Humphrey Bogart, Lauren Bacall, Anita Ekberg, Cecil Beaton, John Gielgud, T.S. Eliot, Noel Coward, Samuel Beckett and one of the greatest artists of the twentieth century, Francis Bacon.

Francis Bacon was born in Dublin on 28 October 1909 to English parents who moved to London at the outbreak of World War I. The family then went back and forth between England and Ireland, giving the young Francis a feeling of displacement that stayed with him for the rest of his life. He never had a normal school experience as he suffered from asthma and was tutored privately. His father, who worked in the War Office, despaired of his son having one day found him admiring himself in the mirror, dressed in women's underwear. Bacon's mother gave him books by Nietzsche.

In his early years in London, Francis Bacon lived off an allowance of £3 a week from his mother's trust fund. He found that he could eke this out by avoiding rent and engaging in petty theft. He worked briefly as a domestic servant, but became bored and resigned. He was also sacked from a job answering the phone in a women's clothes shop in Soho, after he sent a poison pen letter to its owner.

At sixteen, Bacon left home and travelled around Europe, living in Paris and Berlin. At the height of Berlin's decadent period, he watched Fritz Lang's *Metropolis* and Sergei Eisenstein's *Battleship Potemkin*, which fuelled his imagination. In Paris he was inspired by the work of Picasso, as well as Nicolas Poussin's *Massacre of the Innocents*, which he often referred to in his later work. On his return to London, the artist worked as an interior designer before taking up painting again in the 1930s. In 1936 he offered some of his work to the International Surrealist Exhibition, but it was rejected as being 'not sufficiently surreal.' Bacon would often feel discouraged and would turn to drink and gambling – in the early 1940s he destroyed nearly all his paintings. The turning point came in 1945, when the art world was shocked by *Three Studies for Figures at the Base of a Crucifixion*. The art critic, John

Russell said, 'there was painting in England before the Three Studies, and painting after them, and no one . . . can confuse the two.' Among Bacon's other famous works are pictures of screaming faces, such as Study After Velázquez's Portrait of Pope Innocent X, which was inspired by medical text books, the German Renaissance painter, Matthias Grünewald and stills from Battleship Potemkin.

Many of Bacon's other paintings are of twisted and bloodied bodies. In a 1985 television interview with Melvyn Bragg for the South Bank Show, Bacon talked about 'deforming and reforming' the human body and quoted a line from the Greek tragedian, Aeschylus: 'the reek of human blood is laughter to my heart.' He was also frank about his homosexuality. 'I like men,' he said, 'I like the quality of their flesh.' He described his art as not 'illustrating reality but a concentration of reality and a shorthand for sensation.' Asked by Bragg why his studio was such a mess, Bacon replied, 'chaos for me breeds images.' In an echo of William Burroughs, he told his interviewer that many of his paintings were accidents. Chance, he pronounced, was more important than rational intellect, as it allowed him access to the unconscious. 'I've made images that intellect would never make,' he said. 'I am profoundly optimistic . . . about nothing,' he told Bragg, as the red wine flowed at his favourite Italian restaurant in South Kensington and rational intellect began to disintegrate. 'I believe in nothing,' he slurred. 'We are born and then we die. There is nothing else.'

After his death in 1992, Bacon's paintings continued to sell for colossal sums at auction. In November 2013, Three Studies of Lucian Freud sold at Christie's in New York for $142.4 million. At the time, it was the highest price paid for a work of art.

Apart from his astonishing art, Bacon also earned a reputation as a dissolute libertine, heading a coterie of hard-drinking cronies that included his fellow painter, Lucian Freud and the journalist Jeffrey Barnard, who all staggered in and out of Soho's pubs and clubs in the 1950s.

Bacon first arrived in Tangier in 1955 in a white Rolls Royce, belonging to his friend and benefactor, Peter Pollock. The latter bought a restaurant called the Pergola, which subsequently became famous for serving the finest swordfish and chips on the North African coast. When Pollock died in 2001, he left more than 30 of Bacon's works to the British nation. Paul Bowles remembered the painter as a regular visitor to his apartment in 1955.

> I had long admired his paintings, and when I finally knew him, I extended the admiration to him as well. He was a man about to burst from internal pressures. Even with his articulate description he gave me of his method of work, I was unable to imagine for myself exactly what happened as he painted.

After that first trip, Bacon would revisit Tangier for the next six years. It was for him and many other drunks, a sort of Soho by the sea. 'Tangier is a rather curious place,' Bacon confided to his biographer Michael Peppiatt, 'It's a bit like Muriel's club [The Colony Room in Soho], on a large scale. People come here to lose their inhibitions.'

'As an habitué of the easy-come, easy-go lifestyle of Monte Carlo and other casinos on the Côte d'Azur,' wrote Peppiatt, 'Bacon took to Tangier's cosmopolitan mixture of crooks (which included the leading figures of London's underworld), queers, hopheads, fugitives and remittance men as though he were coming home.'

Bacon was drawn to the strong Moroccan colours and light, but also drew a perverse strength from the darkness of Tangier. 'Decadence and disaster were, in the end, what his paintings fed off,' said Peppiatt. He was also fascinated by Burroughs' cut-up technique in *Naked Lunch* and Ginsberg thought Bacon painted the way Burroughs wrote. 'It was a sort of dangerous bullfight of the mind,' writes Ted Morgan, 'where he placed himself in acute psychic danger of uncovering some secret that would destroy him.' Yet, when Ginsberg remarked how similar the two were, Burroughs replied: 'Bacon and I are at opposite ends of the spectrum. He likes middle-aged truck drivers and I like young boys.'

When Ginsberg met Bacon in 1957, the painter told him that his own reputation was 'a lot of chic shit' and his real love was gambling. He had been offered, he said, a gambling stake for allowing himself to be whipped, with a bonus for every stroke that drew blood.

Near the centre of Tangier, various English expats had gathered for a garden party. People stood on a patio enveloped in bamboo trees above a pond echoing to the sound of frogs. 'I get called up,' one English interior decorator confided in me, 'for every urgent cushion crisis.' The house and garden belonged to Anna McKew, an elegant, older woman who is part of Tangier's English establishment. She came here in 1957 when she was married to Bobby McKew, a gangster with the Billy Hill mob. Later she wed a Moroccan, Ahmed Maimouni, who built the house as well as a studio with pink walls that lies on the other side of the garden wall. Anna told me that when she first came to Tangier she stayed in the Marmara Hotel in the medina and one night, her friends bet her a bottle of Calvados that she would not dare streak naked along the Petit Socco. She won the bet but was arrested. She also said that Francis Bacon rented the pink studio over the garden wall. She remembered him as being, 'social, erudite, witty and bohemian.' Bacon had offered her a few of his watercolours for £25, but she refused. 'It was tourist tat,' she told me, 'to pay his rent. He was simply churning them out.'

At the garden party I also chatted to the portrait painter Lawrence Mynott. He informed me that the English stockbroker, Martin Soames, had a house in Tangier and would arrange things for Bacon when he visited. At the end of one trip the painter had to fly back, but was late for his flight, so Soames drove him to the airport at breakneck speed. As he was running along the tarmac to board the plane, Bacon handed Soames some rolls of paintings, which he had been carrying under his arm. 'Think of these as your taxi fare,' Bacon said. Martin Soames' son Richard later sold the paintings for more than two million pounds. Mynott admitted that not everything he told me could be verified. 'Citation needed, is what they will write on my gravestone,' he added. Mynott also said that on his early visits, Bacon preferred to stay at the Rembrandt Hotel. 'One should always stay in a hotel named after an artist,' Bacon had told him. One time he stayed there with the owner of the Colony Room, Muriel Belcher. Every five minutes or so Belcher would dive into the hotel's swimming pool, but get out almost immediately afterwards.

'Is it too cold for you?' enquired the manager.

'Don't be stupid cunty,' replied Belcher, 'I'm only going for a piss.'

The writer, Robin Cook, recalled one hot afternoon in Tangier in the summer of 1956.

Three o'clock. Terribly hot. Woke parched, so got downstairs from my room in the Minzah somehow (no lift again) and crawled across the courtyard past the potted palms, keeping well clear of the sunlight. I did what I knew I was going to do anyway and steered for the eternal twilight of Dean's Bar, partly to watch him traf-ficking in small purple birds whose bottoms he stuffed with cannabis and sold for export, but mostly for the music which forever poured from an upright piano whose top was four ranks deep in empty glasses. This cigarette-scarred instrument produced an inspired stream of music which I had never known to end before seven in the morning, at which hour the performer would sway and his face collapse gravely into the keys with a faint but haunting discord . . . He had the face of a poet who has dropped in to remark that life after death is tolerable.

The man at the piano was Peter Lacy, a dashing RAF pilot who had fought in the Battle of Britain and who later embarked on a love affair with Francis Bacon.

My glance did linger on a large man in rolled-up shirt-sleeves. He was broad-shouldered, rubicund and definitely looked like an Englishman, except that I thought his eyes probed a little too far, further, in fact, than was good for them. He had a bottle of cham-pagne beside him and was covered in splashes of paint; he leaned carelessly on the counter with his back to the bottles, his crossed legs adorned with a pair of green Wellington boots . . . "Have a glass of champagne," he said lazily.

The man at the bar was Bacon. Another of his biographers, Daniel Farson, said the image of his friend in green wellies in the searing summer heat unnerved him for the rest of his life. A previous relation-ship had already come to an end by the time Bacon met Lacy in the Colony Room in 1952. When the latter moved to Tangier that year, Bacon first stayed at the Hotel Cecil with him before moving, on subse-quent occasions into the Rembrandt, and later renting apartments. In 1956 the painter wrote a letter telling Farson about daily life in Tangier.

I have not been able to finish anything here but have done a lot of preparatory work and feel I shall be able to paint a series I want to do quickly when I get back – I love it here, but not for long. All the Arabs here are so wonderful looking and more especially the Berbers I think they are. They answer to almost everything you like . . . Peter is playing the piano in a bar here and staying on.

'My early impression was of an exceptionally nice man,' Farson wrote of Lacy, 'innately shy, with a slight, endearing stammer which caused him to blink. He was attentively polite in a pleasant, old-fashioned way and because of his reticence, I felt gratified when he included me in his company.'

None of this explains why he later hurled Francis Bacon through a plate glass window, disfiguring the painter's face so badly that his right eye had to be sewn back into its socket.

'Unfortunately,' wrote the art historian John Richardson, 'drink released a fiendish, sadistic streak in Lacy that bordered on the psychopathic.' Richardson believed that Bacon was stimulated by sadomasochism, and this only increased his love for Lacy. 'Bacon loved Lacy even more. For weeks he would not forgive Lucian Freud for remonstrating with his torturer,' said Richardson. Peppiatt said Lacy owned nine rhino whips and that Bacon could be seen stumbling around the streets of Tangier beaten black and blue. Bacon's creative impulses were intimately connected with sexual pain and humiliation and this was something that he would act out with another lover, George Dyer, driving the latter to suicide in a Paris hotel bathroom in 1971. David Herbert recalled Lacy and alluded to this violent side too.

I knew him well. Played the piano in Dean's. I don't think he had any money at all. He was awfully sweet but I remember him getting very drunk. Darling Francis was having his first show and Lacy was so blind drunk that they had a fearful row and Lacy slashed 30 of his canvases. Can you imagine! Yet Francis told me, "You know, I rather enjoyed it." Francis was always being beaten up. It got so bad that our consul general was very upset and got hold of the chief of police, who was a friend, and told him he had to do something about it and the wretched street lighting. He impressed on him that Francis was a very distinguished painter and kept on getting mugged.

A few days later the chief of police returned, patently embarrassed: "*Pardon, mais le peintre adore ça!*"

'Peter Lacy was flinging pictures out of the window wherever they went,' said Peter Pollock, 'He had an uncontrollable rage. Trails of canvas were flung from their hotels. He was drunk and desperate and self-destructive.'

Nowhere is Tangier's darkness and light more deeply reflected than in the strangely compelling, yet appalling relationship between Bacon and Lacy. It was an obsession that the painter also confessed to Peppiatt in one of their conversations in Tangier.

In one way I've had a rotten life because I've always lost the people I've been attached to. That side of things has always been impossible, for me at least . . . I don't know why. I met Peter completely by chance one evening at Muriel's bar. I'd known lots of people before, but, even though I was over forty and everything, I'd never really fallen in love. Well, what Peter himself liked was young boys . . . It was the most total disaster from the start. Being in love in that extreme way – being utterly obsessed by someone as I was – it's like having a dreadful disease. I wouldn't wish it on my worst enemy. And we had these four years of continuous horror, with nothing but violent rows.

Peter was marvellous looking, you know. He had this physique, it was so extraordinary. Even his calves were beautiful. And he could be the most marvellous company. He was a kind of playboy, I suppose. He used to play the piano and sing, and he had that real kind of natural wit, he used to come out with one amusing remark after another – just like that – unlike those people who spend their lives planning what they're going to say from morning to night.

'He said to me once, "Why bother to paint?" Of course, he hated my painting and was always trying to destroy it . . . "You could leave your painting and come and live with me," he said to me once. And I said, "What does living with you mean?" And he said, "Well you could live in a corner of my cottage on straw. You could sleep and shit there." He wanted me to live chained to the wall. Well, as it

happened, I did terribly want to go on painting. It would never have
worked in any case. He was a complete sadomasochist, and kinky
in all sorts of ways.

'I regret that I failed to buy the portrait of P.L. painted in 1962,'
wrote Farson wistfully, 'The Marlborough were asking for £1,000 at
the time, and offered to let me pay in installments.' He may well have
expressed such regret. When the portrait of Peter Lacy went up for sale
at Sotheby's in New York in 2013, it had an estimated sale price of
between 30 and 40 million dollars (it did not reach its reserve price
and remains unsold). It was painted in 1962, just months after Lacy's
alcohol-related death in Tangier. 'By that time, he was drinking three
bottles of whisky a day, which nobody can take.' Bacon confided to
Peppiatt, 'In the end I think his pancreas simply exploded. He really
killed himself with drink. He set out to do it, like a suicide.'

As Bacon was receiving telegrams of adulation at the opening of his
major retrospective at the Tate in 1962, he received another telegram
informing him that Lacy had died. This scenario was eerily replicated
in 1971, when he found out about George Dyer's death at the opening
of his show in Paris.

Back in Tangier, Bacon befriended Ginsberg and Burroughs, although
he was characteristically caustic about them. 'Romantically poor with
their American Express cards,' was how he referred to the Beat poets.
Nevertheless, the artist also stayed at Burroughs' favourite haunt, the
Muniria. Just as Tangier's light and dark brought out the best of
Burroughs, so it seemed to feed Bacon's fascination with beauty and
horror. The two men were filmed in conversation in 1986, for a BBC
arts programme that was never broadcast, probably because of their
language. Bacon told the American that art critics and literary critics
were similar in that they 'know absolutely fuck all.'

Bacon joined in Burroughs' parties at the Muniria, but was wary of
the drugs. 'Francis discovered that only a pinch of majoun made them
high,' wrote Farson, 'and when they experimented with kif Francis'
face blew up like a balloon because of his asthma.'

Allen Ginsberg described Bacon as like a 'satyr, with the looks of an
English schoolboy who wears sneakers and tight dungarees and black
silk shirts and always looks like going to tennis . . . and paints mad

gorillas in grey hotel rooms dressed in evening dress with deathly black umbrellas.'

Bacon recalled an odd request from Ginsberg.

Ginsberg actually asked me to do a picture of him and his lover having sex on their bed, and he gave me all these photos. So I said, "well this could be a bit awkward if you want me to paint you as you're doing it, Allen. How long can you hold it for?" Anyway, the lover wasn't very interesting, I'm afraid, but there was something about this striped mattress and the way it spilled over the metal spindles that was so poignant and despairing, that I've kept the photos of the bed and used them ever since.

When Farson interviewed Paul Bowles years later, the American remembered Bacon working in Tangier.

He had a terrible studio which he rented in a building of such dilapidation that the matchwood lift finally plunged five floors to the bottom where it disintegrated into dust, killing a baby and crippling the mother — Francis told me about it with some relish.

Ahmed Yacoubi also struck up a friendship with Bacon, and the artist let the Moroccan observe him as he painted. 'I don't *ever* allow anyone to watch me work,' Bacon said, 'but in your case I'll make an exception and you can come and watch me slosh the stuff on.' In a letter to Farson in 1957, Bacon wrote about a scandal that was to rock Tangier.

Ahmed has been in a bad way. He had an affair with a German boy of 12 and the father found out and arrived at the flat with two police. He was arrested and put in prison for a couple of days until he was bailed out he had a preliminary interview with a tribunal on Saturday he is in awful state as it has been dragging on for about two months and he does not know yet what is going to happen.

It was Bowles who bailed out Yacoubi, but the affair scared the expat community. 'Francis behaved impeccably,' Farson said, 'sending

two canvases to Yacoubi in jail and keeping Paul Bowles informed
when he left the country, with the warning note "I think you should
be careful."

In a letter dated 2 July 1957, Bacon told Farson about some other,
completely different visitors to Tangier.

All the Billy Hill crowd are here they being charming to me because
they are trying to get me involved in something I will tell you when
I get home so if he should telephone or someone called Charlie
Mitchell would you say you don't know when I will be back as they
are leaving tomorrow it is a terrible nuisance to be in this state as
Charlie is a really handsome east end thug and in the circumstances
would not be hard to make as he likes giving the whip. This has
been a disastrous holiday but in ways quite interesting.

'Charlie Mitchell' was thought to be 'Mad Axeman' Frank Mitchell,
a friend of the Kray brothers. The Billy Hill mob used to do battle
with the Krays. Bacon was in Tangier when Ronnie and Reggie Kray
came out there on holiday. The Krays liked Tangier and Ronnie would
later decorate his flat in Walthamstow with Moroccan drapes and
rugs. In a crowded restaurant, Bacon saw the brothers force a man to
go down on his knees and kiss their shoes. 'Deep down I hated the
idea of what they did to people,' he said. And yet he was fascinated by
them.

These gangsters I happened to know, the Krays . . . were really
curious. Of course they were dreadful, just killing people off and
so on, and it's a good thing they've been put away, but at least they
were really different from everybody else. They were prepared to
risk everything. One of them was quite mad. The queer one, Ronnie.
I would never have known them if this actor I used to see, Stanley
Baker, when I was living for a bit in Tangier, hadn't come round to
me one day and said, "Francis, I've got these friends over from
England and can I bring them round for a drink?" And I said yes of
course. So then he turned up with the whole dreadful gang of
them. I suppose he thought it was terribly smart to know them.

In Tangier, Bacon was asked to perform a strange favour by Ronnie Kray.

The really nasty one of course, came to me and said, "Francis, I've got this friend" – he'd fallen for some Spanish boy – "and I don't feel I can take him back to the hotel, can I bring him round to your place?" So I said, "Well, as it happens I don't think hotels here mind about that sort of thing." But he said he was worried about the impression it might make, though you would think that after cutting all those throats he wouldn't have cared. Anyway, I had a place with lots of rooms at the time so I said, "If you want to you can bring him here." Well, he did, and after that I never saw the end of him. Naturally. He always seemed to be there.

If Ronnie was grateful, he had an odd way of showing it. Some time later, one of the Krays' heavies came to burgle Bacon's workshop in London.

One of the ones who worked for them broke into my studio and stole some paintings once. I suppose he'd been told they were worth a lot of money – the newspapers had printed a story about their selling for colossal sums. Anyway he'd been hanging around the studio for some time. He just wanted money I think, because at night there used to be this tap-tap-tap on the door, the whole time, tap-tap-tap, well it went on and on, and I was too bored by the whole thing to go down and open up to him. I could probably have given him something and he would have gone away. It was a great nuisance because he took some pictures that I terribly didn't want to let out of the studio because they were very bad. Well, you know how these things are: there was just no trace of them at all. And then about a week later, I had to go and see my framer, Alfred Hecht. And there he was, showing Alfred the pictures. He'd just that moment been trying to see whether he could sell them. When I came in he took them and ran out. But that wasn't the end of it. It never is with that kind of thing. The next day I went back to the studio in the afternoon and I found them all in there, the whole gang of them, just sitting around waiting, and there was that really nasty one saying to me how long it had been and how nice it was to see me again and so on. Of course I didn't know what to do, so I asked them whether they'd like a cup of tea. And they said they would, so I made them some and we all sat round and they were terribly polite, and just sat there drinking their tea.

The artist was too scared to tell the police and only managed to get the paintings back when they eventually turned up at auction, where he had to pay equally colossal sums to retrieve them. Even after the Krays were eventually put behind bars in 1969, Bacon was still not free of them. 'I still hear from them,' he told Peppiatt, 'they send me these paintings they do there. They're very odd. They're always of these kinds of soft landscapes with little cottages in them.'

Now that Lacy was dead, Bacon had lost his *raison d'être* to be in Tangier. The city had lost its fascination for him and apart from anything else, he did not want to end up in prison.

'Certainly a lot of people I've known very well have died,' Bacon confessed to Melvyn Bragg, 'they were generally heavy drinkers. Life becomes more of a desert around you . . . If you have a very strong feeling for life, its shadow, death is always with you too.'

Perhaps it was not surprising that such a talented yet enigmatic painter would be drawn to Tangier, the city of light and darkness, freedom and addiction. 'It sounds a vain thing to say,' Bacon told Peppiatt, 'but by a series of accidents, they were just accidents, my life has been extraordinary. Much more interesting than my paintings. It's been a ridiculous life as well, of course.' Just as Burroughs and Gysin had stumbled upon the cut-up technique by accident, chance had played a major part in Bacon's life. At the start of his career, when he was short of money, he painted on the reverse side of already used canvases. He then found that this unprimed side made his paintings more dramatic, as paint could not be removed from this 'wrong side.' Bacon's life was a ridiculous one, but it was very suited to Tangier. 'Nothing he put on canvas,' observed Peppiatt, 'could ever match the dark reality of his private life.'

ELEVEN

Joe Orton

They have no right to be occupying chairs reserved for decent sex perverts

Otmane and I walked along the crescent-shaped bay, its promenade flanked by 1960s tower blocks, palm trees and ubiquitous cafés. 'We have a saying in Tangier,' Otmane said, 'between a café and a café . . . there is a café.' The bars and nightclubs lined the beachfront like a surreal strip from a Hollywood boulevard, their names on gaudy signs and neon lights: Club 555, Discotheque Snob, Miramar, and Oxygen. 'You won't find much oxygen there,' Otmane said. When I enquired if prostitutes worked inside, he looked as if I'd asked whether the Pope was a Catholic. He told me that in his youth it was almost impossible to be seen walking outside with a girl, so this pushed sexuality underground and led to an increase in homosexuality. He said that men also worked as prostitutes in the nightclubs. Sometimes, he said, it was obvious as they wore garish clothes and make-up, but at other times it was more hidden. 'There is still a fear that they might be beaten up and there is still prejudice against homosexuality,' he added, 'which is not officially acknowledged.' One particularly raunchy establishment had been owned by a former mayor of Tangier, who just happened to be an MP for the governing, conservative Islamist Party. The Party of Justice and Development (PJD) frequently rails about the immorality of modern Morocco, and has denounced Marrakech and Tangier as "cities of sin." 'We live with contradictions,' Otmane said.

We came to a café, The Windmill, took our seats, ordered coffee and looked at five flat windows, which gave the impression that they

were large TV screens projecting scenes from the beach. We gazed out
onto a series of horizontal lines: a blue sky, a turquoise strip of sea and
a yellow line of beach, its edges blurred by sand whipped up by the
wind. Otmane told me that locals are obsessed with the wind; it is
often the first thing they talk about after they greet each other. Like
Eskimos and snow, Tanjawis have many different words for wind:
Scirocco, Norte, Chergui and Gharbi (also known by their Spanish names
Levante and Poniente). 'People think they are lazy, but it's because they are
affected by the wind. El Norte gets into people's souls, makes their
muscles ache and they wake up very late.'

The interior of The Windmill consisted of a pale yellow room
supported by robust columns. The upper floor had a low and ornate
ballroom ceiling. The empty chairs and tables were all facing the same
way – out to sea – giving the impression that The Windmill was not
actually a bar, but a cruise ship heading for Gibraltar. An endless loop
of soporific muzak wafted from speakers embedded in the ceiling and
hysterical Spanish football commentary burbled from a television.
I went to the toilet and passed a dapper smiling man, with Yves Saint
Laurent style spectacles and platinum hair. As he came closer, I realised
he must have been nearly 70. Apart from him, the place was deserted.
On one of the walls hung an old portrait of Hassan II, trying, unsuc-
cessfully, to look relaxed in a polo shirt and golf slacks, which were
slightly too short for him.

The Windmill was frequented by Americans such as Truman Capote
and Tennessee Williams, but also by two unlikely Englishmen: Kenneth
Williams, of the Carry On films, and Joe Orton. The English playwright
had first visited Tangier in 1965, the year that Williams acted in Orton's
play Loot. Williams holidayed in Tangier many times and in The Kenneth
Williams Diaries he recorded an early encounter with Orton in 1966.

Went down to The Windmill, chatted to Iain and Terry and met
Mohammed and Hassan. The latter had two front teeth missing. Joe
Orton and Ken H. came and were deeply offended because a woman
appeared on the sun terrace. "It's a bloody disgrace," said Joe and
went off for a swim. We had lunch there and then made our way to
the Pergola for the 3 o'clock appointment with Warren Beatty. He
turned up there at 2.45 sitting down to lunch with Kraut royalty, so

we got the bum's rush. I flew back to The Windmill and saw Mohammed and invited him back to tea instead. He has a face like a Byzantine portrait . . . An incredible young man called Paul who lives at Blackheath talked to us and kept using expressions like: "It's no life for a white lady, darling."

Kenneth Williams drank at The Windmill but stayed at the Rembrandt.

I was ensconced in the Rembrandt by 9 o'clock. It is hard to explain the fascination of this place. Above all, there is the feeling of ease – the feeling that you don't have to bother about what people think, and, out of season like this, there aren't those ghastly package tourists about, and no one nudges you as you approach . . . The people are marvellous . . . I got off to sleep, woke up, and found myself peeing all over the writing table in the hotel room! Luckily there were newspapers on it, so it was them that became wet.

Williams' diaries reveal a love-hate relationship with Tangier. He was both intrigued and repulsed by it, as he may also have been about his sexuality.

Everyone at the Rembrandt was charming and the welcome was delightful. And it happened *again*!! that feeling of "It is wonderful to be back in this place" – the sight, sounds and smells of it all are enchanting to me.
      . . . Never has a holiday become so utterly boring and dreary as this . . . I went down to The Windmill and chatted to the same old crowd . . . I left the party at 1 o'clock when I returned to the Rembrandt. It has been a rotten holiday with undertones of unpleasantness and the ever-present hatred of the natives here. It is certainly time to go.

In Tangier, Williams was disparaging about the 'dreary English queens,' but also admired the youthful Moroccan boys. The master of innuendo had an obviously camp stage persona, but would not openly admit he was gay. That is not surprising as homosexuality was not decriminalised in Britain until 1967. His diaries are also full of absurd, indiscreet gossip and even the dreary queens provided great comic material.

> Dickie B. told a marvellous story about Michael D. turning up at a grand house, in drag as the Queen Mother, and the butler saying "Oh no sir – you can't come in – she's here already."

Although, like many Tangier tales, this story may have been apocryphal, it is not inconceivable. I was told that David Herbert was a great friend of the Queen Mother and from time to time he would entertain her in Tangier. Like Williams, Orton also kept a diary and much of it centres around The Windmill, where he and his friends would meet up. The café acts almost as a stage set.

> After changing, we went down to The Windmill, a beach place run by an Englishman (Bill Dent) and an Irishman (Mike). The Windmill is right along the beach and so is very quiet. Bill D. gave us a long talk about his health – he has shaking fits, he looks thinner than last year. Kenneth Halliwell says, with some truth, that what most of the Tangier regulars suffer from is drink.

So begins a remarkable chronicle of life in Tangier in 1967. Three hundred years after Samuel Pepys, Orton's diaries also record the excesses of British expatriates in Tangier, as Kenneth Williams remarked:

> I told Joe, "It's marvellous the way you remember dialogue as well as the accents! You really capture the flavour of the personality you're describing." Joe said, "Yes, I've started a diary." I said, "Pepys put all his references to sexual matters in code so that no one would know." Joe said, "I don't care who knows."

This brief exchange encapsulates Williams and Orton, the former being more guarded about his sexuality.

> When I came thro' the customs today, the officer said "Hallo Mr Williams – your third visit to Morocco isn't it?" And I said yes, and

he said "What's the attraction?" and I said "Well, it's very sunny . . ." rather lamely.

Orton on the other hand was desperate to shock at all costs. The editor of *The Kenneth Williams Diaries*, Russell Davies compares the two.

All in all, there seems to have been much more talk than physical contact – an enduring imbalance in Williams' life . . . Later in life he tended to run away from the offer of a loving intimacy, preferring – or needing – to settle instead for the masturbatory mechanics of "the tradiola" as he called it . . . He felt freer abroad, though his adventures in Morocco must be judged timorous when compared with those recorded by his friend Joe Orton.

John Lahr, who edited *The Orton Diaries*, put it much more bluntly: 'Williams affected outrageousness; but Orton lived it.'

Orton had willed himself into the role of rebel outcast: beyond guilt or shame. At 34, already with a criminal record for comically defacing public library books, Orton had rejected the world of conventional work, conventional sex, and conventional wisdom. He was an iconoclast who believed there was no sense being a rebel without applause.

John Kingsley Orton was born in Leicester on 1 January 1933. By 1967, he was at the peak of his literary powers. He had written *Entertaining Mr Sloane*, *Loot*, *The Erpingham Camp*, *Funeral Games* and was starting *What the Butler Saw*. 'He was on top of his form, full of fun and writing like the young master he knew himself to be,' writes Lahr, 'His literary style and his life acquired a new amperage.'

Orton's plays caught the era's psychopathic mood, that restless, ruthless pursuit of sensation whose manic frivolity announced a refusal to suffer. The diaries are a chronicle not only of a unique comic imagination, but of the cock-eyed liberty of the time – a time before the failure of radical politics, before mass unemployment, before AIDS.

Orton and his boyfriend, Kenneth Halliwell, flew out to Tangier on 7 May 1967 and drove straight from the airport into town, where they rented an apartment at 2 Rue Pizarro, in which Tennessee Williams had written *Suddenly Last Summer*.

The actual owner — a gentle French home-femme — showed us around the place. It is furnished in a most "luxurious" manner — antique furniture and mirrors, gilded chandeliers — awful shit, but comfortable. The kind of taste I abhor, but as I am staying in Tangier for two months I want privacy, comfort and quiet. If I have to have a flat decorated by a gentle French queer, it's a small price to have to pay.

Orton was initially wary of using this apartment for his hanky-panky with local boys and preferred to go to another one belonging to a friend, Bill Fox.

Ridiculous day. Mohammed (1) outside beach bar from eleven to two. I'd arranged to meet him at three. Found Bill. Got the key to flat. Bill said, 'When you've finished bring the key to me at the restaurant across the road.' I went back to The Windmill. No sign by now of the boy. No sign at 3.15. Decided to scrub the idea. Went in search of Bill to give him the key back. The restaurant was closed, it being Sunday. Couldn't find Bill. Walked up and down the street. Met Kenneth coming home, who said my life was one long round of ridiculous complication. Then we saw Bill and a good-looking American called Gerry. I handed Bill back the key. The American came back to the flat with Kenneth and I. I had promised to give him a stick of hashish candy. I gave him half a stick, then Larbi arrived. We all drank tea. The American said that Bill had a youth from Meknes coming at five and why didn't I come over and have a threesome. I said "OK", Kenneth being occupied with Larbi. We walked long the Rue d'Espagne and met Mohammed (1). It was now 4.30. I'd arranged to meet him at three. The American suggested we take him to Bill's. I said, 'But he won't want the flat full of Moroccans,' so we parted from Mohammed (1). We got to the flat. I waited till 6.30. No boy turned up.

But Orton need not have worried about having to use Bill Fox's flat. The place on Rue Pizarro became more like the set of one of Orton's comedies.

Bill Fox told me that the Baron Favier (from whom we rent our flat) likes to dress young men up in military uniform. "One night," Bill said, "he picked up a sailor in uniform, he took him back, made him take off his naval uniform and put on a military uniform before he could have him."

Even so, Orton had to be careful not to arouse suspicion in the apartment. He seemed to enjoy this illicit aspect of his assignations and could not help his descriptions descending into farce.

When the time approached for the boy to come, I realised that the Fatima [the housemaid] hadn't yet left and was showing no sign of leaving. She'd left her coat and kitchen shoes behind the door and gone downstairs to her mother. I couldn't lock the door leading downstairs because she wouldn't be able to get back. Yet, she could at any time appear in the apartment. All the elements of farce were present. It needed only for the boy to arrive, have to be concealed in the bedroom, the Fatima and her mother appear in the flat, Larbi and perhaps Nasser to turn up, plus the Baron to turn up with some complaint and then all it needed was a title.

Besides the comings and goings in the apartment, Orton also recorded scenes and conversations in cafés and restaurants, where his comic timing and ear for dialogue come across. One such cameo was at the Café de Paris, where he had joined a table of friends, including a retired schoolmaster, Nigel.

I sat next to a rather stuffy American tourist and his disapproving wife. They listened to our conversation and I, realising this, began to exaggerate the content. "He took me right up the arse," I said, "and afterwards he thanked me for giving him such a good fucking. They're the most polite people." The American and his wife hardly moved a muscle. "We've got a leopard-skin rug in the flat and he wanted me to fuck him on that," I said in an undertone which was perfectly audible to the next table. "Only I'm afraid of the spunk, you see, it might adversely affect the spots on the leopard." Nigel said quietly, "Those tourists can hear what you're saying." He looked alarmed. "I mean them to hear," I said. "They have no right to be occupying chairs reserved for decent sex perverts."

Orton befriended the Reuters correspondent George Greaves, who knew all the city's gossip.

George Greaves rang and suggested we go out to dinner this evening, it being rather dreary weather. K. and I arrived at his flat in the Rue Goya at a quarter to eight . . . We went out to dinner and met Dai Rees-Davies (M.A. Oxon), reputed to be *persona non-grata* in England. He looks like a frog and has only one eye. "He takes it out, you know," George said later, "takes it out and frightens the shit out of these kids. I remember once I was having dinner with him and he took it out and wiped it. It slipped from his hand and fell straight into the pudding."

By the mid-1960s, Tangier's reputation as a resort without sexual restrictions for homosexual visitors had firmly re-established itself. Perhaps not since the days of Pepys had there been such an expansive catalogue of sex in the city.

Orton had met Halliwell at RADA in 1951. Orton was 18 and the latter was 25. The playwright admired him for his education, money, literary knowledge and *savoir-faire*. He became an acolyte of the older man, who would turn out to be a control freak. A former flatmate noticed that Halliwell kept Orton on a tight leash. Another friend said that Halliwell would pretend to be Orton when he picked up the phone, to find out what people were saying about him to Joe. 'Tight' is the word that comes to mind for Halliwell,' said *Loot*'s director, Charles Marowitz. 'He could never unclench.'

By 1967, Orton's star was rising but Halliwell's was descending. He could not cope with being eclipsed by his protégé. Halliwell's self-esteem was dangerously low and shrinking all the time. 'Orton was now the writer,' Lahr observes, 'Halliwell, who had nurtured Orton's

skills and ambitions, was increasingly a factotum.' Orton's lewd account
of his adventures in Tangier was not written to protect readers' sensi-
bilities. 'The mischief is aggressive,' writes Lahr, 'but the culprit is
invisible, the work of a trickster with a strong rage and a weak ego.'
Orton's behaviour enraged his partner, breaking any illusion that they
were still a couple. A friend of Orton's, Penelope Gilliatt, observed the
seeds of their destruction.

> The household they had was a fake household and Joe knew this.
> Joe knew the fakery well enough to kick it about and endanger it as
> much as possible by staying out late, by promiscuity, by every
> means he could, to see how far he could drive Halliwell.

Orton was having fun in Tangier, but Halliwell was not. He
compared Orton's sexual adventures to his, which were largely
limited to masturbation. He was still in love with Orton, but the
romance was not reciprocated. Halliwell knew he was about to lose
his lover but could not accept it. Orton had been his creation, but by
1967, like Frankenstein, he had become bigger than his creator. At the
start of their holiday, Halliwell tried desperately to cater to his lover's
whims.

> We went down to the beach early today. It had cleared up. Clouds
> were passing over the sun, but enough heat to be pleasant. We were
> hailed with "Hallo" from a very beautiful sixteen-year-old boy
> whom I knew (but never had) from last year. Kenneth wanted him.
> We talked for about five minutes and finally I said: "Come to our
> apartment for tea this afternoon." He was very eager. We arranged
> that he should meet us at The Windmill beach place. As we left the
> boy, Kenneth said, "Wasn't I good at arranging the thing?" This
> astounded me. "I arranged it," I said. "You would have been standing
> there talking about the weather forever." K. didn't reply.

A few days later, Orton went off for a mint tea with a boy called
Abdullah, whom the Englishman called 'Paddington,' as the Moroccan
said he had worked there. When Orton returned, the situation
deteriorated.

I went back and faced Kenneth in such a rage at The Windmill. "Where've you been? You have been gone an hour and a half. I was nearly out of my mind with worry." With that, on the terrace of The Windmill, he burst into tears, to my own embarrassment.

Halliwell hoped that by sharing boys with Orton the two Englishmen might be able to reignite their relationship, but the tactic backfired. On 3 June, a day of wind and cloud, Orton wrote that, 'provided one spent the time drugged or drunk, the world was a fine place.' Just as William Burroughs was not sure which Arab boy he was sleeping with, so Orton found it difficult to keep track of his conquests. Several of them seemed to be called Mohammed.

"I have very good English," said the boy, whose name was inevitably Mohammed, and he produced a battered book, Colloquial English for the Beginner . . . "We must make a date," the boy said. "I'll see you sometime," I said, refusing to make any more dates. My life beginning to run to a timetable no member of the Royal Family would tolerate.

To distinguish the Mohammeds from one another, Orton gave them nicknames. One of them was known as 'Mohammed Yellow-Jersey.'

Yellow-Jersey and I had it off in the bedroom. How incredible it is, I thought later, as I watched him take a shower, to really see a nude fifteen-year-old. That small waist, sudden jutting of the bum; it wasn't just sex, it was an aesthetic experience.

Like Burroughs, Orton was an outsider and both saw Tangier as a playground in which to enact their desires. 'To them Tangier was little more than a bordello,' Mohamed Choukri wrote, 'an endless beach or a huge sanatorium.' Like the American, Orton was also unimpressed by the self-importance of the Tangerinos and was determined to satirise them. His humour derived from the incongruity between their pomposity and his lewdness. 'The English colony have succeeded in turning a fair-sized hill near Tangier into a replica of a Surrey backwater,' he said.

Twisty lanes, foxgloves, large pink rambling roses, tennis courts and gardens watered by sprinklers. Only here and there does the presence of a palm show that Africa is waiting. We drove through an olde English garden and were welcomed by a man called Kevin, who is, I was later told, a millionaire. He was also a bit fattish. I'd say he was in his early thirties. He had a Moroccan youth with him . . . We were led into a large entrance hall differing from that of the British Museum entrance only in that there was no postcard stand. The vast interior was decorated with urns and hubble-bubbles which were fastened to the floor. On the second floor was one big living-room, several small lavatories and something for preparing drinks. I saw no bedroom. The view from the terrace was beautiful. The town lay spread beneath us, and the bay and the mountains in the distance, a soft, almost purple light covered the whole scene . . . The conversation was deathly dull as a whole. I believe, without the aid of the drugs, it would have been unbearably tedious.

The purple haze may not have been weather related, but more to do with drugs. Orton was also popping Halliwell's librium and valium pills: 'They are excellent and make me feel wonderfully relaxed and confident,' he wrote, 'as though the whole of creation was conspiring to make me happy.'

Apart from the aristocrats, Orton also encountered many with less *bona fide* credentials.

We met Nigel again later, at dinner. He had a curious man with him, the Marquis of something or other. A man who said a pipe of opium was pure heaven, and who I suspected was wearing a toupee, though I couldn't be sure. He took us back to his house and name-dropped, "I remember the Duke of Windsor saying his mother, the Queen Mary never had a new dress in thirty years. And I was there when Madame de Gaulle made her famous gaffe, you know. Somebody asked her, "What are you looking forward to when you retire?" "I am looking forward most to a penis," she replied. After a pause somebody said, "Oh, oui, happiness, madame?"

The Marquis' house was crammed with junk. It looked like a Chelsea antique shop. Rubbish from the rag-bag of eighteenth-century culture. Mirrors with the original glass — so cracked that to see one's self in them was to have a vision of what one's face might look like on the Day of Judgment, the marks of the grave upon it . . . We sat drinking and he told us of "the Princess Marina," and "What do you think of the Earl of Snowdon? Do you not think he's an unhappy man?" "The royal family is a noose," I said. "You don't have to put your head in it. If a man does so, he must expect to be unhappy." "Ah oui," said the Marquis, shrugging his shoulders and trying to look like a character in Proust.

Later, George Greaves informed Orton that this was a 'phoney marquis . . . a dirty bit of the South of France trade from way back.' Besides the graphic descriptions of sex with local boys, Orton was also a sharp-eyed observer of Moroccan behaviour. One of those who gave Orton plenty of comic material was Halliwell's lover, Larbi. Although he and others have a certain cartoonish character to them, they also provide snapshots of ordinary Moroccan life, through an irreverent lens.

We went home. We found Fatima had done all the weekly work and left all the clothes in water and bleaching solution, in the bath. Also that the stove didn't work. Larbi arrived and, when we told him that the stove didn't work, he grinned and said, "I make it work, I fuck it good, yes?" He showed his cock. Laughed. Went into the kitchen and found that the Fatima, for some reason not able to be explained, had turned the gas off at the mains.

A day trip to visit Larbi's parents in Ksar el-Kebir is painted with a mixture of disrespectful remarks and well observed details of Moroccan life. In the simple family house, you feel like a fly on the wall, but one that is prone to laughter.

The taxi had dropped us outside a small shop. Larbi took us inside and introduced us to a dour Moor, who didn't seem over-anxious to see us. "Ma famille," Larbi said with a genteel nod. We shook hands with the man who Larbi said was his uncle, and bought a packet of biscuits. Larbi bought a loaf and some horrible *beurre crale* which tasted like fermented camel-spew and indeed my guess might not have been wild. After saying something which didn't sound at all welcoming, the Moor shopkeeper bid us farewell.

We walked through some streets, across a railway line and up to a terraced house. We were welcomed by a young girl kissing our hands, and then a fat woman (Larbi's) mother appeared and, behind, an ugly woman (auntie) and a youngish woman (their Fatima) and a small child . . . Larbi's mother made us a cup of mint 'tay.' I wanted to piss and Larbi led me behind a curtain off the hall. I found the usual native-type lavatory. Two raised places for the feet and a hole in the floor for the shit to drop through. Absolutely no precautions were taken for the old and infirm in their toilet. As George Greaves once remarked, "If I got my arse that low they'd have to bury me in that position."

A remarkably small incident, that might go unnoticed by others, provides a pithy vignette of life in the streets of Tangier.

Left the house at 12.30. Found a strange old man sitting at the foot of the steps eating sardines out of a tin. He seemed surprised to find the door opening and two Europeans treading him down. He recovered his composure and held out his hand for money.

Another of Orton's favourite holiday activities in Tangier was consuming unusual cakes. Just as they provided sex, the Moroccan boys also provided copious amounts of hashish, often rolled into pancakes.

A Moroccan, called Nasser, promised to make me some hashish cake. So today I followed him for miles into some Moroccan district . . . We found his house and I sat outside whilst he went in. He came out with a bag of stuff and asked for three *dirhams* for the hashish. He went back and returned with a packet of what looked like heather. Then we went in search of some special butter. He stopped at one stall in the market and asked to taste some. He gave me a piece to taste. It was very hot. Probably goat or some other incredible animal. He bought a piece. And a piece of round, flat, white cheese. I thought this odd for a cake, but he tasted it and gave me a piece as well. We got back to the flat eventually and he began to make the 'gateau.'

The next hour or two seemed rather vague. I remember Larbi and Kenneth taking my clothes off and I did a belly dance to rounds of applause. I then put my clothes on and had a wrestling match with Larbi, and knocked over a rubbishy antique piss-pot or something, which was fortunately made of unbreakable teak or something, and didn't smash.

I came back to the house at one to begin slaving over a hot stove with these wretched cakes. Nasser has made enough fucking mixture to drug a regiment.

The Fatima, who steals food at an alarming rate, yesterday gobbled a large slice of hashish cake I left purposely in the cupboard. An hour or so later she fell silent and morose.

Under the influence of the homemade cakes, the conversations between Orton and his friends became more random and surreal.

K. and L. appeared at last. Went to dinner about eight. But before then we both had a fit of the giggles and the sudden mounting hysteria that gives away the hashish-swallower as surely as a hole in the back gives away a sword swallower. "We can't go anywhere too respectable like this," Kenneth said, after we had all had hysterics over some weak joke. We decided on Nino's as being the kind of restaurant where we could disgrace ourselves without too much damage being done. The rest of the evening was rather strange. I remember meeting George Greaves again on the Place de France . . . Later again I said to Nigel how like a frog Dai Rees-Davies looked. "Yes," Nigel agreed, "he does look rather like a frog." "But perhaps he isn't really a frog," I said, turning to the plate-glass window of the Café de Paris behind us. "If we threw him through these windows he'd turn into a handsome prince."

Frank told me a story about a soldier who was in a military hospital and one of the nurses came from behind the screen and began laughing. "What are you laughing at?" her friend said. "The patient in there has 'Son' tattooed on his penis," the nurse replied. "Oh, it read Sachatuon when I saw it," her friend said.

But perhaps the drugs and the novelty of Tangier were beginning to wear off. Orton and Halliwell now discussed the fleeting nature of happiness 'and of how it couldn't, surely, last. We'd have to pay for it. Or we'd be struck down from afar by disaster because we were, perhaps, too happy.' Once again we are confronted by the light and darkness of Tangier and how one can quickly morph into the other.

Frank Holroyd was among the eccentric characters Orton sketched in his diaries. He was an elderly professor who had retired to Tangier with an unusual hobby.

I went down to The Windmill. Frank, who arrived at 11.30, an hour after me, had a tale to tell of how he was making a *papier-maché* mask of Kevin's boy "because I collect beautiful boys' faces you know." "What about their cocks?" I said. "Well they can't stay hard long enough for the plaster of Paris mould to set," he said, bitterly. "I've tried, you know, to discover whether there isn't a quick-drying plaster."

Talked to Frank. "My mask of that young Moroccan," he said, "came out rather well. I'm engaged on doing the eyes. I colour them the best I can."

Larbi turned up at five. We took him to Frank's flat to watch my mask being made. An unnerving experience for me. Under the influence of drugs the plaster being put over my face didn't bother me much – though I had an overwhelming desire to laugh at the ridiculousness of it all – but when the time came to fill in my ear, thus taking, away my *sound* as well as my vision by half, I found the whole thing got very frightening and sinister. Suddenly I wasn't in control anymore.

The fact that the *papier-maché* mask story is written in fragments and interwoven into the narrative of *The Diaries*, makes them even more hilarious. This quirky sub-plot would hold its own in an episode of *Seinfeld*.

On 4 June, Orton flew back to London for three days to attend the premiere of The Ruffian on the Stair. The reviews were lukewarm, and he felt deflated on his return. Back at the apartment, he was annoyed to find that Halliwell had taken Mohammed, one of his boys, to bed. The playwright fell into a sulk: perhaps 'because of the nervous excitement of the last few days and the plane journey,' he supposed himself to be 'very depressed. Tired. Behaved rudely to Kenneth who is getting on my nerves.' The holiday continued, punctuated by intermittent sniper fire between Orton and Halliwell, as well as sex with various Mohammeds. 'Even sex with a teenage boy becomes monotonous,' Orton wrote on 25 June. 'Neither Kenneth nor I will be sorry to leave on Friday.'

"Do you remember inventing a wildly funny joke?" Kenneth said. "When?" I said. "Last night while we were trying to get a meal." "Oh yes," I said, "about a vicar with a large congregation, but a very small organ." "It was funnier last night," Kenneth said.

On 27 June, Orton noticed that Halliwell had given Larbi a pink shirt. He had originally bought it for Orton, and when the latter casually told Larbi about this, Halliwell took offence. Orton's taunts of sexual inadequacy had a startling effect on Halliwell who became 'violently angry after this' and attacked Orton, hitting him about the head and knocking a pen from his hand. Both left the apartment in a rage. When Orton returned he found his boyfriend:

Lying in his bed in a towel dressing gown, looking tight-lipped. I realised that it was no good talking to him, the "sore" would come sooner or later. I'd just settled down for the night when the door opened and Kenneth entered. I was selfish, I couldn't bear not to be the centre of attention . . . The holiday had been too perfect. I was determined to spoil it somehow. "And when we get back to London," he said, "we're finished. This is the end!"

Halliwell had another sulking fit the next day and lost his temper with their maid, throwing her clothes out of the apartment.

On 30 June they flew back to London. On arrival, Orton told Halliwell, "the party's over." Early in the morning of 9 August 1967, in their tiny, shared flat in Islington, Kenneth Halliwell beat Joe Orton to death. He picked up a hammer and smashed his lover's cranium with nine blows. Halliwell then took 22 sleeping pills and washed them down with grapefruit juice. On the desk in their room, a note was found: 'If you read his diary all will be explained. K.H.' it said, 'P.S. Especially the last part.'

The short lives of Halliwell and Orton, masters of comedy, had unravelled like a Greek tragedy. 'Morocco,' wrote John Lahr, 'slaked the tension that was always erupting in Orton's life between his emotional needs and the society's social and sexual taboos.'

The prospect of Halliwell's leftover-life drove him crazy. Halliwell beat out the brains that poked such wicked fun at the world, then took his own life. In murder, Halliwell was imitating their art . . . Death made them equal again, linking Halliwell finally and forever to Orton. In the anarchy of his farces, Orton took revenge for the fretfulness of his desires and his disillusion. Now Halliwell did the same.

A week after our stroll along the corniche and our visit to The Windmill, I was back in London. Otmane emailed me to inform me that most of the beachfront bars, nightclubs and cafés that had been such a large part of Tangier's glamorous, yet seedy past, had been confined to history. They had been bulldozed, partly to make way for the luxury marina funded by petrodollars from the Gulf and partly because Morocco's governing party, the PJD disapproved of them. This rather prudish political entity had waited for the holy month of Ramadan before ordering the bars' removal, thus taking their revenge on the City of Sin.

TWELVE

Mohamed Mrabet

Paul's apartment was becoming more and more like a lunatic asylum

The *Librairie des Colonnes* sits on the Boulevard Pasteur, like a jewel in the dust, as it has done since 1949. Its windows are framed by red columns and adorned with discreet black and gold art deco lettering. The Librairie is one of the great cultural centres of Tangier and one of the oldest bookshops in Morocco. Jack Kerouac and André Gide came here to find inspiration, Mohamed Choukri more or less lived in its reading room and Paul Bowles used it as a post box. Rachel Muyal, who managed the shop from 1973 to 1999, explained that since Bowles did not have a telephone, journalists would phone up and ask her to pass messages to him at the Immeuble Itesa. 'I still have some of the notes that I sent and there's writing on the paper from Paul Bowles, with his signature, saying "tell him to come at five o'clock." It had been a paper shop, but in 1951 it was bought by the French publishers, Gallimard, who recruited members of one of Tangier's rich Jewish families, the Gerofis, to manage it. From that time, until their retirement in 1976, Yvonne Gerofi and her sister-in-law Isabelle, ran the Librairie as a boutique, art gallery and literary salon, as John Hopkins recalls in *The Tangier Diaries*.

Angus Wilson takes tea chez Mme. and Mlle. Gerofi, who run the Gallimard bookshop here in Sin City. *Thé à la Belge* consists of whiskey and chocolates at five o'clock in the afternoon. The library ladies are thrilled to have a distinguished *homme de lettres* in their salon.

"Encore du whiskey, Monsieur Wilson?" Isabelle asks in her little bird voice.

"Avec plaisir!" The old boy's face is getting red.

In 2009 the bookshop was bought and meticulously restored by Pierre Bergé, the former partner of Yves Saint Laurent. Bergé was also a friend of Jean-Paul Sartre, Jean Cocteau and Albert Camus, with whom he shared a jail cell after they were arrested at a demonstration. Bergé died in 2017, but his life could have ended much earlier. In 1948 the 18-year-old left his family home in La Rochelle and headed for Paris. On his first day he was walking along the Champs-Elysées when he saw a man fall through a French window, grab hopelessly at a shop sign as he fell though the air and come crashing down on the pavement at Bergé's feet. The next day he read in the newspapers that the falling man was the poet, Jacques Prévert, who had stumbled through the open window of his apartment and missed the walking man by inches. 'I have always considered it an omen,' reflected Bergé, 'that the same day I got to Paris, a poet fell on my head.'

'Tangier has been created,' Josh Shoemake said, 'not just by architects and planners, but by fictions and memories.' Many of these are housed in the Librairie des Colonnes. Inside its walls thousands of books in several languages are immaculately presented in cedar wood cabinets and shelves complete with sliding stepladders. Here I met Simon-Pierre Hamelin, a French writer who manages the bookshop. We went upstairs to his office. Hamelin is impossibly handsome and unmistakably French. He nonchalantly lit a cigarette and began to talk about literature, like a character from a Truffaut film. He said he had been working on a novel called *Manaraf* with Mohamed Mrabet, Tangier's greatest storyteller. When they finished *Manaraf* in 2009, Mrabet was very sick and told Hamelin the book would be his last. In it Mrabet describes his craft.

> When I tell a story I don't know where or why it began, how it will continue or when it will end. A story is like the sea, it has no beginning and no end, it is always the same and still it keeps always changing.

Like Bowles before him, Hamelin was fascinated by Mrabet and was drawn to the rhythm of his stories. It was difficult, Simon-Pierre

told me, to reproduce the storytelling experience in writing. Fixing
the tales to the page, he said, somehow diminishes them.

> When you collaborate with Mrabet, it's like learning to the play the
> guitar. You need to listen to him telling stories a thousand times
> before you get a feel for the music. His gestures can mean so many
> things. First, you have to learn his language. When he tells stories
> he makes up his own language. He mixes Arabic, French, Spanish
> and English and in some of these tongues his vocabulary is quite
> poor, so you have to try to find better words. You really need to
> listen to him for ages before starting to work with him. When we
> wrote *Manaraf*, the publishers said to me, "Oh my God, it's like the
> *Iliad* and the *Odyssey!*" But that's the way they tell stories in this part
> of the world. In the novel he says he died but was later saved by
> a fish and was reborn. After his death, a fish became his father and
> a tree became his mother. It sounds crazy of course but it's very of
> this place. The stories are always the same in a way and there are
> very few characters. There is always a witch and there are monsters
> that are a mixture of humans and animals. It's like jazz music – you
> can follow so many different paths from the beginning to the end
> of the story.

But working with Mrabet, Hamelin explained, was never easy.

> For two months I would visit him for several hours every day. It was
> quite difficult, because at that time he was smoking *kif* all day. The
> morning would be ok but by the afternoon he would forget what he
> wanted to say.

Hamelin also found that Mrabet was unable to explain or contextu-
alise his writing.

> When we finished recording the stories, he turned to me and said,
> "where is the book?" He did not understand the publishing process.
> He is unable to speak about his work. You know the way other
> writers talk incessantly about literature and their ideas and whether
> they are influenced by Victor Hugo etc. Well he just doesn't care! It's

just a story. That is all. He says the stories come from the fish. He says, "The fish came one day to visit me, told me a story and now I am giving it to you." It's very refreshing when someone says, "I don't care about all that other stuff. This is my story and that is all I can say." I remember once, I introduced some journalists to him and they were asking him all these complicated questions and he could not answer them. They would ask things like "what is your concept of womanhood?" "I cannot speak about women," he told them, "I will talk about my woman." And then he would talk about his wedding. Whenever I brought journalists to see him there was always the same problem. He would first ask for money and then he would tell the same stories – always the same ones! You can imagine it was very difficult for them.

Having spent countless hours with storytellers in Marrakech and having had equally frustrating experiences as the journalists who had encountered Mrabet, I decided that it would probably be better for all concerned if I gave the opportunity to interview him a miss. A few trips to Tangier later I was telling Otmane how elusive Mohamed Mrabet was, when he casually mentioned that he knew Mrabet's family. 'I can set up an interview for you,' Otmane said.

So, a couple of days after this we took a taxi to the quartier Souani, a down-at-heel part of Tangier, set further inland from the more glamorous coastal strip. The taxi drove us along Avenue Sidi Mohamed Ben Abdellah, which used to be the Boulevard de Paris. The road is lined by anonymous pale yellow apartment blocks, vacant lots, cafés, banks, car body shops and alleyways sprayed with graffiti. Just off the main boulevard we found a four-storey building on an incline. We entered and climbed a narrow stairwell encased in walls that were plastered with Spanish tiles. Inside, was a tiny windowless apartment with cream coloured walls, an old radio, a bulky television, seashells and starfish, picture frames, paint pots and etchings. The room smelt of turpentine.

Beyond the first room was an even smaller one, sectioned off by alabaster columns and an Alhambra style arch. Sitting on an L-shaped silvery divan beneath his paintings was a small birdlike man in brown corduroy trousers and a black woollen jumper. This was Mohamed

Mrabet. He is small and wiry, but I suspect he is as sprightly as a mountain goat from climbing those staircases.

Mohamed Mrabet was born in Tangier in 1936, or so he thinks. His family had moved to Tangier many years earlier to escape poverty in the Rif. He was one of 12 children. His father, who also had 12 other offspring with a different wife, worked as a pastry chef in the Minzah Hotel. This was Mrabet's first contact with foreigners. He was enrolled in a Qur'anic school at the age of four and left secondary school without being able to read or write. 'I was 11 years old. I said goodbye and I left.'

His autobiography, Look and Move On, dictated by Mrabet but written by Bowles, begins with a tale of violence, setting the tone for the rest of the book.

I was playing in the street outside my house. A bigger boy came and hit me, and I ran into the house crying. My father was sitting in the courtyard. He glanced up.

"What's the matter?"

"Another boy hit me," I sobbed.

"Oh, he did, did he?!"

My father seized my arm and began to pummel me and kick me, and he hurt me much more than the boy had.

"The next time you come back and tell me somebody hit you, you'll get worse than that! Why do you think I work so hard to see that you get enough to eat? So people can beat you up in the street? If anybody hits you, hit them back."

Mrabet's life was beset by violence. He was a wild man. He seemed to act on impulse and seek out pleasure without considering the consequences, like Meursault in Camus' L'Étranger. He told me why he acted on an impulse to leave school.

When our French teacher started telling us things, I understood nothing. One day this French man, who was called Monsieur Titago, wrote something on the blackboard and asked us if we could read it. He wanted all the children to write down what he had written. I could not make out anything he had put on the blackboard, so I just closed my exercise book and fell asleep. He came over to me and hit me on the head with a stick, hurting me very badly. There was a little staircase in the classroom next to the blackboard and I got up and pushed him down it. After that, I picked up a chair and hit him. The teacher grabbed me, but I climbed through the window to the street outside.

Despite the propensity for violence in Mrabet's autobiography, we also catch glimpses of a very sensitive child.

In the Zoco de Fuera, I went to the man who sold canaries. My father had some males, I told him, and I want to try and breed them.

"I've got four fine females," he said.

I bought them and took them home. I had two large cages and I built partitions into them to make rooms. I put two females and one of my father's males into each cage . . . I fed them and cleaned their cages and gave them water. No one ever saw or touched them but me.

One morning as I sat in my room I heard little voices. I jumped up and went to the birdcages. There were new-born canaries in each one of them, and they all had their beaks wide open . . . I was so happy that I decided to say nothing to my father about it. From then on, I took great care of the young birds. I could think of nothing else. I was in love with them.

In Look and Move On, Hamelin says, you can read Bowles' words but hear Mrabet's voice.

In the book we have the story of Mrabet but it is in the writing style of Bowles. When you work with Mrabet, you have to mix things up. It's like a puzzle and it can be very confusing. Bowles' Maghrebi Arabic was not that good, so the two of them spoke in Spanish.

In his book, Tangier: City of the Dream, Iain Finlayson draws parallels between Mrabet and his contemporaries, Mohamed Choukri and Larbi Layachi.

The three principal native novelists of the city, all born under an international administration, all thoroughly disadvantaged by their early circumstances, can reasonably be taken as representative of a large underclass of the city which was at least overlooked, if not positively repressed, by the French and international authorities. An old, residual bitterness, amounting to a smouldering hatred, particularly for the French, still haunts the attitudes of many middle-aged and elderly Tanjawis.

The British were less openly rude than the French, but still regarded themselves as superior to the locals. 'They knew their place,' was how one elderly lady described those Moroccans, mainly domestic servants, she happened to encounter in Tangier, 'they were lucky to have a job.' For many Europeans, the Tanjawis were virtually invisible and their poverty ignored.

Hamelin said that Mrabet honed his storytelling craft by hanging out in Tangier's cafés.

Mrabet learnt some stories from his grandfather when the two of them would go fishing, but most came from the cafés. There used to be some very good storytellers in the city's cafés. Sometimes these old guys would speak for an hour every day for two weeks. They were like TV serials. Mrabet remembered these tales really well because he spent almost his entire life in cafés. That is how he learned to tell stories. When the storytellers disappeared in the 1970s and '80s as radio and television came in, they stopped. But Mrabet carried on telling stories to Bowles, to friends and sometimes to tourists.

Mrabet's stories were reminiscent of those early Picasso collages in which he glued fragments of newspaper articles onto the canvas.

He would mix contemporary facts, which he had learnt from all these foreigners and then he would insert them into traditional stories. And he's still doing that today. It's strange. During the Iraq War, for example, he would put some new material into his stories and create a whole new Mrabet reality.

In his apartment, Mrabet showed me photographs of himself as a young man. There is one where he is holding a fish and standing in the sea, like Daniel Craig in *Casino Royale*. His jet-black hair is dripping wet and he is smiling, proud of his body.

On one occasion, Otmane and I hailed a taxi and travelled south-west from the centre of town along la Route des Belgiques. Ten minutes later we disembarked in Mascouche, a middle-class suburb named after a hill where Mrabet used to live. Embedded in the forest are some desirable villas. Otmane said it was quite rural in the old days and that the fields were speckled with sheep. He explained that there was also a Protestant mission that dispensed medicine before the English Hospital was built in the Marshan in 1886. We trudged up the hill watched by swallows, who perched like musical notes on the tele-phone wires. In the distance we could see the forest of Rahrah that was receding like the hair on the head of a balding man. On the left was a mansion that had been almost completely demolished. Its columns were buckled and steel rods grew out of concrete as if they were whis-kers on a dead cat. It looked more like something out of Aleppo in Syria. Otmane informed me that this was another drug baron's house that had been destroyed, in dubious circumstances, before it was finished. At the crest of the hill was a blue, red and white children's crèche, the *Terre Imaginaire*, designed like a boat. Here we took a left at the Rue Nador and walked down past the British Language Centre. We veered left along the wide Route de Boubana past an old riding school. As we approached a new development on our right, Otmane said, 'There are people living here who came to Tangier with holes in their shoes. They became rich overnight through trafficking. You can write that in your book and say that I told you that!'

At the Golden Tulip hotel we took another left and walked towards Tangier's golf club. The entrance was an ugly, green, modernist arch with a large golf ball embedded as its keystone. It could have been designed by Dali, Miro or Picasso, if they had been insane enough to take up the game.

Founded in 1914, the Royal Country Club of Tangier is the oldest course in Morocco and one of the oldest in Africa. Like Tangier itself, the course has seen better times. Its heyday was in the 1960s, after Hassan II commissioned Henry Cotton to redesign it. The golfing king loved to play there too, until an insurrection in the Rif caused him to fall out of love with Tangier. Today, the green serenity is punctuated by the arthritic swings of the odd expatriate, accompanied occasionally by some of Hassan's former henchmen from the 'years of lead.' Now they pass their retirement ambling along quiet, undulating fairways, lined by cypress and eucalyptus trees.

It was here, at the age of 16, that Mohamed Mrabet blagged his way into a job as a caddy. He was to work here for four years.

> The only place I liked to go regularly was the golf course at Boubana. I would walk there and talk with the caddies while I waited for my turn to go around the course. It was quiet and shady and very green, and I would often stay the whole day, until evening.

The caddies were not old enough to remember Mrabet. The oldest we could find was 71-year-old Omar, who first came here when he was also 16, two years after Mrabet had left. Omar did add though, that his father had caddied for the Sultan Abdelaziz after he had been deposed. Originally, the sultan built nine holes for British golfers. The land is extensive here and no doubt developers would love to get their hands on it. Otmane complained that too many apartment blocks had been built around the golf club and were 'swallowing it up.' Beyond the course there used to be a cricket pitch and polo field. Omar said that during the reign of Hassan II, Abdelaziz's family tried to reclaim the land, but the king refused. He made a decree in perpetuity that no one should touch it. This, Omar told us, could not be proved, as it was never written down. At this point Otmane reminded me that there are two histories to Tangier: one real and the other imaginary. The writers, he said, had relied on the latter. 'Tangier is a like a woman,' he added, 'she does not give herself easily to you.'

The original clubhouse still stands although it has been extended. Inside, I found wooden racks for golf shoes that looked more like rabbit hutches. Even before the club was created, the land here was reserved for the Tangier Tent Club. Founded in 1892, it was the first club in Morocco, a place for diplomats to camp and engage in the noble sport of 'pig-sticking,' essentially hunting on horseback for pigs. The prey did not stand much chance. In the club bar were many black and white photos, including several portraits of Hassan II, looking simultaneously amiable and menacing and one of Prince Andrew, looking smug, as usual.

In 1956, with money he earned from caddying, Mrabet rented a two-roomed house or *mahal* in Mascouche, with a friend called Araiba for 50 pesetas a month.

My father let me take all the canaries to the *mahal*. I knew where I was going to put them. Just inside the door of the house there was a large entrance hall, like an indoor patio. I hung the cages there and filled the hall with flower pots of all sizes. With the big plants and the small plants it looked beautiful.

He told me how he managed to make ends meet after work dried up at the golf club.

I found work in a restaurant and washed the dishes. I would go to work at four in the afternoon and come back the next morning. I also spent a lot of time at the port. At that time, Tangier was international and all the boats came in from everywhere. It was the best city in Morocco. Ooh, la la. There were many Americans and Europeans, like a big "*salade nicoise.*" It was "*magnifique.*" During the day there were not many people, but in the bars and cafés after ten at night until three in the morning, there were people everywhere.

One night, at the Café Central in the Petit Socco, Mrabet met two of those Westerners, an American couple, whom he calls Reeves and Maria. They were actually Russ and Anne-Marie Reeves, and they leased the Hotel Muniria (Tangier Inn) where Mrabet later worked for them as a barman.

The visitors, who had arrived in the city two days earlier, went to see Mrabet's house where they admired the canaries, the plants and the goldfish he had bought. The couple then asked him if he would like to come back to their apartment. Mrabet was hungry. At dinner, like the main character in *The Tiger Who Came to Tea*, he demolished mounds of bread and jam, salad, fruit, a whole chicken and an entire bottle of mayonnaise. Then, complaining about the heat in the airless apartment, he nonchalantly took off his shirt. Reeves and Maria admired his chest, and Maria remarked that his nipples looked like those of a girl. 'In the first place,' Mrabet announced, 'I haven't made love very often yet, and in the second place, I come from a very healthy race.'

He had sex with Reeves before spending the rest of the night with Maria. The next day Mrabet fell ill – undoubtedly due to the mayonnaise – and went home.

> I opened the door and the first thing I saw was two cages lying on the floor, with two canaries dead inside them. I went into the other room. One of the fishbowls was broken and the fish were spread out on the rug.

When he confronted Araiba, his housemate told him that a girl he had brought back had got drunk and caused the damage. The two of them argued, began fighting and Araiba stabbed Mrabet in the stomach. He had to be treated in the Spanish Hospital. Several days later, when the wound had healed, he went out with another friend, Stito, to a bar called La Mar Chica. 'All the Europeans stared at us,' he remembered. They sat down at an empty table, ordered vodka and brandies, and were chatted up by an Englishman called Albert, who was with a large African man, whose job was to keep an eye on four Spanish boys.

Albert enquired if Mrabet and Stito wanted to come back to his place outside Tangier for 'a little party.' They agreed among themselves that if things did not look right they would trash the place. The soirée involved Albert, the four Spanish boys, the African man, a Moroccan from the South and several Englishmen. As Finlayson notes it 'quickly degenerated into a sadomasochistic homosexual orgy.' When the southern Moroccan started having sex with almost everyone at the party, Mrabet took offence.

> Happy with any American or Jew or Englishman, or any filthy Frenchman, yes? They come here and you show them your back-side and everything else you've got. And they take pictures of you doing your work, and sell them later in Europe. And you like that?

Mrabet flew into one of his rages and went for the Moroccan, grinding his vodka glass into his chest and slashing its broken edges against his face. The other participants in this short-lived orgy looked on in horror as Mrabet continued to beat the shit out of him. The brawl adjourned to the garden where the ineffectual Albert tried to intervene, but was thrown into a row of flowerpots. Mrabet smashed one of the pots over Albert's head. The other guests hastily made for their cars. Surprisingly, Mrabet got a lift with one of them back to the city, where he and Stito were dropped off on the Boulevard Pasteur. From there they walked to the Café Central for a restorative beer and ham sandwiches.

By coincidence, Maria was passing by the café and whisked Mrabet back to her apartment. This eventful evening culminated in him and Maria having a row. The latter insisted that she wanted to save Mrabet from his darker, more vicious self. He agreed to change his ways, but not until he was 25. Maria then suggested that the two Americans would look after Mrabet as if he were their own son. This was his response:

Don't tell me you think of me as your son. That's not what you mean. You mean you both like to have me with you in bed, that's all. And I like to play games in bed. But it's not very important to me. I like to drink and smoke kif, but I don't think much about love. Love ruins you faster than anything else. Half the Europeans who live here in Tangier like to live with young Moroccans. When the old English ladies go back to London they leave their boyfriends behind, and you see the boys wandering around the streets looking like ghosts.

I got up, went to her bedroom, and put on a pair of pyjamas. I washed my mouth and my hands and my feet, and got into bed. The window was wide open, and a soft cool breeze blew into the room. I could hear the waves on the beach, and see the lights of the ships in the harbor. Beyond, there was a whole fleet of fishing boats out in the Strait, each one with its bright lights.

Mrabet reached a pragmatic compromise with Maria and Reeves: they would have sex with him and he would get money. By the time their triangular relationship came to an end, he had enough to buy a house. Mrabet first travelled to Marrakech with Reeves and Maria. He was struck by the beauty of the Red City with its palm trees and pink walls, although the bedroom in the Hotel Tazi was 'like a furnace and there was not a breath of air anywhere.'

Back in Tangier, Mrabet still received money from Reeves and Maria and performed various favours, not all of them sexual in return.

One day, Reeves came in and asked me to get him some kif. He had promised to send some to a friend of his in Madrid.

"How much kif?" I asked him.

"Just one kilo, but he wants it already cut, and without any tobacco."

I went down to the Zoco de Fuera to a stall run by a friend, and bought a kilo of kif. Another friend helped me clean and cut it, and then I took it to Reeves. He made a package of it, addressed it, and mailed it to Madrid, to a professor of painting who lived there.

Ten days or so later, Reeves came into the apartment very much excited. "You know that friend I sent the kif to in Madrid? They've put him in jail for six months, and he's got a three thousand dollar fine. For that little package. And something worse. We've got to leave Morocco and go back to the United States, right away do you want to come?"

So in 1959 the three of them set sail from Casablanca to New York.

I stood on deck watching the lights of Casablanca. Soon they were out of sight. I went down to the bar. Reeves and Maria were playing cards. I sat down and had a drink. Then I went up on deck again. There was nothing to see, not a light anywhere. I stood there thinking that if the ship would only sail close to a point of land somewhere, I might jump over the rail and swim ashore.

When they arrived in New York, Reeves and Mrabet were interrogated by a customs officer about the package that had been sent to Madrid.

He brought out a box and opened it. I looked in and saw a pile of sheaves of Ketami kif.

"Do you know what that is?" he said.

"It's kif."

"You have it in Morocco?"

"It grows everywhere," I said. It grows along the rivers, and the livestock are always eating it and going crazy. You can buy it and sell it in cafés, too. People smoke it everywhere . . . I smoke it all the time. It's not bad for you. It makes you very hungry afterwards, and you have to go on eating for a long time."

They all laughed. Then they opened my valises and looked through them. I had some tubes of penicillin powder to dust on my feet. They took them out, brought a glass of water, and poured some of the powder on top of the water. They were holding the glass up to the light and looking at it.

"That's for between my toes", I said.

Mrabet stayed with the couple in an apartment near Central Park. 'For a while I watched the traffic moving down in the street,' he said, 'The big park was in front of me, green and full of trees.' He describes the Big Apple in a childlike, 'innocent abroad' manner, sounding like a fish out of water, or Paul Hogan in Crocodile Dundee.

We went out together, into the street. All I could do was look at the height of the buildings there. I kept trying to count the number of floors of each new one we saw. All those big buildings, all those thousands of cars and people! All those bars and restaurants! And the streets were wide and long. I could only stare at everything, and then stand, watching the lights change from red to green.

While Reeves went to visit his parents in Iowa, Mrabet stayed in New York with Maria. But he drove her crazy by frequently wandering off to the wrong parts of town, getting drunk and hanging out with girls in bars and he could not understand why Maria was jealous. He behaves in an 'I am a camera' way with his shutter wide open and provides us with a disarmingly honest snapshot of New York in the '50s.

We went through a quarter where there were many black people. They did not live as well as the white people, and I felt sorry for them . . . The big difference is that the black man is poor. And the white man wants him poor, so that he'll do the work the white man doesn't want to do himself.

Maria became so exasperated by his behaviour that she packed him off to Iowa. What follows next is even more comic than his short stay in New York. It is like the French exchange from hell, or a scene from *Meet the Fockers*.

Two days later, Maria got her car out of the garage and drove me to the airport. I kissed her good-bye and got onto a plane. There was nothing to see until I got off again. Reeves was standing there waiting for me with an old woman who looked like a witch. "This is my mother," he said.

Reeves' strict and clean-living mother was even more difficult to live with than Maria. Mrabet instantly offended her.

Reeves' mother stared at me. "So you smoke cigarettes too?" she said.
    I laughed. "I smoke cigarettes and I smoke kif, and I drink alcohol. And I love to stay up all night and look for girls to sleep with."
    She put her hand over her mouth.
    After a while Reeves' father came in. He was a short man with glasses, and his jacket was too long for him. He seemed old. Perhaps he was sick. He stared at me when he shook hands with me, and his eyes said that he did not like me.

Reeves Senior insisted that Mrabet got his hair cut, so he had it shaved like an American G.I. and on the way back from the barber's he bought a pack of beer.

I went and got a can of beer and drank it. Reeves' mother came into the kitchen while I was sitting there with the can on the table. She threw up her hands.

Things went further downhill when Mrabet cooked some robins he found in the garden. No one replied when he announced that breakfast was ready. Reeves took him to stay in his sister's house, but Mrabet did not enjoy himself any more there, only finding solace in the arms of a rich woman he met at a swimming pool. He flew back to New York where Maria was glad to see him again, but he felt homesick for Tangier and a few days later she bought him a flight home.

Back in his home city, he felt relieved that he was not being closely monitored. He was proud of his independence. He had a house, plenty of clothes and wads of cash. But without Maria and Reeves' supervision, Mrabet was prone to get into trouble. He beat up an Italian boy who was harassing a Moroccan girl. The only problem was that the boy's father was a police inspector in Tangier. To escape the police, Mrabet had to lie low. To do this, he lived in a cave.

At the foot of the Old Mountain Mijdou and Hassan [his friends] went into the *baqal* and bought food supplies and candles. I kept walking toward Merkala Beach, and they caught up with me. Then we went westward along the coast. We passed through Agla and kept going in the direction of the Cape. Finally we came to a cave in the rocks above the sea . . . I daubed some tar around the walls of the cave to keep out insects and snakes.

Mrabet spent weeks living there, surviving on shrimps he caught with a basket. He also befriended a local Riffian farmer who gave him other supplies.

As time went on Hassan and Mijdou did not come as often as they had in the beginning, but I had everything I needed in order to live. Whenever I caught fish, the Riffian would carry it to market and sell it for me. The summer passed, and the first rains fell. The days when it rained, I stayed in the cave. It was dark and damp, and there was not much I could do, but sit there and smoke *kif*.

After three weeks his friends said it was safe to return to Tangier as the police inspector had taken his whole family back to Italy.

After this, Mrabet decided to give up alcohol so he 'threw out all the liquor and beer and wine in the house,' but carried on smoking kif and spending time on the beach.

On one occasion, Otmane and I took a walk along the corniche and headed west. A new wide highway swirls around the coastline from the ferry terminal, lined by a walkway that is perfect for young lovers and joggers. We ended up at Merkala Beach.

Otmane used to spend his summers at Merkala and Oued Lihoud (Jews' River) and it was here that he first learnt to swim. Many others would also head there to swim, sunbathe and fish. There was an area where the children played football, but now there is nothing, just the odd lost youth sniffing glue. The new road is designed to reduce traffic congestion but seems to have reduced Merkala to a modest patch of sand strewn with flotsam and jetsam. Merkala does have quite a nice backdrop; a few white villas on a green hill to the west, but their lush gardens are fenced off from the undesirables by a stark concrete wall. Someone had spray painted an image of a football fan waving a scarf with the word 'Hercules' on it. At least the vandals, unlike the town planners, have a sense of history.

Otmane said there used to be several beach cafés. One famous one in the 1960s was run by a dark-skinned Tangerine nicknamed 'Merri.' This man had never been given permission to build a café, but, in typical Moroccan style, he went ahead anyway. Merri also worked in the contraband business, smuggling hashish to boats that left Tangier under cover of darkness. In the 1980s Merri got into a fight with someone and killed him. Merri himself later died in prison. 'He was a bon viveur,' Otmane concluded, 'but he was also wicked. When he passed away people were relieved.' A man with a dark side, committing a murder in the blazing sun on a beach, seemed to encapsulate Tangier in a single sentence.

The seawall that buttresses the highway is itself supported by a jumble of boulders sloping down to the Atlantic. Three young men were casting their fishing rods into the water. One was doing a very convincing impression of a seagull. 'The fishermen used to know the name of every rock,' my sage companion added enigmatically. 'If a Tangerois leaves the city, he is like a fish out of water.' By now, Otmane was sounding more and more like Eric Cantona. He recounted a

legend about a rock near here, Lala Jamila, that protrudes from the
water. 'Unmarried girls should not swim towards the rock or wild sea
monsters will ravish them.' Mrabet also had a strong memory of an
unmarried girl at Merkala.

There were many days on the beach, but I remember only one.
I had been walking along the hard sand at the edge of the waves. At
one point I turned and went up onto the soft sand where it was dry.
I spread out the towel and threw my shirt on top of it. Then I took
off my trousers and sat on the towel. There was a large family near
me, spread out all over the sand. One of the girls was as beautiful as
the sun.

Zohra el Allali was just 14. She lived with her family on the Marshan
and worked in a factory making women's lingerie. Mrabet began to
court her. Unfortunately, she was already engaged to another suitor
from Casablanca, and after a bride price had been settled between the
two families, Zohra left Tangier.

But something else happened at Merkala. In the spring of 1964,
looking out over the sand and the waves, he met Paul and Jane Bowles.

One spring day I was sitting on the terrace of Merri's Café on the
beach at Merkala. A Nazarene man and his wife were there with
their Moroccan maid. I sat looking out at the beach, smoking kif and
sipping tea.

Mrabet was smoking his sebsi so intensely that Jane called across to
him. They struck up a conversation. Mrabet told Jane that they had
met twice before at parties in Tangier. This tallies with what he told
me in his apartment.

I was working in the kitchen of one of those big houses on the Old
Mountain. It belonged to the wife of the painter, James McBey.
Every Saturday they would have a party and invite almost all the
Europeans who lived in Tangier. One Saturday night I was working
in the kitchen and they laid out a big table in the garden with lots
of plates, glasses, bottles of alcohol and so on. There were so many

Europeans there. I saw a woman on her own, smoking a cigarette
and holding a glass. I went up to her and said "good evening." She
looked at me and answered in Arabic. I asked her why she was on
her own. "Oh it's better for me," she replied, "there are many
Europeans here who talk a lot about things that don't interest me."
She said her name was Jane Bowles. She drank a lot and I fetched
more glasses for her. She looked very ill. She told me her husband
had gone to the south of Morocco to record music. "That's magnifique!"
I said, but she gave me a funny look, that of a woman who is not
happy.

It was at this point that Mrabet told her the first of many stories.
Jane was entranced. When the three of them met weeks later at
Merri's, Mrabet also told Paul that he had spotted him before, fishing
on the rocks with Capote, Burroughs, Gysin and others. Paul compli-
mented Mrabet, saying that Jane had loved his stories. They walked
back into town and invited Mrabet to their apartment. Over lemon
tea, and another pipe of kif, the three began to talk. Mrabet said he was
unemployed. Bowles told him he was a writer. 'How's he going to
write with a head full of kif?' Jane asked.

Days later, Mrabet returned to the apartment where Bowles showed
him a book with a photograph of Larbi Layachi on the cover. Layachi
worked as a watchman at the beach café and knew Mrabet, and the
latter knew that Layachi was as illiterate as he was. Bowles explained
how Layachi had dictated his narrative into a tape recorder and played
an extract. Mrabet was unimpressed. 'Larbi was talking about taking
care of sheep. It was not interesting, and it was probably all lies,
anyway.'

What appealed to Mrabet most about the reccordings though, was
making money out of them. So, when Mrabet came back a few days
later, he asked Bowles if he could do the same. This is what Mrabet
told me:

One day he invited me to come to his place and record my stories.
"I will speak to a man in America and he will publish them over
there. He will pay you money." Of course I knew nothing about all
of this – translating, publishing, selling and contracts. "Money for

words?" I replied, "no, that can't be!" I needed to earn a living so I would go to his place. He gave me a large machine with a microphone and I began to tell stories, from ten in the morning until three in the afternoon.

Jane spoke good *Darija* but Paul's was not so good. So I would tell him the stories in Spanish and Paul would then write it down by hand in English. After that, he would go to his room and type the stories. That's how it went.

They were stories I had heard in the cafés. In the old days I used to go to many cafés in Tangier and at that time television did not exist. There was radio and people used to listen in the cafés to follow what was going on, for example, in Egypt during the time of Nasser. But after the news they would turn the radio off. I remember there was one particular old man who was about 80 years old who would tell fantastic stories. They would last for about half an hour and there were even some very long tales that were more like a novel. For these, he would come back every day and tell them for at least a week. I also listened a lot to my grandfather and I invented many things in my head. Eventually, I began to make up stories myself very easily and quickly. My stories are about the sea and what lives under the sea. But I also talk about things that exist on the land, but they smell bad. The creatures in the sea are *magnifique*, beautiful, marvellous, but those on the land are very stinky!

One day later, I'm here in my house, in my studio, like this, and someone pushed my shoulder. I look over; it's the fish. And he said, "I am the fish, your friend, whose life you saved, and I bring something good for you."

He told me four stories. That's how it happens. He comes, he tells stories. He told me lots of stories. His name is Mehend.

With money often at the forefront of his mind, Mrabet embarked upon a long campaign to persuade the American writer to buy him a car. Bowles eventually relented. By this time Jane was ill. She watched the relationship between the two men grow stronger, but did not get in their way. She said she liked their new friend, but Mrabet could feel some resentment from her.

One night I began to tape a story that went on and on. For about three months I told a little every day. Sometimes Jane came and listened while I talked. I could see that she did not like to have Paul spend so much time working on my tapes and typing them out in English. She wanted him to write his own books.

The story was turned into a novel. *Love With a Few Hairs* was published in London by Peter Owen in 1967. Five years later, Owen would also publish Mohamed Choukri's *For Bread Alone*. 'I realised I was dealing with a vampire,' Choukri wrote, recalling the pitiful financial recompense he received from the publishers. *Love With a Few Hairs* is about a Mr David, a European who ran a hotel in Tangier, and Mohammed, a diffident 17-year-old Moroccan. The two become lovers and all is going smoothly until Mohammed falls in love with Minah, a local, young girl, who does not feel the same way about him. Mohammed sees a witch who makes him a *tseuheur* or love charm. It works. Minah marries Mohammed and the two are happy together until her mother smells a rat and breaks the spell. When Minah falls out of love with Mohammed, he leaves her and returns to Mr David. Iain Finlayson believes that *Love With a Few Hairs* is a perfect snapshot of what was happening in Tangier at the time.

If any one story deftly sums up the collusion between Moroccan and European Tangier, it is *Love With a Few Hairs*. The character of the sentimental, glad-handed, homosexual expatriate Mr David, romantically in love with his young Muslim, is typical of the European settler being willingly taken for a ride by a young Moroccan who skillfully plays him for his personal advantage.

Finlayson does not dwell on the fact that Moroccan boys like Mohammed were clearly exploited by the likes of Mr David for sex. Before *Love With a Few Hairs*, most stories set in Tangier had been written by Western writers from their slightly jaded perspective. Mrabet's novel was the first to be recorded in an authentic local voice and was original and fresh. And since Mrabet could neither read nor write, we have the stripped-down language of a natural storyteller. Between them, Mrabet and Bowles produced more than a dozen published novels and collections of short stories. 'Mrabet's Tangier is a secret city to which non-Moroccans still have very limited access,' writes Finlayson, 'the secret city is mental as much as material.'

But Mrabet's memories of working with Bowles are contaminated by a bitterness about money, that he still holds today and which kept cropping up in my interview with him.

> Paul translated about 35 of my stories. He sold them and kept all the money. Peter Owen wanted to publish my books, so he could steal my stories too. I don't know if he is dead or alive, but he's a big thief.

Mrabet also told me that Mohamed Choukri's book For Bread Alone was stolen from the experiences that Mrabet had recounted to Bowles.

> Choukri began to turn up every day at Paul's place and sit down with both of us. I would tell them about my life. Choukri had this little book and would write things down each time I spoke. One day he came and said to Paul, "I have a novel which needs to be translated." Paul agreed. Then one day Choukri was with us. I was in the kitchen and Paul came to me and whispered: "You know all of this book, is exactly what you told Choukri?" "Yes, I know," I said. When Choukri wrote that such and such happened to his family, he was actually talking about my family. It became For Bread Alone. That is how it happened. Choukri became the greatest writer in Morocco and Mrabet became the greatest fool!

This bitterness may not have been at the forefront of Mrabet's mind when he spent time with Paul and Jane though. In Look and Move On he describes a typical day with them.

> I began to go every morning to the apartment and call for Jane. I would drive her to the market and we would buy the food together. In the afternoon I would take Paul to the post office. Sometimes I bought bait, and we would take sandwiches to the

beach. Then I would fish, while Jane and Paul lay on the sand and talked. If she did not come with us, he would walk for miles along the empty beach. He was glad to get out of town into the fresh air.

Millicent Dillon describes her first encounter with Mrabet at Bowles' apartment in the Immeuble Itesa.

He was still very muscular, and there was a raw, sensual quality in the way he moved. Immediately he took over center stage. He spoke English haltingly and, when he could not find the right word, moved to Spanish and occasionally to Darija, a Moroccan dialect. Whether laughing or telling a story – frequently a story involving violence – the energy of his feelings poured forth, unmeasured.

He's a mythoman. He doesn't understand the difference between fantasy and reality, especially with kif. He allows it to affect him. He likes that, making an embroidery in his mind, which he then speaks of as if it were true.

I remember Mrabet's rages as immense, almost mythic in scale, a fury unleashed at anyone he felt had caused him injury, beginning with individuals and expanding to whole classes of beings – Jews, Americans, women. And yet, after such a rage, he might suddenly relent.

John Hopkins told me that Bowles' apartment was always filled with Mrabet's strong presence.

Mrabet was there, stripped to the waist with all his muscles bulging. He had a huge knife for chopping kif. Mrabet scared a lot of people who did not understand him. He spoke in Spanish and pointed his knife at people. It was razor sharp.

Bowles recalled another incident involving Mrabet.

At one party given by John Hopkins there was a group of Jilala musicians to entertain the guests . . . Thus it was that Mohammed Mrabet, whom John had innocently invited to the dinner party, began to dance along with other guests. But being a Jilali, his participation soon passed from casual to compulsive, and before long he was in a deep trance. The musicians, far from being disposed to interfere, were delighted to have found an adept among the guests. Still, the rest of us had not noticed what was going on at the far end of the terrace. Suddenly there was a crash, and an explosion of burning embers showered over the dancers. I stood up. Mrabet had a long curved knife in his hand. John also saw him and he and three other men tackled him. In the melee on the floor among the glowing coals, John managed to get his knee dislocated and spent the next week in bed.

'It was like wrestling with ten men,' Hopkins said to me. Mrabet did in the end marry the girl he had fallen in love with at Merkala. There were, from the outset, problems with the relationship. When Mrabet discovered Zohra was about to get married, his approach was not subtle. He drugged the would-be bridegroom and slept with the man's fiancée. He then cut his hand with a penknife and splashed blood on the bed sheets. Zohra and Mrabet undressed the drugged man and left him on the bloodied bed. Three days later, the newlywed husband uncovered this deception and went to challenge Mrabet, who beat him to a pulp. The next day the husband and wife were divorced and Mrabet quickly married Zohra who was now pregnant with his child. The marriage did not go well. Feeling used and abused, Zohra started to poison Mrabet's food. He also found pieces of paper with cryptic messages, written by his mother-in-law, under the furniture. Then tragedy struck: their baby died. Mrabet came up with an idea. He decided to purify his house by exorcizing the djinn that had put a curse on it.

Mrabet went to see a fqih, who told him that Zohra had accidentally splashed water over herself from a brazier on the patio. 'At that moment,' the fqih told him, 'there was a small djinn in the fire, and the water surprised him, and he threw the ashes that were in the brazier against her leg.' The only solution was to cut the throat of a black rooster and burn two papers. The fqih also gave Mrabet water to run on Zorah's legs. In this way the household would be purified by its walls being white-washed and its corners sprinkled with milk. Mrabet's marriage, says Finlayson:

Can perhaps be broadly interpreted in terms of his wife's hysteria, his own resentment at any restriction on his personal freedom of action and thought, and the undoubted distress of both of them at the familiar Tangier tragedy of infant mortality which robbed them of all but four of their 16 children.

The description of the death of his first child, Nadia, in Look and Move On is particularly sad.

One night Paul and I were busy translating a story. We had nearly reached the end when someone rang the bell. When I got up and opened the door, I saw my little brother Abdallah standing there.

"What's the matter?" I asked him.

"Your baby's dead."

When I got home I found the house full of women. In the bedroom I looked at Nadia and saw her lying there dead. I kissed her on the forehead and covered her face.

In the other room the women crowded around me. I looked at them.

"Haven't you got anything to do?" I asked them.

They stared at me. "Why? What do you mean?"

"It's bedtime now," I told them. "We're not going to stay up all night are we? The baby's dead. There's no use in losing our sleep. You all go home now, and come back in the morning and cry some more. And each one of you can think about her own life . . . And you can all get together and cry. Not about the baby, but about your own lives."

Mrabet and Zohra's second baby, Fatima Zohra also died: Look and Move On ends with a trip to the cemetery.

I kept moving ahead between the rows of stones until I came to the two small graves of Nadia and Fatima Zohra . . . I sat smoking and watching the twilight grow over the valley. The silence let me think back to the time when I was a child . . . I did not even remember that I was sitting between the two graves . . . I walked out into the empty road, and kept going.

Like Tangier, Mrabet's memoir is itself a mixture of light and shade, a combination of the melancholic and the hilarious. Besides the sojourn in America, other comic interludes centre around Bowles' guests.

Paul's apartment was becoming more and more like a lunatic asylum. Whenever there were crazy people in Tangier, they came to see Paul. Sometimes a letter would arrive for him from America, and he would say: "Another letter from somebody I don't know who's coming here!" And the next time I would go to see him new people would be there.

And I would shake hands with them and wait to hear their first words. Then I would know how crazy they were. There was an Englishman who smoked kif while he drank his alcohol. He would take off his trousers and go in his underpants and his raincoat to drink in the bars . . . There were usually groups of hippies sitting around on the floor, and their hippyas were with them, half asleep, with their hair covering their faces. When I saw them all together, looking so crazy, I could only shake my head and say to myself: "Now it's really a madhouse."

The craziest man of all was an American named Alfred. One day when I went to Paul's he was there. I looked through the beaded curtain and saw a bald man sitting on the couch. I had never seen him before. He glanced up and saw my head sticking through the curtain. His eyes grew very wide, and he threw himself to the floor and began to scream: "Paul! Paul! They're going to kill me!"

Mrabet remembers that Alfred Chester was particularly paranoid about a sweet potato plant that the Moroccan had placed in a jar of water and which began to climb like a creeper up to the top of a bookcase.

Even when the sweet potato died and I threw it out, he would still look at the place where it had been and yell, and when Paul told him: "It's been dead for weeks, Alfred," he would say: "How do I know it's really dead?"

In September 1967, Mrabet travelled with Bowles to California, but, as had been the case with Reeves and Maria, the trip made him extremely homesick. In Tangier he could do whatever he wanted, but beyond it, he felt like a prisoner. In the United States he suffered racist abuse from Americans and even Hispanics. As he walked around Los Angeles in Moroccan robes, Mrabet attracted the wrong kind of attention. One night he and Bowles were stopped by a policeman who asked 'what sort of an outfit is that?'

Today, Mrabet is still married to Zohra and proud of his two surviving daughters and two sons, whom he shares the four-storey building with. 'I have four children and ten grandchildren,' he said, 'I love God and God loves Mrabet. I really am very happy. I started making paintings, thank God, although no one ever taught me.'

I bought one of his etchings; it was of weird, twisting sea monsters intertwining like yin and yang in a sea of stories. None of his art is comfortable and much of it is very dark. 'The picture alludes to the dark side of Morocco that people rarely choose to paint,' writes Diana Wylie about another of his paintings, Hand of Fatima, 'It seems to express the mysteries of God's dangers and our efforts to stop them.'

Mrabet also told me one of his tales. It was about himself, but set in Madrid in 1810. He is poor and walks around the city asking people to give him bread saying, 'He who gives me a loaf of bread, God will help him, and be with him.' Some people give him a whole loaf, some give him half and others a quarter. One day he sits outside a big house. A tall man looks down from his window and throws Mrabet a loaf of bread. Mrabet sells the loaves, but keeps the halves and quarters. This carries on for 30 days. After this, the man in the big house asks Mrabet what he did with the loaves. Mrabet tells him he takes home the halves and quarters but sells the complete loaves to buy provisions for his family. The man invites Mrabet inside and asks him who buys the large pieces of bread. Mrabet says he sells them to a cobbler. So the man asks his servants to fetch the cobbler. When the craftsman arrives, he admits that he bought 30 loaves for one peseta each from Mrabet, but inside each loaf he found a diamond. The cobbler takes out a small bag containing 30 diamonds. The tall man then produces 30 pesetas, hands them to the cobbler and dismisses him. The householder goes upstairs to find a box for the diamonds. He empties the jewels from the bag into the box and beckons to Mrabet to come upstairs. He hands him the box and wishes him well, but just as Mrabet starts to descend the staircase, he trips and falls, rolling all the way down. The man looks down to see Mrabet on the floor below, with arms and legs outstretched. The diamonds are strewn, glittering around him and there is blood pouring out of Mrabet's ears. There are also bloodstains on the wall, which say: 'I made him poor, but you enriched him. I took away his life. Now just you try and bring him back to life.'

Otmane and I thanked Mohamed Mrabet and said our goodbyes. We shut the door and stood on the landing. I told Otmane that I loved the story, but was not sure what it meant. 'He is foreseeing his own death,' Otmane said. We made our way down from the apartment to the bright streets of Souani outside, taking care not to slip on the stairs.

THIRTEEN

Brian Jones

Let's jump in the Bentley and go to Morocco

From the Rue de la Liberté, the view of the El Minzah hotel is unpromising, but when you pass through the security gate, you step, Aladdin like, into another world. In Arabic, *Minzah* means a 'place of pleasure.' You are greeted by bellboys in *tarbouch* hats, mustard jackets and baggy *Sarouel* pantaloons tucked into long black socks. Their elfish outfits infantilise them; even the octogenarian porter, who showed me my room, looked more like an eight-year-old. Beyond the reception desk, one half of a wide marble staircase sweeps up towards the first floor bedrooms, while the other leads past a grandfather clock down to an Andalusian patio. Here a porticoed arcade surrounds the open courtyard, populated by orange trees, breakfast tables draped in blue tablecloths and a white marble fountain, often visited by sparrows. 'I only ever met the King in my swimsuit,' recalls a regal Italian lady. 'Lots of writers lived here,' a large American boasts to his wide-eyed companion, 'like Paul Bowels,' pronouncing his name like 'vowels.' The walls are covered with Spanish blue *azulejos* tiles and black and white photos of celebrities who have passed through: Winston Churchill, Rita Hayworth, Aristotle Onassis, John Malkovich, Francis Ford Coppola, Jacques Cousteau, Yves Saint Laurent, Farrah Fawcett, Rex Harrison, Cubby Broccoli, Rock Hudson and Jean-Claude Van Damme.

The original building belonged to Ion Perdicaris, whose capture by Raisuli was described by Walter Harris. According to *Lord Bute's Palace* by Andrew Clandermond and Terence MacCarthy, Perdicaris' house was no humble abode, but 'the constant venue for diplomatic balls, operas, theatrical performances, and charity dinners, and was the beating heart of expatriate social life in the White City.' In the late 1920s a Scottish aristocrat, John Crichton-Stuart, the 4th Marquess of Bute, bought Perdicaris' mansion and demolished it. He instructed his architects to respect the Andalusian style of the previous building and the hotel was officially opened in 1930. Glowing reports of social occasions were written up in the *Tangier Gazette*, perhaps because it too was owned by Lord Bute.

Beyond the patio lies the El Korsan dining room with its receding Moorish arches and a veranda looking out across the port. To the right is the Caid's Bar where a portrait of Sir Henry 'Caid' MacLean by John Lavery stares accusingly at the guests. Rachel Muyal told me that during World War II spies from America, Britain, Spain and Japan would all stay at the Minzah at the same time, eyeing each other suspiciously over their cocktails. 'Sometimes one feels frightfully peckish,' pronounces an Englishwoman nibbling nuts at the bar. Like the rest of the hotel, the drinks: Johnnie Walker, Drambuie and Chivas Regal, are of another time. 'Do you know Bunny Guinness?' This unprompted question that is directed at me, comes from a man who has probably drunk all three. He wears a navy blazer and burgundy corduroys, and props himself up against the padded top of the bar. My answer disappoints him.

Outside lies an azure blue swimming pool, often empty apart from the odd seagull, embedded in a tranquil green garden of palm and eucalyptus trees, geraniums and roses. On the far side is the El Minzah Wellness Centre, a gym and spa housed in a modern extension decorated with incongruous Ionic columns. It is a strange glass and stone block that peers over the *Terrasse des Paresseux*, like a spaceship full of hyperventilating astronauts.

From my bedroom balcony I look out over the garden, the palm trees and the harbour beyond as starlings circle in the darkening sky. At night, the trees are lit up like frosted broccoli and the dogs bark in the darkness. The corridors in the main building are lined with raffia panelling and the occasional musket. The ceiling is decorated with Islamic coving. Often there are empty chairs occupying vacant spaces, giving the place a disappointingly soulless atmosphere. I spot a fire

extinguisher on the wall waiting, perhaps, for Keith Richards to hurl
it through a window if he ever passes this way again, as he and Brian
Jones did in the late 1960s.

Like Bowles, Burroughs and Gysin, Brian Jones was a classic outsider.
A misfit even among the rebellious Rolling Stones, this emblem of
Sixties counterculture has been described both as a genius and an
insecure attention seeker. Like Gysin, he never achieved the same level
of success as his collaborators. Unlike Mick Jagger he could not handle
fame; unlike Keith Richards he could not handle drugs, but like
Jonathan Dawson and so many others who stayed in the White City,
he was perfectly suited to Tangier.

In *Brian Jones: The Making of the Rolling Stones*, Paul Trynka says he was a
visionary who changed the face of rock'n'roll.

> His contrariness, his vulnerability and his unhappiness prompted
> his estrangement from the establishment, and ultimately would
> underpin the values of the band, which challenged the establish-
> ment so provocatively . . . Brian Jones was responsible not just for
> the musical inspiration of the Rolling Stones, but their dark magic,
> too. His frustration and angst were the inspiration for the Sixties
> counterculture. Brian Jones, as much as any single figure, helped
> destroy the rotten, complacent establishment.

Lewis Brian Hopkin Jones was born on 28 February 1942 to middle-
class parents in Cheltenham (weirdly Cecil Beaton would later refer to
Tangier as 'this Oriental Cheltenham'). At the age of three, Brian's
younger sister, Pamela, died of pneumonia. It is difficult to imagine
the psychological impact this would have had on his parents. It
happened to my own family and, like Brian's mother and father, mine
hardly ever talked about it. When he was four, an attack of croup left
Brian with asthma for the rest of his life. As Francis Bacon had also
found, asthma had a profound effect on Jones' self-esteem and often
led to isolation from other children. 'He would have to go and sit
quite separate from his friends with his back to a tree,' writes Laura
Jackson in *Golden Stone*, 'this enforced isolation turned him into a
dreamer.' The image of him sitting against a tree is reminiscent of

Paul Bowles sitting in a garden in the midst of a party, removed from everybody else.

In 1959, Brian left school in disgrace after getting a 14-year-old girl pregnant. The baby, who was given up for adoption, would be the first of six illegitimate children. As Burroughs had found with Florida, Jones found Cheltenham stifling, so he moved to London where he immersed himself in the jazz, rhythm and blues scene. In May 1962, Brian placed an advert in a local flyer for musicians to join him in a band at a Soho pub. Among those answering the advert were Mick Jagger and Keith Richards, who remembers the occasion in his autobiography, *Life*.

> I went to the Bricklayers Arms, a seedy pub in Soho . . . As I get there the pub's just opened. Typical brassy blond, old barmaid, not many customers, stale beer. She sees the guitar and says "Upstairs" . . . I walked up those stairs, creak, creak, creak. In a way, I walk up those stairs and come down a different person.

Signs of resentment from the other members of the band soon began to bubble to the surface. While acting as the Rolling Stones' first manager, Brian awarded himself five pounds more than the others, much to their chagrin since they were broke, and they never forgave him for it. 'The slow decline of Brian Jones,' writes Trynka, 'started with a five-pound note.' When a new manager, Andrew Loog Oldham, arrived on the scene, that arrangement came to an end. Oldham decided to make Jagger the star of the show and Brian's role would diminish, leading to an increasing sense of isolation. 'The cunt who gives me trouble,' was how Oldham described him. Brian became increasingly withdrawn as the animosity increased between him, Mick and Keith. Brian's health began to suffer with his escalating consumption of drugs and alcohol, which in turn fed into a vicious circle of insecurity. 'As you can see,' remembers the journalist Chris Welch, 'the Sixties wasn't all peace and love.' The American DJ Scott Ross remembers an incident in New York. There was a knock on Brian's hotel room door. It was Bob Dylan, who greeted him with the words, 'how's your paranoia meter now, Brian?'

In the winter of 1963, at a cottage in Hampshire, Brian attempted to slash his wrists and when that failed, tried jumping out of his bedroom window. 'The silly sod was so drunk he'd forgotten the window was on the ground floor,' recalled a friend.

Brian Jones first went to Tangier in August 1965 with his then girl-friend, Linda Lawrence. They were invited to stay at the Minzah Hotel by the art dealer Robert Fraser. 'Groovy Bob' was the embodiment of the emerging Swinging Sixties, in 'London's combination of aristo-cratic decadence and gangster chic,' as Trynka writes. Fraser's biogra-pher Harriet Vyner says he was attracted to Jones as 'the most culturally adventurous of the Stones at that time. Robert was an authority on cool and esoteric subjects . . . he was drawn to wayward energy and talent.'

It was on a photo shoot with Linda in the palace in the Kasbah, that Brian first met Brion Gysin, who was a friend of Fraser's. Someone had tipped off the press that Brian was going to propose to Linda, but in fact, Jones used the holiday to tell her their relationship was over. As journalists and photographers followed the couple everywhere, the holiday unravelled and they returned home separately.

On 28 August 1966, Brian flew out to Tangier again, with one of Robert Fraser's friends, Christopher Gibbs. With them was Brian's latest girlfriend, Anita Pallenberg. She was a fashion model descended from generations of Swiss-German painters. She spoke four languages, knew her own mind and was drop dead gorgeous. She remembers the first night they spent together.

There had been some kind of disagreement within the Stones. Brian against the others and he was crying. He said, "Come and spend the night with me. I don't want to be alone." So I went with him. Almost the whole night he spent crying.

Brian and Anita would, says Trynka, 'become the Sixties' hottest, most dangerous couple, celebrated for damaging each other.' 'One time in Paris I remember they were so sexually stimulated they could hardly leave the room before starting to shag,' recalls Pete Townshend, 'Brian was living on a higher plane of decadence than anyone I would ever meet.'

Brian was besotted with the cool, headstrong Anita, who could crush Mick with a single word and terrified Keith. Brian was also, according to Trynka, besotted with Tangier.

Certainly his trip to Tangier that August was a little set-piece in his life, a demonstration of both his power and his helplessness. The city was the perfect location for the scene. Tangier had a uniquely twisted, depraved history, and boasted its own special brutality . . . Brian loved the city, the way the pavements were crowded with people in native dress, their donkeys plodding alongside them, the streets full of shit and exotic sounds . . . Somehow, Brian's time in Tangier seemed to epitomise his key character traits – the most outgoing Stone and also the most unreliable. He was the Stone who had travelled the most . . . yet by the time he hooked up with Gibbs and Anita at the El Minzah, he'd become addicted to the whole star trip, staying in luxurious hotels, leaving clothes strewn around and lapping up the attentions of complaisant Moroccans.

In Tangier, Brian and Anita's relationship grew ever more destruc-tive, as Bill Wyman recalls.

The trip was quickly marred by tensions between Brian and Anita. This couple, so magnetically drawn together, began squabbling about almost everything – both in the privacy of their room and publicly in restaurants. There were stories of fights and after seven days, Brian returned to London with a broken left wrist in a plaster cast.

Explaining why he was wearing the cast, Brian said, 'I fell on a slip-pery bathroom floor and trapped my hand under my hip and the bath.' The truth, however, was darker, as Christopher Gibbs said:

Brian, Anita and I were staying at the Minzah. I couldn't say whether he was lashing out in general, or trying to hit Anita – and I'm sure he couldn't either. But he was in a rage. They had a fight and Brian broke his arm; when he went to hit Anita he struck an iron window frame instead, snapping his arm, so that we had to put him in a nursing home . . . They fought about everything – cars, prices, restaurant meals. Brian could never win an argument with Anita, although he always made the mistake of trying. There would be a terrific scene with both of them screaming at each other. The difference was that Brian didn't know what he was doing. Anita did know what she was doing . . . He had too much too young. He was the most selfish, the most spoilt, the most wilful, the most thoughtless, demanding, wheedling, maddening, sweet and charming person. He had just enough charm to get away with being an absolute nightmare. Just. Because he *was* a nightmare. There might have been a sensual buzz to it, and there was a sort of chemistry – but it was destructive.

Brian and his broken wrist were ferried by ambulance to the Clinique Californie, where he stayed for nearly a week. Trynka said Brian 'often expected people to clear up after him, like a toddler.' Following the failure of Gysin's 1001 Nights, Hamri opened another restaurant of the same name in Asilah. When Brian visited it he displayed more of this spoilt behaviour.

Brian was a pain, turning up to dine at the restaurant, then after praising the food extravagantly complaining that he had problems changing his currency and would have to pay for the meal next time. The wealth, the presence of flunkies and the plentiful supplies of hash simply acted to amplify his selfish traits.   \

Back in London, Brian had a brief dalliance with Marianne Faithfull, who said sex with him was 'half-hearted and unsatisfactory.' Nevertheless, Brian and Anita moved into a new flat, described by Trynka as 'one of London's most legendary rock star pads,' 1 Courtfield Road, South Kensington, with memories of Tangier on its walls.

Brian took to his new home, with its cavernous lounge and minstrel gallery in heavy oak, and huge Moroccan tapestries to drape around the vast rooms, which he kept very dimly lit.

On 5 February 1967 *The News of the World* accused Mick Jagger of taking acid. 'The stage was set,' writes Trynka, 'for a showdown between the straight world and the alternative world.' Mick sued the newspaper for libel. A week later most of the Stones left for a quiet weekend at Redlands, Keith's home in Sussex. Brian was supposed to have been there, but stayed in London after a row with Anita.

On 12 February, 20 police officers descended on Redlands. Mick and Keith were inside. The Stones always believed that the raid had followed an insider tip-off. But discovering who had alerted the police was like a game of whodunnit at a murder mystery weekend. Those at Redlands at the time included Keith, Mick, Marianne, Nicky Cramer, Robert Fraser, Christopher Gibbs and the photographer Michael Cooper. There was also another guest, David Schneiderman. His name and nationality is not clear. Cooper recalled that Schneiderman had 'a whole collection of different passports in different names.' The Stones knew him as, 'the Acid King', but we must assume it did not say that on his passport. 'David Schneiderman was a Pied-Piperish character,' Gibbs said. 'Who the hell he was, and where he came from, nobody knew. He had just popped up. He was able to tune into everybody's wavelength and was seductive, satanic, the devil in his most beguiling of disguises. After the bust he vanished, as devils do, in a puff of smoke.'

After the raid, the band needed to escape from the media. So, in late February 1967, they left. 'We decided to get out of England and not go back until it was time for the court case,' Richards writes. 'And it would be better to find somewhere where we could get legal drugs. It was one of those sudden things, "Let's jump in the Bentley and go to Morocco."'

The idea was that Keith, Brian, Anita and Deborah Dixon (the girl-friend of the film director Donald Cammell), would drive to Morocco via France and Spain. Keith had still not passed his driving test so they employed their chauffeur, Tom Keylock. 'With Keylock at the wheel they all began the long drive down to North Africa,' Wyman writes, 'The intention was to meet Mick, Marianne, Michael Cooper, Robert Fraser and Christopher Gibbs at the El Minzah Hotel in Tangier.'

Keylock drove, Keith sat in the front, and Brian and the two young women reclined on the back seats. It was not long before Keith noticed the friction between Brian and Anita.

Brian's relationship with Anita had reached a jealous stalemate when she refused to give up whatever acting work she was doing to

fulfil domestic duties as his full-time geisha, flatterer, punchbag –
whatever he imagined, including partaker in orgies, which Anita
always resolutely refused to do. On this trip he never stopped
complaining and whining about how ill he felt, how he couldn't
breathe. No one took him seriously.

At first Anita thought Brian's outbursts were funny, but Keith learned
later how dark they had become, 'as the downward slide began,
throwing knives, glass, punches at her, forcing her to barricade herself
behind sofas.' Trynka believes that this road trip also exposed the
complicated relationship between Brian and Keith.

Keith's attitude towards Brian was an unfathomably complex mix
of admiration and resentment. Brian was brave, yet lazy, inspira-
tional yet soul-sapping. Worst of all, he was simply better at some
things – and he still seemed, in a profound way, to be the soul of
the band . . . The atmosphere was heavy, loaded with more than
just the smoke from the cigs and the spliffs, as Keylock drove the
four of them south, the back of the car festooned with blankets and
multi-coloured cushions, Keith keeping the eight-track player
constantly fed with music.

Before they reached Spain, Brian was diagnosed with pneumonia
and spent several days in a hospital in Toulouse. They agreed that the
others would carry on without him and that he would fly to Tangier
later.

Richards was to find out that his band mate had given strict instructions to Deborah Dixon not to leave Keith and Anita alone together,
but after a few more days, the novelty of this adventure had worn off
and Deborah headed back to Paris. That left Keith and Anita on their
own, with nothing between them except sexual tension. Keith admits
that he had always been shy with women.

Anita made the first move. I just could not put the make on my
friend's girl, even though he'd become an asshole, to Anita too. It's
the Sir Galahad in me. Anita was beautiful too. And we got closer
and closer and then suddenly, without her old man, she had the

balls to break the ice and say "fuck it." In the back of the Bentley, somewhere between Barcelona and Valencia, Anita and I looked at each other, and the tension was so high in the backseat, the next thing I know she's given me a blow job. The tension broke then. Phew. And suddenly we're together . . . I still remember the smell of orange trees in Valencia. When you get laid with Anita Pallenberg for the first time, you remember things. We stopped in Valencia overnight and checked in as Count and Countess Zigenpuss, and that was the first time I made love to Anita. And from Algeciras, where we checked in as Count and Countess Castiglione, we took the ferry and the car over to Tangier to the El Minzah Hotel.

'By the time we reached Valencia we could no longer resist each other and Keith spent the night in my room,' recalls Pallenberg, 'In the morning I realised that we were creating an unmanageable situation.'

Keith, Anita and Tom Keylock took the ferry to Tangier. At the Minzah they met up with Robert Fraser and Christopher Gibbs, but it was Brion Gysin who was the most welcoming. He could hardly contain his excitement. 'The Rolling Stones are here!' he yelled at Bowles. The writer was bemused as he had not actually heard of the band, but there was not much else to do that day so he decided to meet them at Gysin's apartment. 'They were very much rolling (in money) . . .' recalled Bowles, 'and very stoned.' The musicians were also introduced to Burroughs and the interior decorator Bill Willis. At the Minzah, Keith was greeted by a 'bundle of telegrams from Brian, ordering Anita to come back and collect him.' The telegrams went unanswered.

We weren't going anywhere except the Kasbah in Tangier. It's boinky boinky boinky, down in the Kasbah, and we're randy as rabbits, but we're also wondering how we're going to deal with it. Because we were expecting Brian in Tangier. We only dropped him off to have treatment. We were both, I remember, trying to be polite, at least for each other's benefit. "When Brian gets to Tangier we'll do this and that." "Let's make a phone call to see if he's all right." And all of that. And at the same time that was the last thing on our minds. The truth was "Oh God. Brian's going to turn up in Tangier and then we've got to start to play a fucking game."

260   BRIAN JONES

Four days later, Anita's conscience got the better of her and she
returned to pick up Brian from the South of France. Back in London,
doctors judged him fit to travel. On 10 March 1967, Brian, Anita and
Marianne flew to Tangier via Gibraltar. The plan was that Marianne
would meet up with Jagger in Marrakech for the weekend. Marianne,
Trynka says, thought Brian was having 'a mental breakdown and a
drugs breakdown all in one.'

So they decided to drop acid on the flight to Gibraltar. It was there
that Marianne noted one of the most beautifully bizarre and unlikely
incidents of Brian's life. Still high on acid, he decided they should get
a cab out to the Rock to see the Barbary apes, pampered creatures on
a small nature reserve overseen by the British military garrison. His
plan was to play them a tape of his Mord und Totschlag [Pallenberg's first
movie] soundtrack. The three of them approached the animals with
respect, bowing to them before Brian pressed the play button on his
portable recorder. The beasts seemed positively alarmed by the
impressionistic sounds and scampered away, screaming. Brian, says
Marianne, became hysterical and started sobbing.

If you turn right out of the Minzah, walk about 50 yards and then
take a sharp right down a steep paved street, L'Escalier Waller (featured in
a scene in the James Bond film, Spectre), which leads towards the fish
market, you will find the Saveur de Poisson restaurant and a row of hole-
in-the-wall kiosks.

One balmy night, I joined the queue of diners outside. Once inside,
you are offered neither a menu nor any choice at all, just fresh fish.
The restaurant is cramped and lit only by basketwork lanterns dangling
from a low ceiling. The walls are decorated to the halfway point with
blue and white tiles. Above that level, the yellowing walls are cluttered
with gourds, worry beads, clocks, pots, plates, amateurish paintings
of maritime scenes and a stuffed swordfish. The owner, Mohamed
Belhadj, better known as Popeye, has been running the Saveur de Poisson
for 23 years. In his white skullcap, he hands out wooden ladles for the
fish soup and talks to the customers, but he also has the habit of occasionally eating off your plate with his fingers. He does not take much
of your food, just the odd shrimp.

Popeye is one of those people whose age is almost impossible to guess. He also claims to be a doctor (some say a witch doctor). He brings herbs and spices from the Rif, which, he says, improve your sex life. Jonathan Dawson informed me that Popeye once threw him out of the restaurant because 'there was nothing wrong with me.' 'First time anyone told me that,' added Dawson, 'Someone said I had so many split personalities that I could attend a group therapy session by myself.'

Where the *Saveur de Poisson* is now, there used to be four such hole-in-the-wall kiosks. In one of these, Keith and Anita met a man called Hole-in-Head and subsequently spent many hours completely off their heads. On Brian and Anita's previous visit to Tangier in 1966, Christopher Gibbs had introduced them to this hashish dealer, Achmed Hamifsah, but they called him 'Achmed Hole-in-Head', because he knelt down to say his prayers so often, that he had a dent in his forehead. Christopher Gibbs told me about that first encounter.

After Brian put his arm through the window frame in the Minzah, Anita and I went for a walk and we met a very small Moroccan carrying a Chinese jar on his shoulder and he kept beckoning to us. So we followed him and we walked up those steps. When we had almost reached the top, he pulled his key out, opened the door and we went in. There was this almost empty, very small shop with a low ceiling. He sat down on a little bench and pulled out a box of Berber jewellery. Then he pulled out another box. In this one was a pipe and a whole lot of hashish. Now this was almost unknown at the time, as all the Moroccans smoked kif – the grass cut with black tobacco – whereas hashish is the resin. Then he did this terribly showing off kind of thing they do – he took three pulls on the pipe and then blew an enormous smoke ring that made a smacking noise.

He used to send hashish abroad stitched into slippers, and he became hugely successful. So about two years later he had four of these shops and he was trading in a big way. He was surrounded by lovely Norwegian girls. He was jolly good fun. He told stories from the more obscure and questionable *hadith* of the Prophet. The shop was just a room with four-poster beds and lots of mattresses in different types of Moroccan velvet on top of each other. There were bits and pieces for sale and flaked-out loons, who were travelling the world, were all lying about saying "come and give me another pipe."

Achmed was very fit. He was small and wiry and he could walk on the beach standing on his hands. He also did a lot of staring at the sun and praying, so he had this hole in his head. But after a while the police got fed up with him and put him in the slammer. After that he became a holy man. Popeye took over all his premises and started The *Saveur de Poisson* there.

'Kif' Richards remembers Achmed as the perfect host, bringing them mint tea and a *sebsi* stuffed with hashish.

He was somewhat on the spiritual side, and as he gave you your pipe he would usually tell you some thrilling adventure of the Prophet in the wilderness. He was a good ambassador for his faith and a cheerful soul. Also, a typical Moroccan shyster. He had gaps in his teeth, and he had this great smile that never left. Once he started smiling, it was there all the time. And he kept looking at you. But he had such good shit, you kind of went to the land of milk and honey there. And after a few rounds of this, it was almost as if you were on acid. In and out he went, bringing sweetmeats and candies. And it was very difficult to get out. You think you're going to have a quick one and then do something else, but very rarely would you do anything else. You could stay there all day, all night; you could live there. And always Radio Cairo, with static always off the tuning.

Tangier was Keith's first experience of Africa and he fell in love with the city. He felt that he had been teleported back in time: 'You either went "How weird," or you went, "Wow! This is great,"' he remembers. The Café Baba near Bab al-Assa in the Kasbah is one of the oldest in the city. As you enter, you are immediately hit by the pungent aroma of hashish. Here, Moroccan boys and girls sit smoking on its narrow terrace overlooking the medina. Coffee tables are covered in etchings of sharks and fishing boats. On one of its turquoise walls is a photograph by Michael Cooper of Keith holding a cigarette in one hand and a *sebsi* in the other. It reminded me of a joke I had heard: 'Every time you smoke a cigarette, God takes a minute of your life away, and gives it to Keith Richards.' When Brian and Anita came back to Tangier, Keith writes that things became even more bizarre.

Some incident at Achmed's, in which Marianne found her sari (the only item of clothing she had packed) unravelling and herself suddenly exposed naked in the Kasbah caused panic to set in – especially in Brian, who ran back to the hotel, seized with fear. There they huddled in the corridors of the Minzah Hotel on straw mats, grappling with hallucinations.

'When the party drove down to Marrakech to continue their holiday,' writes Wyman, 'things degenerated quickly.' Keith says that by the time they reached the Red City, Brian sensed something had happened between him and Anita.

We're pretending barely to know each other. "Yeah, we had a great trip, Brian. Everything was cool. Went to the Kasbah. Valencia was lovely." The almost unbearable tension of the situation. That was recorded by Michael Cooper in one of his most revealing photographs, and a chilling image in retrospect, the last picture of Anita and Brian and me together. It has a tension about it that still radiates – Anita staring straight at the camera, me and Brian looking grimly away in different directions, a joint in Brian's hand.

There is another photo by Michael Cooper, one which shows Cecil Beaton snapping Richards as he lies shirtless beside the pool of the Es Saadi Hotel in Marrakech. 'Fair Cecily' was a friend of the Queen Mother and a frequent visitor to the hotel. In his diary, Beaton paints the following portrait of the Stones.

It was a strange group. Three Stones, Brian Jones. Dirty white face, dirty blackened eyes, dirty canary-yellow wisps of hair, barbaric jewellery. Keith, an eighteenth-century suit, long black velvet coat and the tightest pants. Mick was very gentle with perfect manners.

At the Es Saadi, Brian and Anita's relationship hit rock bottom. The physical sparring soon started again, but Brian often came off the worse. In one fight with Anita, Brian broke two ribs. Watching the tragedy unfold, Keith felt he could no longer be a bystander.

Then Brian dragged two tattooed whores – remembered by Anita, incidentally, as "really hairy girls" – down the hotel corridor and into the room, trying to force Anita into a scene, humiliating her in front of them. He started to fling food at her from the many trays he'd ordered up. At that point Anita ran to my room.

Here, Keith suggested an exit plan to Anita. The plot involved Brion Gysin taking Brian to the main square in Marrakech, the Jemaa el-Fnaa, to record the sounds of musicians with a reel-to-reel tape recorder. Then Mick and Marianne would leave separately and Keith and Anita would pile into the Bentley again, on their 'great moonlight flit from Marrakech to Tangier.' Gysin remembered how Brian collapsed in shock at the realisation that his friends had left him. Shortly after Jones came back to the Es Saadi, he called Gysin.

"Come quickly! They've all gone and left me. Cleared out! I don't know where they've gone. No message. The hotel won't tell me. I'm here all alone, help me. Come at once!" I go over there. Get him into bed. Call a doctor to give him a shot and stick around long enough to see it take hold of him. Don't want him jumping down those ten storeys into the swimming pool.

Brian left Morocco and flew to Paris. Keith and Anita retraced their steps to Tangier. From there, she was the first to fly back to London and face the music with Brian. Keith did not feel that guilty. 'It's said that I stole her,' he writes, 'but my take on it is that I rescued her. Actually, in a way, I rescued him. Both of them. They were both on a very destructive course.'

Others disagree. 'I think the loss of Anita destroyed Brian,' Dave Thomson, one of the Stones' friends said, 'He was totally in love with her. It finished him.' Trynka says Brian felt totally let down by the others.

However painful her abandonment was . . . her leaving him wasn't the shock. It was the traitorous actions of Mick and Keith that devastated him. This was a pair of multimillionaires who'd whinge about a fiver for the next 50 years, yet barely mention how they'd abandoned their bandmate penniless in an alien country. The loss of Anita was terrible; the betrayal by his fellow Stones was infinitely worse.

Back in London, Brian tried to win Anita back. Although he had countless groupies and admirers, he tormented himself with thoughts of the one he could not have. He was depressed and exhausted. Between 1963 and 1967 he had been on 31 tours. Friends remarked that he looked like a ghost. The Stones' accountant, Stan Blackbourne, remembers Brian asking him out for tea, dressed as the Archbishop of Canterbury, while a friend, Keith Altham, said Brian would often show him travel brochures and talk of going away to 'get his head together.' Altham said he suspected though, that Brian would 'go to Tangier or somewhere, where he could get his head untogether.'

On 10 May 1967, at his flat in Courtfield Road, Brian was arrested in another drugs bust. On 30 October he appeared in court. Despite his doctor testifying that Brian needed psychiatric treatment, which he could not get in prison, he was convicted. At his appeal hearing, an appointed psychiatrist, Dr Walter Neustatter examined him. 'He came to my first session dressed in the most extraordinary clothes,' Dr Neustatter told the court, 'which one could only describe as flam- boyant. I think he wore gold trousers, and something which looked like a fur rug. Surprisingly, I found the man inside the clothes quiet and thoughtful, with a courteous manner.' The court set aside the original sentence and Brian was let off with a fine.

After the various drugs trials, Anita and Keith spent the Christmas of 1967 in Morocco. On their way to Marrakech they paid another visit to Achmed Hole-in-Head in Tangier.

His shop was now decorated with collages of the Stones. He'd cut up old seed catalogues, and our faces peered out from a forest of sweet peas and hyacinths. This was the period when dope could be mailed in various ways . . . And over the next couple of years, Achmed would send out large quantities of hashish sealed in the bases of brass candlesticks. Soon he had four shops in a row and big

American cars. All kinds of wonderful things happened to him. And then a couple of years later, I heard he was in the slammer with everything taken from him. Gibbs looked after him and kept in touch with him until he died.

'Tangier was a place of fugitives and suspects,' Keith remembers, 'marginal characters acting other lives.' On the beach he recalls spotting two strange men in suits 'looking like the Blues Brothers.' These were the Kray twins. Ronnie was fond of Moroccan boys. Wearing knotted handkerchiefs on their heads and rolled up trousers, the Krays 'brought a touch of Southend with them.'

Long before the term 'world music' was coined by the likes of Peter Gabriel, it was actually Brian Jones who pioneered this concept. The song *Paint it Black* for example, in which Jones played the sitar, was inspired by his love of Moroccan music. 'I think he would have taken that music another stage further,' says Eric Burdon of The Animals, 'the last time I heard of him, I was driving around in the south of Spain, and I heard, "He's across the water in North Africa, recording musicians."'

In early 1968, Brian set off for Marrakech with a sound engineer, Glyn Johns. Brion Gysin had told Brian about the music of the Gnawa. Brian intended to record as much as he could and overdub it with black American soul music. It was a revolutionary and visionary concept, pre-dating modern sampling methods by decades.

Brian and Glyn stayed at a palatial riad, where they were guests of John Paul Getty, Jr. and his glamorous wife Talitha, who would die three years later of a heroin overdose. 'I tried to get him out of the house,' Johns says, 'and I couldn't manage it. He got out of it, the minute he arrived, and remained that way more or less until we left.' In the end Glyn went on his own into the square to record the music, before persuading the musicians to come back to the house to perform in front of Brian and the others. Johns remembers the Stone with a mixture of respect and frustration.

For me, Brian as a person was an asshole. But I really respected him as a musician. I went out to Morocco with him and taped the Gnawa. Brian's idea was to take the tapes to New York to use black musicians along with it. It was a clever idea, but in the end nothing came of it.

This ill-fated project has echoes of Brion Gysin trying to introduce a prototype of the CD player. Disenchanted, Brian abandoned the Gnawa project before it was finished.

Back in London, Brian was busted for a second time on 21 May 1968, but maintained it was a stitch-up. He was released on bail pending a later trial. It wasn't long before Brian's *wanderlust* resurfaced and he headed to Morocco again. This time, Brian decided to focus on the mysterious musicians in the mountain village of Joujouka.

Under a starlit night sky, a large green and red tent was erected on a hill in the southern Rif Mountains. Inside, sat a dozen musicians: half of them banging *tbel* drums and the other half blowing *rhaitas* or reed pipes. In front of them was a tiny man dressed in a furry costume made from goat hide, wearing a straw hat and dancing like a madman. These were the Master Musicians of Joujouka. In June 2017 I went to the festival in the village to see them for myself.

'The 4,000 year-old rock and roll band,' is how Burroughs described them. 'Their sound empties the brain,' Mohammed Hamri's widow Blanca has remarked, and their music has also been said to heal troubled minds. About 50 tourists from across the globe had gathered here. Many of them were dancing too. As the night wore on, the hypnotic rhythm of the drums vibrated inside their bodies and built up to a crescendo. By wild repeated movements – like Whirling Dervishes – the revellers whipped themselves into an ecstatic trance-like state. When the music stopped, they felt euphoric and cleansed. One of the visitors, Rieko from Tokyo, said she first came here five years ago after both her parents died. 'I was so depressed, I did not think life was worth living,' she said. 'But the music healed me. It brought me energy and I felt I could live again.' She explained that the music allows the dancer to reconnect with the body and disconnect the mind. Rieko said she felt completely in the present; liberated from the sadness of the past.

I had taken a train from Tangier to the town of El Ksar el Kebir, one hour and twenty minutes south of the Mediterranean coast. Fields of golden corn rushed past the window, dotted by blobs of green olive trees. When we reached the station, the Master Musicians' manager Frank Rynne, a languid Irish academic, who lives in Paris, looks like Mick Jagger and sounds like Bob Geldof, bundled us into taxis. From there we took a winding mountain road to the village of Joujouka. It had whitewashed buildings with blue wooden doors and Turkish style toilets. Until a few years ago there was no electricity and a stone olive press was powered by a donkey.

'I came to bury Brian,' an English voice confided in me. Jimi, from Macclesfield, showed me a vial hanging around his neck. It contained earth that he had dug up from Jones' grave. Jimi wanted to bury this earth in Joujouka and then take some Moroccan soil back to Cheltenham.

Despite the fact that Joujouka is a small, remote mountain village, there are actually two rival Master Musician groups. One is led by Bachir Attar, whose father was the leader of the band when Brian visited. Now he seems to spend much of his time trying to discredit this group, which is ironic, because the music is from the Sufi tradition – the mystical form of Islam, which promotes a message of peace.

That evening Frank took me on a tour of the village. He pointed to a rock overlooking the valley and the sea beyond. Here, he said, four winds collide in a hot maelstrom. He then indicated a cave halfway up a hill. This is where the ancient deity Boujeloud is said to live. He is half-man, half-goat and resembles the classical god Pan. It is said that Boujeloud brought the gift of fertility to the village. In the original ceremony a goat was slaughtered and skinned. The pelt was then filled with salt and a local boy would be sewn into the hide. It was believed that the salt, blood, heat and music brought on visions. The teenager would then dance, pursue female virgins and whip them with olive branches. For more than 40 years, the part of Boujeloud at the festival has been played by an unassuming man, Mohamed Hatmi, who runs a local café by day while by night he performs in the tent, whirling, writhing and dancing ecstatically like a teenager at a rave or a modern-day shaman. Two days later I walked with a Japanese couple through thorny bushes and olive groves, for more than an hour in the blinding sun. We clambered up to Boujeloud's cave and sat inside on its smooth, rocky surface. It was as cool as a fridge and as quiet as noise-cancelling headphones. From here we gazed out towards the Atlantic in the direction of Lixus.

Frank also showed me the shrine of a fifteenth-century Sufi saint, Sidi Ahmed Schiech. Inside the courtyard was a fig tree with an iron chain wrapped around its trunk, strangely reminiscent of Pepys' tree in Dar Zero. In the old days, anyone suffering from mental illness would be tied to the tree and the musicians would blast their pipes within inches of the madman's face. This acted as a sort of musical exorcism to drive demons from disturbed minds. It is a type of cosmic meditation, thought to induce states of ecstasy and telepathy in the audience. Another guest, Brian, from America's West Coast, told me he was so distraught when he heard that Donald Trump had won the election, that he put on a vinyl record of the musicians and placed his head directly in front of the speakers to cleanse him of his grief. It did not work.

Back at the marquee I was at first reluctant and too self-conscious to join in with the ravers. Instead, I recorded the music and watched the others from a distance. Their wild movements seemed utterly bizarre to me. Perhaps Nietzsche was right when he said: 'those who were seen dancing were thought insane by those who could not hear the music.' Eventually I began to dance, awkwardly at first, but then the vibrations began to penetrate my bones. I felt as if Boujeloud had taken over my unmusical body and I too danced like a madman under the starlit sky. From the corners of Joujouka and remote mountain villages, the dogs barked, a strange call and response, echoing in surround sound to the rhythms of the 4,000-year-old rock and roll band. Perhaps if we could decode them, we might, as Brion Gysin suggested, have been able to understand their messages.

I walked back to the house where I was staying. An old man from the host family showed me the way. I followed this hooded figure down through the alleyways of Joujouka. The solitary mosque pointed up like a finger towards the heavens and a crescent moon. Tangier's light and dark was encapsulated by the stars winking in the night sky. That night, I slept like a baby with absolutely nothing on my mind. No wonder Brian Jones was inspired by this place.

On 4 July 1968, Brian visited Tangier again with another girl-friend, Suki Potier. Brian stayed at the Minzah with Christopher Gibbs, whose patience was pushed to the limit. One night in the hotel, in a scene reminiscent of those between Brian and Anita, the pair had a massive row and Suki tried to slash her wrists with a broken mirror. The staff, who had seen it all before, called an ambulance, but when it arrived Brian tried to persuade Gibbs to be Suki's chaperone to the hospital.

He was really trying to pass the buck, as was his wont. I wasn't interested. No, get in there mate, this is your baby. They were a disaster area. As you go through life you know the people you can basically rely on. And there are some people who aren't reliable and they were never going to be, either of them.

Paul Trynka sees Brian's experiences in Tangier and Marrakech as symptomatic of his wayward lifestyle.

Brian's trips to Morocco had charted his life: moving on from Linda, his impossibly tempestuous relationship with Anita, that terrible moment when Mick and Keith, the only brothers he'd ever had, left him in Marrakech. During those visits he'd spent more and more time with Mohamed Hamri (running up bills at his 1001 Nights restaurant) and Brion Gysin, who considered Brian something of a *dilettante* (takes one to know one) but bonded with him over music, namely the mysterious, powerful Pipes of Pan from Joujouka.

Brion Gysin first heard the Master Musicians of Joujouka in 1951 when he travelled with Bowles to a Sufi music festival in Sidi Kacem, near Rabat. He was fascinated by this motley collection of men in *djellabas* who had once been the sultan's very own entertainers. Gysin and Hamri opened 1001 Nights in 1954, specifically to bring the Joujoukan musicians to the city. In those days, Gysin was the only person allowed to bring strangers to the village.

Gysin became obsessed with the sounds of Joujouka, and said he would never let the sun go down without listening to them. 'I just want to hear that music for the rest of my life,' he said. Mohamed Hamri was at various times Gysin's friend, student and lover and he also performed the same role for Paul Bowles. When Hamri took Gysin to Joujouka, he discovered, to his astonishment that the music he had fallen in love with was played by Hamri's uncles. When Jones heard about Joujouka, he begged Gysin to take him there.

Brian's interest in the occult, which he had explored with Anita, included a fixation with the Greek God of fertility, Pan. One of Brian's friends, Stanislaus Klossowski, believed that this half-man, half-goat appealed to Brian as it embodied the spirit of rock'n'roll.

Pan is a very dangerous sort of power. The word 'Panic' comes from the name Pan. It's significant that Brian was attracted by the notion of Pan, and at the same time in awe.

Trynka considers that Brian's weird fixations and obsessions would come to 'define the Rolling Stones for ever.'

His fascination with chaos, dark forces and lasciviousness would permeate the band's music and image; Mick and Keith would follow in his wake. Dancing with the devil would come at a high cost. In the process, though, they'd make great art.

On 1 August 1968, Gysin and Hamri set off with Brian and Suki to Joujouka. They were also joined by George Chkiantz, a sound engineer, who brought two of Brian's Uher tape recorders, complete with flat batteries. 'He was totally together,' recalls Chkiantz of his meeting with Brian at Tangier airport that morning, 'and knew exactly what he was doing. He explained we were off to meet Hamri, and couldn't be late.' It is thanks to Chkiantz that we have quite a detailed account of their trip. He was told that they would be heading in two taxis up a bumpy mountain road. Chkiantz was in one car with Brian, Suki and Gysin, who used the journey to wax lyrical about the music.

When Brian, in white robes and Suki, in long trousers and short hair, arrived in the village, the locals were stunned by these strange apparitions. It was as if aliens had landed from another planet. One of the villagers was a young shepherd boy called Bachir Attar.

When Brian Jones come to the village, my little brother Moustapha comes to me and he says: "Somebody come with big hair." I said to my brother, "keep the sheep here, I want to run to see how he

looked. My brother went back to the village. I run and I run to see
my father and I see the man with big golden hair. I shake his hand
and he looked great!

Bachir was in fact the eldest son of Hadj Abdesalam Attar, the
master musician, who had invited Gysin to the village. Brian greeted
Bachir, shaking his hand and kissing his cheeks. He had no idea of the
effect this meeting would have on his young friend, as Laura Jackson
writes.

It was a deep, abiding affection which transcended far beyond the
hero worship of an adoring and impressionable shepherd boy.
Abdesalam and all the musicians found Brian to be someone worthy
of respect – something not lightly bestowed. His whole personality,
zest, and sheer inquisitiveness about their culture and music, his
genuine need to understand them, not to mention his extraordinary ability to pick up one of their ancient instruments and actually
be able to play it, earned Brian their everlasting love.

The guests made a picnic in an olive grove, as one of the taxi drivers
handed over his car battery to Chkiantz to recharge the dead Uhers.
The main performances took place in an open space in the centre of
the village, near the shrine of Sidi Ahmed Schiech. The visitors were
treated to pastoral flutes, women singing outside their houses and an
obscure song that Gysin had never heard before. They were informed
that on the second day they would experience the highlight of the
festival, the performance of Boujeloud.

Brian, Suki and George slept in a whitewashed house with mud
floors beside a courtyard of fig trees, above the main square. Although
they were woken in the early hours by the mysterious sound of several
mountain oboes, Brian slept peacefully that night. George remembers
his travelling companion seemed content, 'considerate and concerned
for people.'

He was so relieved for a moment from the pressure of being a
Rolling Stone. He didn't have to impress anyone. The villagers didn't
give a toss – and he wasn't competing, he wasn't conscientiously

being a bad boy. He'd come because he admired the musicianship and he was here to learn.

Laura Jackson also believes that in Joujouka this troubled soul found peace of mind.

An exchange of souls between him and Joujouka happened that summer, leaving behind in the village, to this day, a reverence for him which sits squarely in sainthood and investing in Brian, something he had long been pursuing – without quite knowing what it was.

On the second day Chkiantz recorded the rhaitas and tbel drums, as well as applause from Brian. 'His hand-clapping we could have done without,' adds Chkiantz. The set was a shorter version of the full-length ceremony, which normally stretches for three nights, like a Wagnerian opera. The rhaitas blared out a constantly changing call and response. The volume of the drums could be heard from miles away. Brian and Suki reclined on cushions. He wore headphones and was said to be completely calm and enraptured. Chkiantz moved between the seated audience, trying to record the sounds on the Uhers without too much distortion. I had a similar problem with my recorder and had to stand quite far away. On the verge of giving up, Chkiantz finally decided to aim two microphones towards the ground and capture vibrations as they bounced weirdly off the earth. As Trynka writes, 'the recordings therefore immortalised both this immense, profound music and the land that gave birth to it.'

Disappointingly, Boujeloud did not appear that evening. Brian wrote in notes for the album cover, that he was not too upset. 'I don't know if I possess the stamina to endure the incredible, constant strain of the full festival,' he wrote, 'Such psychic weaklings has Western civilization made of us.' Brian wrote of the ceremony:

She and the others are singing not to an audience of mortals, but rather they are chanting an incantation to those of another plane, and while we were recording her she hid her beautiful voice behind the drum she was playing. It was not for our ears.

Brian only stayed for a few days, but even during this short visit, he joined in. Brian asked Hamri if he could come back another time to see the full festival and perform as Boujeloud himself. Gysin remembered how 'the most beautiful goat anyone had ever seen – pure white!' was led in front of them. Brian leapt up and shouted: 'that's me!' before the animal was taken away to be butchered. 'It was a powerful moment,' Chkiantz says, 'by then Brian had been smoking too much.' A few hours later, the cooked animal was brought back to them and they ate it with their hands, wrapped in bread. Gysin said that Brian thought the experience was like some sort of Eucharist. 'I see Brian Jones he really likes this,' said Bachir.

He is dancing wild with his headphones and everybody loving him. When I see this big musician from the highest band of the world – he make me think to get our music out into the world. He is the one who brought beautiful things for Jajouka. We all see him as the one who opened the door of the music of Jajouka to the world. Meeting Brian Jones changed my life.

He was a great musician. The greatest musician in the world I can say. Some day, somebody will come to bring out this music of Jajouka to the world and carve the memories of Brian Jones. Somebody will come. I have a feeling for that. Still today the children of the village sing his song and when the musicians wish to pay tribute to Brian, we sing along too.

That song, sung in Darija is called 'Brahim' meaning Brian.

When Brahim Jones was with us the people of the
village didn't know what was going on.
When Brahim Jones was with us we were all very happy.
He recorded our music for the entire world to hear.
Joujouka has power from the Saint, Sidi Hamid
Shiek is buried there.
Brahim Jones left us, but we will never forget
what he did for us.

The following day, the visitors made their way back to Tangier with hours of music on tape. As soon as he was back at the Minzah,

Chkiantz, who had not slept for two nights, crashed out on his bed, but was awoken within a few hours by Brian. Chkiantz staggered into the guitarist's room and plugged in a few cables, as Brian waited in expectation with a few friends. Chkiantz would wonder if he had dreamt that a pallid figure in a raincoat and hat had also been there. Years afterwards it was confirmed that one of the first people to hear the recordings was William Burroughs. In *The Ticket That Exploded*, Burroughs wrote about the 'Pan God of Panic piping blue notes through empty streets.'

Chkiantz finally caught up on some sleep and the next day, Brian and Suki took him on a tour of the city that Brian loved. They went to the Café Hafa before heading off to the beach. Again, Brian displayed his more considerate side, warning Chkiantz not to swim too far out, to avoid a steep gradient in the seabed and strong currents. That hot August afternoon, Chkiantz dozed off again, but when he woke up he saw Brian swimming out into the Mediterranean.

> I remember the economy with which he swam, a fast crawl, very little splashing. He swam out a long way, and waved to us, then swam all the way back. And walked in his own footsteps back to the beach. With currents that strong, it gives you a good idea of what a good swimmer he was.

After three days of exemplary behaviour, on Chkiantz's final night at the Minzah, Brian revealed the other side of his character. He snuck out of the hotel, wandered down *L' Escalier Waller* and scored heaps of hashish from Achmed Hole-in-Head. At dawn the next day, promenaders on the Rue de la Liberté heard shouts coming from a balcony above them. '*Salaam alaikum!*' Brian bellowed, swiftly followed by 'Fuck you!' if the Tangerines failed to reciprocate. Then he passed out, 'without even putting an arm out,' Chkiantz recounts. 'I was thinking Jesus, what's happening? Suki said, "Fuck him, this happens all the time." Then she put a blanket over him.'

Brian left Tangier a week later, looking tanned and seemingly healthier. On his return, Brian played the tapes to himself and others relentlessly, but his enthusiasm for this obscure music received a luke-warm response from the rest of the Stones, who were not interested in such exoticism. Years later, Keith confessed that Brian was the first to bring other people's cultural influences into the band and encourage experimentation. The recordings were finally released in 1971 as, *Brian Jones Presents the Pipes of Pan at Joujouka* with a picture painted by Mohamed Hamri entitled 'Brahim Jones Joujouka very Stoned.' Two decades later, the Stones, who had by this time more or less airbrushed Brian out of their history, admitted that the Moroccan musicians did, after all, have a contribution to make and featured them on the track, 'Continental Drift' on the *Steel Wheels* album in 1989.

As with the pipes and drums of Joujouka, Brian could pick up almost any instrument and play it within minutes. He mastered the harmonica, saxophone, recorder, sitar and marimba, as well as more obscure paraphernalia such as the mellotron, Appalachian dulcimer and vibraslap, but his legal troubles, mood swings and substance abuse left him further estranged from the band and proved too much of an obstacle to their progress. By 1968 he was playing only minor roles on a few pieces. 'Keith and I took drugs,' Mick says, 'but Brian took too many drugs of the wrong kind, and he wasn't functioning as a musician.' On 8 June 1969 they informed Brian that the group, which he had formed, would continue without him.

In East Sussex several years after World War I, a little boy called Christopher Robin explored the woods near his house with his teddy bear Edward. His father A.A. Milne was inspired by his son's adventures in the 'Hundred Acre Wood' to write the *Winnie-the-Pooh* books. Poohsticks Bridge, Galleon's Lap and Roo's Sandpit are all based on real places where his son played. Milne had been injured in the Battle of the Somme and bought Cotchford Farm on the edge of Ashdown Forest to recover from the trauma of the conflict. The world of Pooh, Piglet, Tigger, Eeyore, Kanga and Roo was his escape and his therapy.

In November 1968 Brian bought the farmhouse. It also became his sanctuary, where he could escape the police and the paparazzi, wean himself off drugs and recover from the trauma of leaving the Stones. He converted the sitting room into a recording studio, worked on solo music projects and began to plan another trip to Joujouka.

The garden at Cotchford Farm contains a summer house, a statue of Christopher Robin, a sundial with Pooh and his friends carved on its plinth and a rectangular swimming pool, at the bottom of which,

Brian Jones was discovered motionless at around midnight on 2 July 1969. By the time the doctors arrived, he was pronounced dead. A coroner recorded a verdict of death by misadventure, adding that his heart and liver had been enlarged by drug and alcohol abuse.

I drove down to East Sussex to take a look at Cotchford Farm for myself. Luckily it was on the market, (for £1,895,000, Brian had paid £28,750), so the estate agents showed me around. 'An opportunity to buy not just a delightful family home, but a slice of British history,' gushed the brochure. Not having a spare £1.89 million, I had of course no intention of taking the opportunity to buy it, but pretended that I might do.

It was a crisp, January morning and a watery light filtered through Ashdown Forest. The sixteenth-century listed building was a maze of low ceilings, creaking timbers and wobbly floors. I tried to suppress my sense of being a charlatan, while the estate agent tried to suppress a sense of not having much to say. She randomly opened cupboards and talked about their obvious uses. Jones' contributions to the interior decor included a blue, stained-glass windowpane that made the lounge look subaqueous and a bathroom mirror that made you look thinner. Visiting the House at Pooh Corner shortly before Brian died, the Blues musician, Alexis Korner, noticed that his friend had put on weight, resembling a 'fat, mummified, Louis XIV.'

Outside, I was shown the statue, the sundial and the swimming pool, which was littered with dead leaves. The whole experience made me feel inexpressibly sad. The house had been on the market for some time. Perhaps the ghost of Brian Jones was having a chilling effect on prospective buyers. At the end of my tour, I mumbled something plausible, yet non-committal, which included the words 'think about it' and 'discuss it with my wife.' I then went for a walk in the woods searching for Poohsticks Bridge. I got lost, but a dog walker came to my rescue. She told me she had moved to the countryside, as 'the London of the sixties and seventies was simply no fun anymore,' and now 'taught yoga in Sussex and LA.' She could have been something out of a Stones biography or a Bowles novel. She pointed me in the direction of the bridge. When I found it, I stood on its weathered planks for some time, wishing I had brought my children with me to play Poohsticks.

After Jones' death, Jimi Hendrix dedicated a song to him on American television and Jim Morrison published a poem entitled, 'Ode to L.A. While thinking of Brian Jones, deceased.' 'I hope you went out smiling like a child,' he wrote, 'into the cool remnant of a dream.' Morrison actually drove from Tangier to Casablanca along the Atlantic coast and then inland to Marrakech with his girlfriend Pamela Courson in 1971. Both Hendrix and Morrison would die within two years of Jones, at the same age: 27. Janis Joplin, Kurt Cobain and Amy Winehouse would also follow in their blighted footsteps. The man who supplied Jim Morrison with the heroin that probably killed him was Jean de Breteuil, a former boyfriend of Marianne Faithfull. He later died of an overdose in Tangier.

'For all his weaknesses and hang-ups, his impertinence and terrible behaviour,' writes Bill Wyman, 'he was a pivotal figure. As a symbol of the Sixties that helped to shape us, he was entitled to a free pardon.' 'There was nothing the matter with him,' echoes George Harrison, 'that a little extra love wouldn't have cured.' One of the most poignant insights comes from Shirley Arnold, who worked as a secretary for the Stones.

> Even with millions of girls clamouring to meet him, and ready to do anything for him, he was lonely. He just couldn't communicate with people. Brian couldn't love anybody except himself or his own music. That was his problem. He used to use drugs and drink to try to overcome his deep loneliness.

Lewis Brian Hopkin Jones was buried in Cheltenham cemetery. His blond hair was bleached platinum white, his corpse was embalmed and hermetically sealed in a bronze casket. His body lies ten feet under the earth to discourage trophy-hunters from digging it up.

Like a body rising from the bottom of the pool, conspiracy theories surrounding Brian's death soon began to surface. One was that he had been killed in a fight by Frank Thorogood, a builder hired to renovate the house. Thorogood was one of the few people at Cotchford Farm at the time and was the last person to see him alive. On his deathbed he allegedly told the Stones' driver, Tom Keylock, that he had killed Jones, but Keylock later denied this. The American writer Geoffrey Giuliano is adamant that Keylock himself murdered the musician by holding his head under until he drowned. In his book *Paint it Black*, Giuliano says that the British authorities hushed up the death because Princess Margaret was at Cotchford Farm that night. There is only one problem with this theory. Keylock was not at Cotchford then, but with the Stones at Olympic Studios in London.

A *Daily Mail* reporter believed the cause of death was covered up by police officers the next morning, citing a neighbour who saw documents being thrown onto a large bonfire, but Sussex police said there was no reason to disbelieve the coroner's original verdict and that they would not be reopening the case.

On 5 July 1969, two days after his death, the Rolling Stones performed in Hyde Park, dedicating their performance to Brian Jones. It was the biggest, free, open-air concert held in Britain. 3,500 white butterflies were released from the stage, many of them landing on the heads of the spectators. Mick Jagger read an extract from the poem *Adonais* by Shelley about the death of his friend, Keats.

> Peace, peace! He is not dead, he doth not sleep –
> He has awakened from the dream of life –
> 'Tis we, who lost in stormy visions, keep
> With phantoms an unprofitable strife,
> And in mad trance, strike with our spirit's knife
> Invulnerable nothings.
> – We decay
> Like corpses in a charnel; fear and grief
> Convulse us and consume us day by day,
> And cold hopes swarm like worms within our living clay.
> The One remains, the many change and pass;
> Heaven's light forever shines, Earth's shadows fly.

Tangier Today and Tomorrow

I am sitting in the Café Hafa. The word means 'cliff' and the white-washed terraces are sculpted out of the rocky escarpment and bedecked with green wooden tables and blue plastic chairs. A wasp hovers around my glass of mint tea, takes a sip and falls in. A waiter in a white coat, like a baker or a caretaker from an asylum, walks around selling cakes, macaroons and cocoa leaves. Some Moroccans are playing draughts. Most of them, like the rest of the modern world, stare at their mobile phones. On one table a Moroccan boy is so bored he takes selfies with his toes. Paul Bowles did not even have a landline, just the purple toy telephone to speak to Jane. These boys have everything they need: beautiful girls, kif, mint tea, an azure sea and a benevolent sheltering sky; everything they could ever wish for, except prospects.

From here I look out across the Strait of Gibraltar to the Spanish coast. 'In the old days,' John Hopkins had told me, 'Jewish families would congregate at the Café Hafa and look back across to Spain, imagining the houses they had left behind in 1492. They still had their keys; they were as big as shovels.'

A flotilla of fishing boats makes its way out to sea and tankers leave traces like planes in the sky. 'To avoid detection, German U-boats would switch off their engines and silently follow the current past the Strait of Gibraltar,' Gipi de Richemont had explained. 'The Romans did the same thing. They would fill the sails of their galleys with stones, the ship would sink into the water unnoticed, the current would catch the sail and drag the boat through the Strait.'

The Café Hafa has been here since 1921 and seen all its storytellers come and go. Its walls reek of history and are haunted by literary ghosts. From its terraces, Mrabet, Layachi and Choukri would look at the sea and concoct their stories, tangled up in blue. Mrabet learnt many of his tales from the owner of the Café Hafa, Ba M'Hammed. For Choukri, Tangier would always remain a mystery, 'the key to whose labyrinth is yet to be found.'

This 'Tangier,' for whose foundational origins historians and researchers scrabble in vain, sprang from the Flood, according to Tanjawi legend. The dove returned, Noah cried out 'Tin Ja' (land is here), and shortly thereafter his ark docked near the plateau of Charf. Myth and history merge in Tangier. Yet it never divulges its eternal secret, enfolded in the enduring silence of its memory – a blend of enigma, magic and wisdom.

From the desolate neighbourhood of Mghogha, on the outskirts of Tangier, Otmane had pointed out the Charf to me. Here, half-finished buildings cling to green hills like barnacles on the hulls of ships. 'It used to be a forest,' Otmane lamented, 'now it's a concrete jungle.' Standing near a pile of disused bricks and smouldering rubbish, we gazed back towards the sea and could make out a barrow shaped mound in the distance, with a mobile phone mast on its peak. This is where Sertorius is said to have come across the tomb of the giant Antaeus, or was it a dinosaur? Here, nothing is certain, but everything is possible, as Choukri sensed.

In Tangier, everything is surreal and everything is possible. In Tangier, anyone adept at telling stories can invent anything and it will be believed and he, in turn, will believe the stories told to him by others. Such is the eternal pleasure of living in a land embedded in multicoloured myth. A certain truth has been imprinted in the minds of all those who have ever loved Tangier, regardless of the epoch: as in The Thousand and One Nights, boredom is expelled from its magical kingdom and the grandeur of its myth. Stretching back to the period of Antaeus and reaching up to the most recent conquest, it is a myth that continues to preserve and feed all the legends that are woven in Tangier, and all the stories that are told about it. Everyone who comes to Tangier desires to be its Shahrayar, with the city playing the part of Shahrazad. But the city promises subjugation, expulsion, and even death to whoever betrays it, or misinterprets its secret mystery.

'If you ever manage to figure out Tangier,' Hopkins had said to me, 'you will be the first person in history to do so.' Tangier seems to be suspended in unreality. It escapes definition and defies categorization. Unraveling its secrets is about as easy as decoding the barks of Brion Gysin's dogs. Tangier has been hailed as a paradigm for international cooperation and a cradle of creativity, but it is also a kind of museum of failure, a graveyard of ambition. 'There were a lot of phoney writers,' Hopkins confided, 'who tried to write "The Great Novel," but they never got anywhere. They started smoking and wrote the same line over and over again.'

From the Café Hafa I can see the sunlight sparkling on the waves of the water and the white terrace walls that are too bright to look at without sunglasses. This is Tangier's light side, but on the other side of the city, on the cliffs of Malabata, I had once seen nothing but darkness. Ten years earlier, as a BBC reporter, I had climbed into a cylindrical metal lift and descended down a shaft into the depths of the earth. Here, men in blue coats, yellow helmets and head torches were pushing a trolley along a single track towards a wall of rock. They were trying to dig a tunnel between Morocco and Spain. Hercules had split Europe and Africa apart and now engineers were trying to join them together again, but like many Tangier stories, this strange idea never became reality. A lack of resources and political will meant that the two continents would remain tantalizingly close, but forever apart. 'Many things have changed,' wrote Lotfi Akalay, 'but the essential things have stayed the same. We are separated from Europe by 14 kilometres and as many centuries.'

Everything in Tangier is light and darkness: the lighthouse at Spartel and the tunnel at Malabata; the white walled buildings and the shadows in the alleyways; Jones' genius and paranoia; Orton's playfulness and shame; Gysin's creativity and failure; Burroughs' addiction and redemption; Bowles' imagination and fascination with depravity; Matisse's depression and romance with colour; Sertorius' victory and assassination; Hercules' strength and flaws. Tangier is known as the 'White City,' but it is also, as Choukri wrote, 'a city haunted by shadows.' Perhaps in the end Tangier is us. It reflects humanity itself.

Down by the corniche, the old order of dark alleyways, drab staircases and creaky lifts has been usurped by the bright, clean lines of shiny steel, concrete and glass. These are the new giants of Tangier, proudly looking down on the ambitious new marina. 'An old port, with a new vocation!' beams a billboard next to the harbour. 'Tangier is like a beautiful woman,' Otmane said, 'dressed in ugly clothes.' 'For me, it's a disaster,' exclaimed Gipi de Richemont, 'They could have built a Saint-Tropez, but they're turning it into Dubai.'

They should have kept the fishermen there. If you want to have a great lunch, go to the pier, to those little fishermen's restaurants. Ask them to put up a table for you. You can see the fishermen working, you can see the Kasbah. You are in a dream. You will have the freshest fish for 50 dirhams. It's amazing. You can bring a millionaire there and he's happy. But no, what do they want to do there? They want to build a stupid, modern harbour with a bloody telepherique – from the harbour to the Kasbah – it's a joke. We have winds up to 150 kilometres per hour. I'd like to see it in the wind.

I suggest to Gipi that maybe the breath of Hercules will blow the telepherique away. 'They don't understand that the pleasure of being in Morocco is to walk, to talk, to look at the shops and take tea. They don't understand that, because they never do it.'

Everything is changing. Madame Porte's, once famed for its pastries, intrigue and espionage, has been turned into a McDonalds. Will the older generation of Tangerinos stay on? 'It depends what happens here,' Christopher Gibbs told me, 'If there were no more storytellers, no more dancing and no more old ladies from the Rif sitting outside selling vegetables, I wouldn't really be interested any more.' Above all there is an overriding sense that the party is over. 'The magical days are gone,' wrote Choukri 'destroyed by the population explosion, by wars, economic crises and the collapse of social values and liberal governments.'

But others do not see it that way. 'They have always said that Tangier is finished,' Rachel Muyal said to me, 'but it's not. People say Tangier is this or that. They say it's black or white. But it's not. Actually it's grey.' Maybe the city that has survived waves of invasions by Carthaginians, Romans, Vandals, Byzantines, Arabs, Portuguese, British, Spanish and French can now endure a new wave of development? 'Tangier is having a real renaissance,' Jonathan Dawson told me. The money started pouring in after King Mohammed VI arrived here in 1999, reversing years of decline under his father. 'When I first came, it was dead in the water,' he said. 'There was nothing: no internet, just a bit of Gibraltar television. Now it's booming. It's on a roll.' And he remembered a time when he went to visit Marguerite McBey, towards the end of her life.

I used to go up to her house on the Old Mountain for lunch and I would ask her the same question you just asked me. "What do you think of Tangier now?" Of course she'd been there since 1930. Well, she looked me straight in the eye and she said: "Darling I loved it then, and I love it now."

Select Bibliography

Akalay, Lotfi, *Ibn Battouta: Prince des Voyageurs*, Casablanca: Editions Le Fennec, 1998.

Tanger: C'est Tanger, Tangier, Frogeraie, 2014.

Ben Jelloun, Tahar, *Silent Day in Tangier*, London: Quartet, 1991.

——— *Leaving Tangier*, London: Penguin, 2009.

——— *This Blinding Absence of Light*, London: Penguin, 2005.

Ben-Srhir, Khalid, *Britain and Morocco during the Embassy of John Drummond Hay*, London: Routledge, 2010.

Bidwell, Margaret & Robin, *Morocco: The Traveller's Companion*, London: I.B.Tauris, 1992.

Booth, Stanley, *The True Adventures of The Rolling Stones*, London: William Heinemann, 1985.

Bowles, Jane, *Two Serious Ladies*, London: Peter Owen, 1965.

Bowles, Paul, *The Sheltering Sky*, London: John Lehman, 1949.

——— *Let It Come Down*, London: John Lehman, 1952.

——— *A Hundred Camels in the Courtyard*, San Francisco: City Lights, 1962.

——— *Collected Stories*, London: Penguin, 2009.

——— *Days: A Tangier Diary*, New York: Harper Perennial, 2006.

——— *Let It Come Down*, London: John Lehman, 1952.

——— *Their Heads are Green*, London: Peter Owen, 1985.

——— *Without Stopping*, New York: Ecco Press, 1985.

Bryant, Arthur, *Samuel Pepys Volume 3: The Saviour of the Navy*, Cambridge: Cambridge University Press, 1933.

Burroughs, William S., *Naked Lunch*, New York: Grove Press, 1959.

——— *The Letters of William S Burroughs, 1945-59*, London: Penguin, 2009.

——— *Rub Out the Words: Letters of William S Burroughs, 1959-1974*, London: Penguin, 2013.

Carr, Virginia Spencer, *Paul Bowles: A Life*, London: Peter Owen, 2004.

Ceballos, Leopoldo, *Historia de Tanger*, Cordoba: Almuzara, 2013.

Choukri, Mohamed, *For Bread Alone*, San Francisco: City Lights, 1973.

In Tangier, London: Telegram, 2008.

Clandermond, Andrew & MacCarthy, Terence, *A Room with a View: A History of the Grand Hotel Villa de France*, Tangier: Minville, 2012.

———— *By Royal Appointment: A History of the Continental Hotel*, Tangier: Black Eagle Press, 2012.

———— *Lord Bute's Palace: A History of the Hotel El Minzah*, Tangier: Minville, 2012.

———— *Beyond the Columns: A History of the Librairie des Colonnes*, Tangier: Black Eagle Press, 2013.

Codrington, Tessa, *Spirits of Tangier*, London: Arcadia, 2008.

Croft-Cooke, Rupert, *The Tangerine House*, London: Macmillan, 1956.

The Caves of Hercules, London: WH Allen, 1974.

Davies, Ethel, *North Africa: The Roman Coast*, London: Bradt Travel Guides, 2009.

Dillon, Millicent, *You Are Not I: A Portrait of Paul Bowles*, Berkeley, University of California Press: 1998.

Drummond-Hay, Alice Emily, *A Memoir of Sir John Drummond Hay: Sometime Minister at the Court of Morocco*, London: John Murray, 1896.

Farson, Daniel, *The Gilded Gutter Life of Francis Bacon*, London: Vintage Books, 1994.

Finlayson, Iain, *Tangier: City of the Dream*, London: Harper Collins, 1992.

Geiger, John, *Nothing Is True Everything is Permitted: The Life of Brion Gysin*, New York: Disinformation Company, 2005.

Grant, Michael and Hazel, John, *Who's Who in Classical Mythology*, London: Hodder and Stoughton, 1979.

Green, Michelle, *The Dream at the End of The World: Paul Bowles and the Literary Renegades in Tangier*, New York: Harper Collins, 1991.

Gysin, Brion, *Brion Gysin Let The Mice In*, West Glover: Something Else Press, 1973.

Hamri, Mohamed, *Tales of Joujouka*, Santa Barbara, CA: Capra Press, 1975.

Harris, Oliver, *William Burroughs and the Secret of Fascination*, Chicago: Southern Illinois University Press, 2006.

Harris, Walter, *Morocco that Was* London: Eland, 2002.

Herbert, David, *Second Son*, London: Peter Owen, 1990.

Hopkins, John, *The Tangier Diaries, 1962-1979*, London: Arcadia Books, 1997.

Howe, Marvine, *One Woman's Morocco*, London: Arthur Baker, 1956.

Hughes, Richard, *In the Lap of Atlas*, London: Chatto & Windus, 1979.

Jackson, Laura, *Golden Stone: The Untold Life and Mysterious Death of Brian Jones*, London: Smith Gryphon, 1992.

Jagger, Richards, Watts, & Wood, *According to the Rolling Stones*, London: Weidenfeld & Nicolson, 2004.

Landau, Rom, *Portrait of Tangier*, London: Robert Hale, 1952.

Lane Fox, Robin, *Travelling Heroes: Greeks and their Myths in the Epic Age of Homer*, London: Penguin, 2008.

Layachi, Larbi, *A Life Full of Holes*, London: Harper Perennial, 2008.

Lyautey, Hubert, *Lettres Marocaines et Autres Ecrits*, Rabat: La Croisee des Chemins, 2010.

Mackintosh-Smith, Tim, *Travels with a Tangerine: a Journey in the Footnotes of Ibn Battutah*, London: John Murray, 2001.

McMahon, Aidan, *Tangier Unanchor Travel Guide* Online.

Miles, Barry, *William S. Burroughs: A Life*, London: Weidenfeld and Nicolson, 2014.

Milton, Giles, *White Gold: The extraordinary story of Thomas Pellow and North Africa's One Million European Slaves*, London: Sceptre, 2005.

Morgan, Ted, *Literary Outlaw: The Life and Times of William S. Burroughs*, London: Pimlico, 1991.

Mrabet, Mohamed, *Look and Move On*, London: Peter Owen, 1989.

Mrabet, Mohamed & Eric Valentin, *Le Poisson Conteur*, Manosque: Le Bec en L'Air, 2006.

———— and Hamelin, Simon-Pierre, *Manaraf*, Nieuw Amsterdam, 2009.

———— and Hamelin, Simon-Pierre, *Stories of Tangier*, Casablanca: Editions du Sirocco, 2009.

Naylor, Phillip, *North Africa: A History from Antiquity to the Present*, Austin: University of Texas Press, 2009.

Nutting, Cherie, *Yesterday's Perfume: An Intimate Memoir of Paul Bowles*, New York: Random House, 2000.

Orton, Joe, *The Orton Diaries*, ed. John Lahr, London: Methuen Minerva, 1986.

Pennell, Richard, *Morocco from Empire to Independence*, London: One World, 2009.

Peppiatt, Michael, *Francis Bacon in Your Blood: A Memoir*, London: Bloomsbury Circus, 2015.

Pepys, Samuel, *The Tangier Papers of Samuel Pepys*, ed. Chappell, London: Navy Records Society, 1935.

Pons, Dominique, *Les Riches Heures de Tanger*, Paris: La Table Ronde, 1990.

Plutarch, *Lives, VIII Sertorius and Eumenes, Phocion and Cato the Younger*, Loeb Classical Library, Cambridge, MA: Harvard University Press: 1919.

Rogerson, Barnaby, *A Traveller's History of North Africa*, London: Duckworth Overlook, 2008.

Routh, Enid, *Tangier 1661-84: England's Lost Atlantic Outpost*, London: John Murray, 1912.

Schneider, Pierre, *Matisse in Morocco: The Paintings and Drawings*, 1912-1913, Exhibition Catalogue Washington, DC: National Gallery of Art Washington,DC, 1990.

Shoemake, Josh, *Tangier: A Literary Guide for Travellers*, London: I.B.Tauris, 2013.

Spurling, Hilary, *Matisse: the Master*, London: Penguin, 2005.

Stotter, David, *A Postcard from Tangier*, Saffron Walden: Postal History Society, 2015.

Stuart, Graham Henry, *The International City of Tangier*, Stanford, CA: Stanford University Press, 1955.

Tafersiti, Rachid, *Tanger: Realités d'un Mythe*, Tangier: Zarouila, 1998.

Theroux, Paul, *The Pillars of Hercules: A Grand Tour of the Mediterranean*, New York: Ballantine Books, 1996.

Tomalin, Claire, *Samuel Pepys: The Unequalled Self*, London: Viking, 2002.

Trynka, Paul, *Brian Jones: The Making of the Rolling Stones*, New York: Plume Books, 2015.

Van Lente, Fred, *Hercules (Myths and Legends)*, Oxford: Osprey, 2013.

Vernier, Victor, *La Singuliere Zone de Tanger*, Paris: Editions Eurafricaines, 1955.

Waines, David, *The Odyssey of Ibn Battuta*, London: I.B. Tauris, 2012.

Waterfield, Robin and Kathryn, *The Greek Myths: Stories of the Greek Gods and Heroes*, London: Quercus, 2011.

Wharton, Edith, *In Morocco*, New York: Ecco Press, 1996.

Williams, Kenneth, *The Kenneth Williams Diaries*, ed. Russell Davies, London: Harper Collins, 1993.

Winter, Bert, *The Rogue's Guide to Tangier*, London: Viking,1986.

Woolman, David, *Stars in the Firmament: Tangier Characters, 1660-1960*, Pueblo: Passeggiata Press,1998.

Wylie, Diana, *Enchantment: Pictures from the Tangier American Legation Museum*, Tangier: TALIM, 2010.

Wyman, Bill, *Stone Alone: The Story of a Rock 'n' Roll Band*, New York: Da Capo Press, 1997.

Index